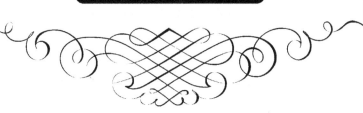

ISBN 978-1-330-79809-6
PIBN 10106785

# 1 MONTH OF
# FREE
# READING

## at

## www.ForgottenBooks.com

By purchasing this book you are eligible for one month membership to ForgottenBooks.com, giving you unlimited access to our entire collection of over 700,000 titles via our web site and mobile apps.

To claim your free month visit:

www.forgottenbooks.com/free106785

English
Français
Deutsche
Italiano
Español
Português

# www.forgottenbooks.com

**Mythology** Photography **Fiction**
Fishing Christianity **Art** Cooking
Essays Buddhism Freemasonry
Medicine **Biology** Music **Ancient**
**Egypt** Evolution Carpentry Physics
Dance Geology **Mathematics** Fitness
Shakespeare **Folklore** Yoga Marketing
**Confidence** Immortality Biographies
Poetry **Psychology** Witchcraft
Electronics Chemistry History **Law**
Accounting **Philosophy** Anthropology
Alchemy Drama Quantum Mechanics
Atheism Sexual Health **Ancient History**
**Entrepreneurship** Languages Sport
Paleontology Needlework Islam
**Metaphysics** Investment Archaeology
Parenting Statistics Criminology
**Motivational**

# INDIVIDUALITY AND DESTINY

## THE GIFFORD LECTURES FOR 1911-12

### SECOND SERIES

MACMILLAN AND CO., Limited
LONDON . BOMBAY . CALCUTTA
MELBOURNE

THE MACMILLAN COMPANY
NEW YORK · BOSTON . CHICAGO
DALLAS · SAN FRANCISCO

THE MACMILLAN CO. OF CANADA, Ltd.
TORONTO

# THE VALUE AND DESTINY

OF

# THE INDIVIDUAL

THE GIFFORD LECTURES FOR 1912
DELIVERED IN EDINBURGH UNIVERSITY

BY

B. BOSANQUET
LL.D., D.C.L.
FELLOW OF THE BRITISH ACADEMY

MACMILLAN AND CO., LIMITED
ST. MARTIN'S STREET, LONDON
1913

COPYRIGHT

# PREFACE

THE present course of lectures is a continuation and application of the argument contained in the previous course, which was published under the title "The Principle of Individuality and Value." I hope that this second series will be found somewhat less abundant in controversial detail than the former, though it, too, inevitably contains many paragraphs and references which time did not permit to be included in the lectures as delivered.

I may observe that the Index has been restricted as far as possible to proper names and special allusions. I do not think that the reader is assisted when subject-headings, set out in methodical order in a very full Table of Contents, are repeated in an Alphabetical Index which is thus made inconveniently voluminous.

I have, as before, inserted the Abstracts which were furnished to the press immediately after the Table of Contents.

BERNARD BOSANQUET.

EDINBURGH, *November* 1912.

259278

# CONTENTS

## LECTURE I

### INTRODUCTORY—THE FINITE, ITS SELF-TRANSCENDENCE AND STABILITY

## LECTURE II

### THE VALUE OF PERSONAL FEELING, AND
### THE GROUNDS OF THE DISTINCTNESS OF PERSONS

## *A.* THE MOULDING OF SOULS

## LECTURE III

### NATURAL AND SOCIAL SELECTION

## *A.* THE MOULDING OF SOULS—*Continued*

## LECTURE IV

### THE MIRACLE OF WILL

# *B.* HAZARDS AND HARDSHIPS OF FINITE SELFHOOD

## LECTURE V

### THE WORLD OF CLAIMS AND COUNTER-CLAIMS

# *B.* HAZARDS AND HARDSHIPS OF FINITE SELFHOOD—*Continued*

## LECTURE VI

### PLEASURE AND PAIN

## B. HAZARDS AND HARDSHIPS OF FINITE SELFHOOD—*Continued*

## LECTURE VII
### GOOD AND EVIL

## C. THE STABILITY AND SECURITY OF FINITE SELFHOOD

### LECTURE VIII

#### THE RELIGIOUS CONSCIOUSNESS

## *C.* THE STABILITY AND SECURITY OF FINITE SELFHOOD—*Continued*

### LECTURE IX

#### THE DESTINY OF THE FINITE SELF

## *C.* THE STABILITY AND SECURITY OF FINITE SELFHOOD—*Continued*

### LECTURE X

#### THE GATES OF THE FUTURE

# ABSTRACTS OF LECTURES

## LECTURE I

### INTRODUCTORY—FINITENESS AND SELF-TRANSCENDENCE

THE general title of the two courses was "The Value and Destiny of the Individual." The first course, "The Principle of Individuality and Value," delivered last year, attempted to show how the reality and value of all things in the universe depended on the degree of their embodiment of the principle of individuality—the completeness, coherence, or self-containedness of the universe. This second course, with the title, "The Value and Destiny of the Individual," is an attempt to apply the principle developed in the first course to finite beings, that is, in effect, to human souls. It discusses in what way the so-called "individual" or human soul works out its destiny and achieves its worth, by and through its membership of the universe, the only real and ultimate individual. The present lecture, on "Finiteness and Self-Transcendence," was intended to give an outline of the course, showing how its sub-divisions are connected with different sides of the nature of finite beings as our principle requires us to analyse it. The human soul has sometimes been thought of as a celestial spark of divinity, sometimes as a crystallisation out of unconscious Nature, or out of a hardly conscious tribal collectivity, sharing the nature of a suffering deity who represents that collectivity. This latter idea goes to meet modern philosophy from the historical side; and these two ideas, even apart, but better if taken together, illustrate our view of the soul as a link or focus, through which the striving of the universe unites the multitude of things and persons in the absolute whole. This conception determines the treatment of the soul in these lectures. We shall first consider, in the following lecture, how the distinctness of particular persons, though practically a fact, shows indications of an underlying unity not generally recognised. After that, we shall consider the soul and its destiny under three principal heads. First, the idea of " soul-making " as the work of the universe, borrowed from Keats, will lead us to speak of the moulding of souls by natural and social selection, and of their self-creation through the miracle of will. Secondly, the life of the finite self in apparent self-completeness and independence, will show itself to be one of suffering and adventure. And, thirdly, as far as through such adventure the soul is driven to self-recognition, or knowledge of its own true nature and dependence in the religious consciousness, the secret of stability and security, even for the finite self, will be revealed. This consciousness is closely akin to the best things in knowledge ; but philosophy depends on it rather than *vice versa,* and it is natural to the healthy mind, as Spinoza says.

# LECTURE II

## PERSONAL FEELING AND THE DISTINCTNESS
## OF PERSONS

THE aim of this lecture is to prepare us for a freer dealing with the distinction between different persons than is commonly held permissible. No one wants to deny it is a fact ; but it is important to recognise what sort of fact it is, and that it presents indications of not being ultimate and irreducible. The common conviction is that the most " personal " part of us is the least capable of being shared or communicated. I am I and not you, because you cannot have my feelings just as I have them, especially my bodily feelings. We cannot " enter into " each other's minds in their immediate quality—each other's sensations, for instance. To realise our personality is to absorb ourselves in our exclusiveness. This amounts to the facts it relies on, and no more. I cannot have your pleasure as you have it. This is true. But, further, there are all sorts of really great things which seem to belong to the man himself, and to no other man, *e.g.* his religion, in which, some say, he is alone with God. These things are called " personal," and set to the credit of what is peculiar and unsharable in the " person." So, for example, with philosophy or art. But this is just con-fusion. What is above, or includes, the social relation, is being confounded with what is below, or has not reached it. The maximum is being confused with the minimum of experience. All these great things are above " altruism," and rest on man's universal nature. They in no way support the exclusiveness of personality. It, in fact, is " personality " in the worst sense ; what we try to avoid. The most real personal feeling is the most universal, like tragic emotion. When we come to consider the material, so to speak, of persons, the objects of their attention and achievements, we see how much they have in common, and how little, from the point of view of what is great in the world, their distinctness seems to matter. Take the development of Christianity, or of the drama, or of the British Constitution, or of mechanical invention. You can distinguish the phases and values in each ; you cannot distinguish what individuals contributed. Their " contents " overlap irregularly ; the clear structure is that of the object. But yet it is these objects which are their life and value. No doubt the relation of each person to them is different ; but his achievement blends with that of others, and his distinctness from them shows as merely external and superficial. There is no rule as to how far " persons " can overlap in their contents. Often a little change of quality in feeling, it seems, would all but bring them into one. It is impotence, and no mysterious limita-tion, that keeps them apart. At their strongest they become confluent, and we see how they might be wholly so.

# *A.* THE MOULDING OF SOULS

## LECTURE III

### NATURAL AND SOCIAL SELECTION

THIS lecture treats, as will also the next, of "The Moulding of Souls." The expression "soul-making" is borrowed from a letter of Keats, in which he condemns the phrase "a vale of tears," and proposes rather to consider the world as "a vale of soul-making," in which pain and trouble are essential. Keats's suggestion is expressed so as to imply the pre-existence of something to be developed into souls, and a survival of souls in a further life after being moulded in this world. Accepting the conservation of all values in the absolute, I do not think these special assumptions necessary. But the view that the moulding of souls is the main work of the universe as finite seems to contain an unquestionable truth. To begin with, I may recall my account of the development of life under natural selection. Its line of evolution, we held, was a summary of the significance of the world, as acting through and upon each living centre under special conditions. It was only as thus regarded that life gives any clue to the nature of the universe. The formation of soul is in the beginning, for our knowledge, indistinguishable from that of living centres, and has been compared to condensation of, *e.g.*, tribal peculiarities of life ; which as consciousness and intelligence emerge, continues as an analogous process, guided by what in the large sense must be regarded as natural selection, *i.e.* the requirement, in every case, of being "equal to the situation" on pain of extinction. How such principles as those of life and mind can elicit special and individual structures from special environments may be illustrated by the case of knowledge, which is an example of a similar process at a higher level. It begins with no detailed apparatus of consciousness, but constructs the whole framework of logic, *e.g.* laws of causation, etc., which have no apparent place in the environment, under pressure of the need for interpreting situations. Mind or soul take shape under pressure of situations, and may be called adaptive variations, if we remember that this does not explain their ultimate nature, but only, given their nature, its particular shapes. Mind or soul, of course, does not start empty, but takes over its content from life. But this content, that of life, has all been elicited in this same way. As a partial expression of the world, formed by its surroundings, soul may be said to be moulded by natural selection, although more especially in the shape of social selection ; for mind has its main environment in mind, and there is far more room for contrivance and initiative than in mere natural selection. But still the dominant law is that of being equal to the situation ; and it models and sculptures the soul. And through this pressure of the world upon them, souls recover their primitive unity with each other, and develop forms of life in which the absolute begins to show itself, and the particular soul to be fused and recast through larger experiences, such as social self-sacrifice, art and science, or religion. And all this has a side of severity, but is the revelation of value.

# *A.* THE MOULDING OF SOULS—*Continued*

# LECTURE IV

## THE MIRACLE OF WILL, OR CHARACTER AND CIRCUMSTANCE

WE spoke in the last lecture of soul-formation through natural and social selection. To-day we are to consider the other side of this process—the self-formation of the soul, or the " Miracle of Will." Mind, in " being moulded," is moulding itself and its environment. It just is the focussing and adaptation by which a range of surroundings, meeting in a single spirit, brings new facts and meanings out of itself. What is the secret or miracle of will? That is, how or why can a mind be sure of remoulding, modifying, "being equal to," any situation in which it finds itself? This is a very difficult question, and it is not answered merely by seeing that mind is in some sense above things, or a condition of experience. Again, it is no use to appeal to blind will. This might make changes, but there could be no occasion for expecting them to be changes for the better. Why can mind always in principle transform things for the better? The secret lies in the fact that mind has always more in it than is before it. Or, in other words, the universe (as Plato urged) is all connected. So for every given situation there is a larger and more effective point of view than that given, and because the spirit of the whole, in the shape of some special want or question, is always in the mind, it can always, in principle, find clues to new possibilities in every given situation. It is like the expert's view of any situation, practical or theoretical. He has instincts and ideas which take hold of points which no one else would see, and make a new thing of the problem. Every mind in its degree is able to do this. Many modern doctrines of logic and ethics converge in this view, which is the essence, for instance, of real inductive theory. This, then, is the secret of the power of will, which people often mean when they ask about its freedom. This principle is simply and clearly illustrated by looking at the detail of a human will, and asking where it comes from, and how, *e.g.* language out of animal sounds, marriage and the family out of animal parentage, the sacrament out of eating together. "Institutions" come out of natural facts. Thinking Will has "elicited" them. This shows the nature of will, and the same sort of thing shows its power. A dozen artisans want to get groceries without a middleman, and found the magnificent co-operative movement. The great social need was in their minds, though not before them. "Circumstance" implies a centre, and the word reveals a meaning opposite to its common use. Really, it is part of a life, and so transformed when understood. Even "physical impossibility" is highly relative, and if we count in resignation and self-sacrifice, can never resist will. Strength of will—*e.g.* resoluteness—is not its power, but may help it. In developing these ideas a very detailed knowledge of moral and social facts has been achieved, to which, and to social improvement, the voluntarist movement has contributed but little, showing the inadequacy of its notion of will. Will, as we said, is one side of the formation of souls.

# *B.* HAZARDS AND HARDSHIPS OF FINITE SELFHOOD

## LECTURE V

### THE WORLD OF CLAIMS AND COUNTER-CLAIMS

WITH this lecture we begin the consideration of the " Hazards and Hardships of Finite Selfhood." The subject of the lecture is the " World of Claims and Counter-claims." Such a world is what we live in, as far as we think of ourselves as finite beings, independent, yet connected by relations of right and duty with God, and Nature, and our fellow-men. We are, then, in lawyers' phrase, " at arm's length " with them. Life, so conceived, is full of hazard and hardship ; of hazard, because these relations of right and duty do not express our real unity with God, man, and Nature, and so have a character of chance ; of hardship, because, being accidental, they are constantly breaking down, and we find ourselves always failing in our " duty " (the source of moral pessimism) and not getting our " rights " (pessimistic sense of injustice). Theism belongs in principle to such a view of the world, regarding God as a creator and governor, under

conditions which involve a future life in order to compensation and moral improvement. Such ideas involve insuperable difficulties, as may be seen from the conception
of a creator of free beings. Morality, considered as duty
to a superior being, other than ourselves, is one form
taken by the contradictions of such a world. Justice,
as a rule of apportionment of goods to individuals—a
standard for which is really impossible to find—is another.
The rules of morality and justice, thus understood, are
perpetually being broken down by our real nature, which
is religious, not merely moral, and based on the unity of
one with another, not on apportionment to individuals.
Thus there is a constant moral pessimism and sense of
injustice arising from the non-fulfilment of our mistaken
demands on God, our fellow-men, Nature, and ourselves.
Our true nature discards the notion of individual merit,
and individual claims, and the expectation of perfectly
realising the supreme will in the individual's finite will
(as "duty"). We can see the total breakdown of the
notion of claims in any enterprise conducted by persons
really unselfish and united. Claims all vanish, and the
"best" people have most to bear, and carry the burdens
of the rest. And this we feel to be right; but it involves
recognising that the rules of the world of claims do not
represent our nature as it is, and in trying to live by them
we are in a perpetual condition of hazard and hardship.

# *B.* HAZARDS AND HARDSHIPS OF FINITE SELFHOOD—*Continued*

## LECTURE VI

### PLEASURE AND PAIN

In the last lecture we considered the origin of moral
pessimism and the sense of injustice, as depending on
false expectations promoted by an inadequate view of our

nature. To-day we are to consider how, in a similar way, pleasure and pain are inevitable accidents of the limitations of our nature, along with our impulse to transcend them. It is not our object to make little of pain ; rather, in a sense, to make the most of it, by showing its connection with the worth of human souls. The root of both of them we take to be the mind's effort towards completeness ; which is attended by pleasure when so far successful, but by pain when it meets with friction and obstruction. Two things follow from this : first, pleasure and pain are not opposites, but are the same kind of experience, and its perfection must include the essence of both—obstruction, but overcome. And secondly, it is not true that pleasure corresponds to good and pain to evil, each to each, throughout life. Man is so limited that expansion towards the good is as likely to bring pain as pleasure. Yet, knowing the ground of pain, viz. the obstructedness of activity, we know its limit, and that it actually depends on life and activity, the conditions of pleasure. Thus our theory, while accepting pain as inevitable, would not admit as possible total and unmitigated misery. Still, in problems of optimism and pessimism, we should refuse to attempt judgment by quantity. Pleasure and pain are only incidents in the self-development of souls, and the success or completeness of this is the criterion of value. We see this in the place occupied by suffering in great religions, and in the necessity of accident and death. The rationale of it is that it is only in confronting the extreme of contradiction that the value of souls is universally and substantially affirmed. We see, in this way only, what values will stand the supreme test, and what will not.

## *B.* HAZARDS AND HARDSHIPS OF FINITE SELFHOOD—*Continued*

## LECTURE VII

### GOOD AND EVIL

THIS is the third of three lectures under the heading " Hazards and Hardships of Finite Selfhood," and is on the subject of " Good and Evil." Good and evil are ventures of the finite self in the same way as pleasure and pain, but differ from these by involving an attitude of the self as a whole in its desire for satisfaction. Good is an advance towards what would really satisfy the self ; evil, all that is, under given conditions, inconsistent with this. Thinking of " good " as what we ought to aim at, we tend to treat " goodness " or virtue as the only good. But this makes virtue seem too wide or good too narrow ; and the truth seems to be that the recognised virtues or duties deal with the central goods, such as the maintenance of life and society, and so are classed as morality *par excellence* ; but other kinds of order in the self, *e.g.* knowledge and artistic power, are also moralities, though not noticed as such, because more or less unessential to life (less so than we think). But as morality, thus understood, rests largely on " gifts," we see that the individual, though responsible, is yet dependent on the universe—a fact recognised in religion. Moral good—the venture of a finite being towards perfection—implies evil to be overcome. The reason is that no finite good can satisfy a creature's whole wants ; the creature therefore makes, out of the unsatisfied wants, a secondary self, hostile to the central self which agrees with humanity and society. This secondary or evil self is only evil because it conflicts with the good self, and so with its own self. Its objects of desire are, as it were, good in the wrong place—*i.e.* aims which have nothing in common but opposition to the central good self, but are not originally bad in themselves. Thus we can conceive that if readjusted in a perfect experience they could cease to conflict with good, and so could be no longer evil. And thus good and evil exhibit the venture of the finite spirit, striving to pass its limits towards perfection.

# *C.* THE STABILITY AND SECURITY OF FINITE SELFHOOD

## LECTURE VIII

### THE RELIGIOUS CONSCIOUSNESS

THE previous lectures of the present course have spoken of the finite individual, such as ourselves, with regard to his formation by the world, and the adventure of his life as an apparently separate being. The present lecture begins to point out how there comes to him, in and through those experiences, a feeling and conviction of belonging to a reality in which all that he really cares for is permanent and secure. This conviction is the same thing with recognising his own genuine nature, as a creature which is an eternal spirit revealing itself in time and space, and it is gained and verified in the very stress of hazard and hardship, which arises out of this twofold being. It asserts, therefore, the true structure of reality, and is present so far as this structure is rightly asserted through unselfish devotion to interests beyond oneself. In this wide and true sense the conviction in question is the religious consciousness, of which devoutness or worship is the essence, and of which what is called " religion " in the traditional sense is only an intensified form. In it the finite creature possesses perfection by faith and will, involving self-surrender. It is the content of the highest philosophy, but philosophy is not necessary to it; nor does it involve the assertion of any facts or doctrines referring to a future in this or another world, or to the "supernatural" in the popular sense. The stability or the security of finite selfhood is in this recognition of its own true nature, which extends over the whole adventure of life, and is reinforced by it.

# C. THE STABILITY AND SECURITY OF FINITE SELFHOOD—*Continued*

## LECTURE IX

### THE DESTINY OF THE FINITE SELF

ALL discussion of this subject presupposes for us the general principle that our self, like everything else, is here and now an element in the Absolute, and therefore the question of its continuance can only be a question of the kind or degree of its transformation in further temporal appearance (if any). There is little to say of direct reasons for anticipating one kind or degree of transformation rather than another. But there is a good deal to say in criticism of our own supposed desires for continuance, in the way of pointing out the result of attempting to reduce them to consistency with one another, or in other words, of ascertaining what they amount to if we are clear what we mean. We may find that their meaning, thus elucidated, agrees with our general convictions.

Reviewing, first, the ideas of continuance in human memories and in the effects of our actions, of Metempsychosis, and of Nirwana, we note that they are not negligible considerations, but yet that their great influence is only explicable by their acting as symbols of some more profound conviction; which we take to be that of the safeguarding of what we really care about by and in the nature of the universe.

Pursuing the question what destiny we can seriously
and self-consistently desire, we find that simple prolongation of a life like the present probably comes back to the
idea of a cycle of lives (already considered); while the
demand for a better state raises the problem of a conflict
between our personal identity and transformation towards
perfection. An analysis of T. H. Green's insistence on
personality results in the suggestion that it is rather *a*
personality than *our* personality (what is called by our
proper name) that is essential, and that there is no
repugnance against something *more* than, but only against
something *less* than, personality. What matters, it seems,
is the survival of what we really care for ; which, as we
know even from common sense, may be something beyond
and different from our present self as it stands.

# *C.* THE STABILITY AND SECURITY OF FINITE SELFHOOD—*Continued*

## LECTURE X

### THE GATES OF THE FUTURE

M. BERGSON has said that "the Gates of the Future are
wide open." Dante has alluded to the day when they
shall be shut. Both doctrines seem to make unwarranted
drafts upon the future. For one, however bad the world
may be, there is ahead an infinite real progress in which
it may grow better. For the other, there is a far-off
divine event in which a final good will be realised,
counterbalancing all evil.

To us it seems clear that a comprehensive philosophy
must satisfy both the demand for progress in the finite,
and that for an eternally realised perfection. It seems
clear that a series may be a necessary element of a whole
which can never *as such* be expressed in a series ; but that

xxxii   *ABSTRACTS OF LECTURES*

if the whole is a series and no more, perfection is by the hypothesis excluded ; and equally so, if it is laid down (a self-contradictory postulate) that at some future time the finite is in its own right to achieve and possess perfection.

In our view, the demand for an actual progress to infinity means that the finite has only half recognised its own nature ; while true self-recognition involves abandoning the pretension to possess perfection in its own right. This recognition, which is the religious attitude, is, we suggest, what really matters in the progress of finite beings, and is the main lesson to be learned from the advance of mechanical civilisation, and its failure, as such, to bring satisfaction.

The advance towards such recognition has been, we may say by way of illustration, the most important change in man's history in the past, being one with the achievement of true freedom.   It has actually arisen, in a great

# LECTURE I

## INTRODUCTORY—FINITENESS AND SELF-TRANSCENDENCE

1. IN the present course of lectures I am to speak Two points from previous lectures. of the finite self, its worth, and its destiny. In this introductory lecture I will first recur to two points in the essence of the finite, which were discussed in the previous series, and having pushed each of them a little further, I will then sketch the general argument on which we are entering to-day.

i. The finite individual soul seems naturally to Mind and externality; our view not a Dualism. present a double aspect. It looks like, on the one hand, a climax, or concentration, of the nature beneath it and the community around it, and on the other hand a spark or fragment from what is above and beyond it. It is crystallised out of the collective soul of nature or society, or it falls down from the transcendental soul of heaven or what is above humanity.[1] In both cases alike it has its share of divinity—in the one case through the suffering deity, in the other through the Olympian deity or from the stars.

[1] I am drawing both on Hegel's psychology (cf. *Principle*, p. 178) and on such ideas as are expressed in Mr. Cornford's *From Religion to Philosophy*. The two views are very noticeable in both Plato and Aristotle.

B

Both of these conceptions might illustrate our point of view. We think of the soul as, on the one hand, a nisus towards unity on the part of a world on its own level or below it; on the other hand as an element contributing to the absolute, isolated only in appearance by an impotence[1] which constitutes its finiteness.

In conjoining the essences of these descriptions I do not think that we are liable to a charge of dualism. The natural is necessary to the spiritual, and nothing is to be gained by minimising the distinction between them so long as it is clear that their difference is such as to promote a complete identity. Thus when we maintain that consciousness actually works in and through the systematic adaptation of a certain type of matter, we are not really adopting any one of the three dualistic doctrines, parallelism, interaction, epiphenomenalism.[2] It is a different thing to say that consciousness, as the universal susceptibility, appears within certain special transactions on the part of matter, when highly organised and systematised; and to say that it forms a separate and isolated entity, whether as a parallel series or as an interacting subject, or as an epiphenomenal effect which has no reaction. The point, as it appears to me, is that in all these theories consciousness is conceived on intentionally dualistic lines, as a repetition or duplication of neurosis in a different medium, or within a different attribute. Neurosis is taken as in space; and psychosis as the same thing over

[1] *Principle*, Lect VII.

[2] The phrase "akin to parallelism" appeared in one of the abstracts in *Principle* (p. xxv.), but only by comparison with interaction. Cf. *ibid.* p. 175.

again, repeated without any reason, in the form of feeling or conation or cognition. Then the psychosis may be taken as an inert concomitant, or as in causal reaction with the neurosis, or as an effect which has no reaction. But in all these conceptions the central idea is the same. The neurosis is there and complete without the psychosis. But there is a psychosis also, in relation or out of relation with the neurosis, and there is a problem about its supply of physical energy.

Nothing of this kind applies to what I was attempting to express in the previous lectures.[1] It seems to me that the fertile point of view lies in taking some neuroses—not all—as only complete in themselves by passing into a degree of psychosis. The question of duplicating a neurosis by a psychosis does not arise. There can be no problem of a special supply of energy for the psychosis. It is one thing to say that a series of psychoses reproduces in conscious form the physical events within the nervous system, raising the question of relations or no relations between the two series. It seems to me altogether a different thing to say that *e.g.* the weighing of a situation, begun in a certain balance of nervous tensions or inhibitions, has to complete itself in a conscious form, before the neural crisis can end in a motor reaction representing the logical solution. It is not repeating in another attribute what has happened in one; it is completing in a non-spatial activity what, having its source in spatial combinations, yet could not be completed by their means pure and simple. The change from

---

[1] *Principle*, p. 203.

spatial to non-spatial togetherness is, of course, inexplicable.   But empirical evidence seems to be in its favour, and, after all, externality is always for mind and not self-existent.[1]   So the question is merely how and when an externality which is the object of mind becomes a focus in which mind appears.   It plainly must happen ; and the only necessary precaution is to make no superfluous assumptions in explaining it.   On one view what happens in consciousness is an amplification of the neurosis inherent in its special nature ; on the other it is something alien and additional.   On the former line it is naturally taken as within the physiological cost of the neurosis ; on the latter as having an equivocal position outside it.[2]

What is certain, and what matters to us, is that the finite self is plainly a partial world, yet possesses within it the principle of infinity, taken in the sense of the nisus towards absolute unity and self-completion.   It is both a concentration of externality and a fragment of the Absolute.   It has the lawfulness and routine of the logical spirit, working towards totality within a fragmentary context.   The essential for philosophy is to dismiss as self-contradictory all attempts to set the creativeness of mind in opposition to its systematic law-

[1] Perhaps too little importance was attached to this in *Principle*, p. 211.

[2] Cf. Dr. Lloyd Morgan's forthcoming work on *Instinct and Experience* with reference to the different uses of the term "mechanical." It is plain that highly organised matter $a$ has a routine of its own, which is highly predictable, and $\beta$ is capable of forming systems which modify in the most elaborate way the response to stimuli. I do not think that philosophers can be bound to say whether physico-chemical laws can explain these properties. But if not, what seems to be wanted is some conception of a secondary mechanism. Cf. "Vitalism," by E. S. Russell, *Scientia*, ix. xviii. 2.

fulness. The precise laws of the externality which forms the store-house of acquisitions and adaptations for every centre of experience—and these things, as stored up, must necessarily take an external and so far non-psychical shape [1]—are not, as it seems to me, a fundamental question for philosophy.[2]

ii. The view which we have just reiterated of the reasonable spirit that works within the finite being is essentially one with our conception of creative freedom.[3] And it will repay us to pursue this subject a little further, so as to throw light on the one really plausible objection that is brought against the latter.

*" Every theory of volition determin- istic "—not true.*

*Any* theory of volition, it is urged, must give the victory to determinism. A theory, it is said, involves an explanation or rationale, and this again is enough to bring to bear the hypothetical neces- sity which belongs to science. If you can say that freedom has this or that *modus operandi*, or nature, or essential nisus or principle, then you have set up a necessity according to which it must behave. If there is anything that freedom is, then, in principle, for every case, there is something that it must do. Give it any nature you please, and that nature becomes its bondage. It does not matter *what* theory you make about it, unless it is a theory that it cannot be theorised. If you make any theory about it at all, you determine it by the principles of that theory, and then it is freedom no longer. Its

[1] Cf. *Principle*, p. 215.
[2] The pure mechanical theory has been criticised, I believe effectively, on its merits, if supposed to be more than an illustrative hypothesis. Cf. *Principle*, p. 109.
[3] *Principle*, Lect. IX.

only nature is to be new at every point, to exclude repetition,[1] to defy logic.

Now this objection appears at first sight to tell against our view with peculiar force. For we certainly have ventured to say not merely *that* mind is free and creative, but *how* it is free and creative. We are at a further stage than the current discussion of freedom and its opposite. And in saying how it is free, no doubt we should be accused, according to the view just mentioned, of subjecting it to necessity. It *must* pursue the logic of the self; it *must* work out its nisus to the whole ; it *must* struggle in some form towards self-consistency and self-realisation. It is the very thoroughness of our view that exposes it to this special attack. If we had stopped at an earlier point, and merely maintained in the abstract that mind is self-determined, we should have told much less truth, but we should have escaped this formidable difficulty.

Is there any account of volition against which this objection tells unanswerably? I think there is more than one. Any account which in affirming self-determination unduly limits the self, does tie freedom's hands by the very definition of its liberty. A psychologically Hedonist theory, an egoist theory, which considers the self in part only, an indeterminist theory, which affirms necessity through contingency, and therefore external necessity—all these in explaining freedom do really explain it away.

But the very same objection which we feel

---

[1] On the relation of intelligence to repetition see *Principle*, p. 141, with note and reference.

against these partial dogmas, as they seem to us, is widely felt against the necessity of logic, which to us is merely the same as the impulse to the whole. This hostile feeling is a remarkable fact, and bears witness beyond a doubt to the defectiveness of logical theory as well as to the perverseness of common sentiment.[1] Logical necessity is felt, and no doubt has often been represented by those who believe in it, as a something mysteriously imposed, which mind must obey perhaps unwillingly,[2] instead of being the inmost life and spiritual order of mind itself. This is merely because text-books and typical examples on the one hand have restricted it to very partial abstractions which no one recognises as the natural working of mind, while on the other hand there are moods to which all reason and coherence, even those of great art, not to speak of great philosophy, come as foreign and as a bondage.

The case against identifying freedom with the principle of reason rests on this opposition. And it amounts to a postulate that there can be no theory of a self-determining spiritual process. If it can be theorised, it cannot be self-determined; so the assumption must run. In assigning it a nature, you have assigned it a necessity; and in assigning it a necessity, you have destroyed its self-determina-

---

[1] An able writer, speaking of Parisian culture under the influence of recent philosophy, says, " Men are everywhere busy, consciously or unconsciously, lifting the jewel of human vision out of the mire of logic " (*New Age*, May 11, 1911). It sounds like an intentional caricature of the great passage in which Plato speaks of διαλεκτική as rescuing the spiritual organ of vision from the mire of sensuousness and ignorance. I do not know whether it was so meant.

[2] I owe the remark to Professor Cook Wilson. I do not for a moment suggest that he would agree with my application of it.

tion.  *Any* nature is looked at as a bondage by
contrast to all possible natures.

Now let us consider, for example, the case of
science itself—the spirit which animates the body
of the exact and natural sciences.  There has never
been a doubt that its nature and procedure can be
theoretically understood.  And yet it is a typically
free or self-organising procedure.  I do not remember to have seen the question raised whether
or no the future course of science can be predicted ;
and if not, why not ?  But plainly the answer is the
same as we gave to the same question in relation
to individual will.[1]  Its behaviour could only be
predicted by being achieved before it is achieved ;
that is, in so far as a mind could be possessed
beforehand of the endowment which enriches the
growing point of thought at every crisis, along with
the situations it will have to meet.  The course of
science itself, then, is predictable only in the same
mode and degree as that of conduct.  It is the very
type and essence of mental freedom—mind con-
structing its totality with no regard but for the
fitness of its materials.

Yet again in every step it determines itself in
accordance with a logical need.  If any advance of
science is not logically necessary, it is null and
void ; it is not an advance of science at all.  Its
structure is the type of a pure necessity without
remainder.  It theorises itself, one might say, as it
goes along.  It exists by giving the reason for
being what it is.  You cannot determine it *ab extra*
by bare logic ; that is true ; but that is only because
it is so thoroughly determined in itself.  It is not

[1] *Principle*, p. 115.

applied logic.  But it is the logical life of which logic is the theory.  Here the postulate that there can be no valid theory of a self-determining spiritual process is obviously false.

So with free-will.  We have maintained not merely that there is free-will, but that we know its nature and the way in which it seeks the whole. It is this thoroughness of the theory that exposes it to attack.  " If you can predicate anything at all of the will, it ceases to be free."  And we profess to predicate of it the inherent nature of reason—the absolute demand for totality and consistency.

For to us, on the contrary, it seems that that of which nothing can be predicated can have no interest.  There can be no continuity between its beginning and its end.  But what we care for is the completeness of what we have begun, developed in accordance with our own inherent demand. Therefore freedom for us means the nisus to the whole, the ἔρως or spirit of union, which is at once logic and love.  And its character as such we drew out in the previous lectures; and its necessity is nothing but mind acting out its own nature.  This necessity is no limitation of the self, but the very force and secret of its self-maintenance and self-expansion ; and the theory which identifies it with freedom lays on the latter *no necessity which is narrower or other than itself.*

2. We now proceed to sketch our further doctrine of the finite.  The last year's course of lectures was an attempt to familiarise ourselves with the principle of ultimate reality, and to establish it as the standard of value.  The argument on which we are entering to-day will treat of finite minds, such beings as

ourselves, and endeavour to attain some connected survey of the value and destiny that belongs to them as participants in such a universe as we have outlined.

Best under-
stood from
continuum i. If any one wishes to-day to make a study of any human being, from a primitive savage to an Athenian citizen, or from a Northerner or Southerner in the American Civil War to a London dock-labourer on strike in the twentieth century, the first thing he attempts is to place himself in the medium or atmosphere of the mind he is studying; in the collectivity to which the man belongs, and of which, in the main, his consciousness is a function. The student of philosophy should not be less thorough than the student of anthropology or of society, and indeed it is this obviously sound method which has determined the sequence of our discussions. We thus make short work of a difficulty with which we are apt to be confronted—the difficulty of understanding how the countless minds and incidents and objects scattered abroad in our everyday world can ever be raised and unified into a single experience. Who is going to bring them together? Is there a mind outside them that will achieve it? And if there is a mind that can understand them all as an aggregate, is not this just an experience of its own, which will leave them all in fact and existence what they were before?

But if we only consider how any competent thinker will to-day discuss the soul of the savage or of the citizen, we shall see how much more fertile is the idea of dissociation than that of aggregation. Perhaps, indeed, as a question of exposition I have laid even too much stress on the idea of upward transformation.[1] Dissociation and deformation, rather than unification and transformation, are the keys to the study of the finite. Ultimate reality is for our argument what the social collectivity is for the social student. If the infinite has existence only through the finite, the finite is intelligible only through the infinite. The difference, as I have said, is only one of exposition. The arguments which disclose the nature of reality are the same in essence, whether we start from the imperfect creature or from the principle of perfection. But if we retain throughout the former as our point of departure, we grant it by this custom a position of absoluteness which hampers our reasoning at every step. It is as if, after establishing the community of will, tradition, habits, and ideas throughout the social whole, we were in a further treatment to drop out all this that we had learned, and to accept the "individual" *wie er geht und steht* as if no common spiritual forces were working within him, and behind his self-contained appearance.

Thus we approach the study of finite self-conscious creatures, prepared to find in them the fragments of a vast continuum, fragments in a great measure unaware of this their inherent character, just as the unreflective citizen will believe in his own absolute independence and self-existence, as merely limited by that of others through a few external contacts. This false claim to absoluteness, with the want of recognition which is its cause, condition the whole character and being of the finite mind. It is able, as we have seen, to concentrate in itself and to represent only a limited

---

[1] Cf., however, *Principle*, pp. 383, 388.

range of externality, and in this limited range it is always inclined, just because of the limitation, to suppose its being self-complete. But yet, belonging as it does to the continuum of the whole, and unconsciously inspired by its unity, it is always passing beyond its given self in the attempt to resolve the contradictions which infect its being and obstruct its self-satisfaction. This double being *is* the nature of the finite. It is the spirit of the whole, or of ultimate reality, working in and through a limited external sphere. Its law is that of the real; its existence is the existence of an appearance. The whole of our argument, in attempting to exhibit its worth and destiny, will consist in nothing more than expanding the conception of this double nature.

Double implication of term "Appearance." ii. Before we approach the detailed discussion of the finite, it will be well to say a word on the meaning of contrasting it as relatively unreal with the absolute as real. The opposition of "appearance and reality" is familiar. I only propose to explain our attitude to it in order to avoid what I think false implications.

To "appear," or "to be apparent," has a curiously double significance. It means on the one hand to be obvious or self-evident. " It appears from the evidence"; "it was supposed to be so, but it now appears to have been otherwise." " It is plainly apparent." On the other it contains the well-known antithesis to truth or reality. " It appears to be so, but the fact is otherwise," " The sun appears to move round the earth," and so forth. Further examples are needless.

The double significance springs from this, that what "appears" is on the one hand, for whatever cause or reason, in fact selected so that it stands out and is clearly discerned, or is such as to be clearly discerned.[1]   But on the other hand, in so standing out, it is implied to be partial, to correspond to special conditions, falling within those of some whole which we accept as normal and complete.   We find both implications together in such a phrase as "make his, or its, appearance," which may be said of an actor or of an epidemic.   The person or thing, we imply, *is* somehow or somewhere over and above the appearance, but at some time or place which is noteworthy, he or it stands out and produces itself in a special manner.   Here we have no implication whatever of error or illusion.   What "makes its appearance" is really there in its appearance, and what "appears from the evidence" or what "is plainly apparent" is *as a rule* meant to be taken as an outstanding truth.

But the implication of illusion readily arises from the distinction which all these phrases contain,[2] the distinction between the conditions of such a selected or outstanding reality and those of reality as a relative or ultimate whole.   The appearance is distinguished from the reality by its selected or partial conditions contrasted with those which are relatively or absolutely complete.   And if you take the object as it is under partial conditions for the object as it is under the totality of conditions, you get the general illusory character of which all appearance as such always goes in peril; just as, if you take an

---

[1] For this qualification cf. Bradley, *Appearance*, p. 485.

[2] "Appears *from the evidence*" is after all a *special way* of standing forth.   It may be an introduction to saying "but the evidence is false," judged, *e.g.*, by the whole circumstances.

appearance under one partial set of conditions for another appearance under another equally partial set of conditions, you get the ordinary error of mistaking one everyday object for another.

This double nature of appearance, with the peril but not the necessity of total illusion, is the reason why the finite world is the world of appearances, and explains its character. It is the world of outstanding and obvious realities as particularly conditioned within the whole; while the only unconditioned real is the whole itself within which all conditions are included. Finite minds and objects, then, though appearances, are not inherently illusions. But for and as finite minds they are always in so far illusory, as it is impossible but that they should have ascribed to them and ascribe to themselves a false character of self-existence. For no finite mind can go far in grasping the conditions of any piece of reality, and this applies to itself; and yet all that is finite has working in it the nature of the whole. And therefore, as we saw in the previous course, both finite mind itself, and its appreciation of objects, are always passing beyond themselves and fluctuating up and down the scale of reality, that is, in seeing and being more or less nearly as the whole demands.

This seems to be why, so far as we can understand, if there is to be a perfect system with detail and differentiation, there must be finiteness and infinity, and why there can be no infinity without finiteness, and why all finiteness is self-contradictory when considered as self-existent (*i.e.* as apart from infinity). We shall see how and how far the finite can remedy this its inherent vice.

Thus we can already answer in general terms the irrepressible general question which lies at the root of the whole theoretical tendency towards critical censure of the universe. " If the Absolute is so perfect and so excellent, and the finite is so full of evil, surely the postulate of perfection would have required that the Absolute experience should have been real without the finite—the perfection without the imperfection." But the point just is that each—the perfect and the imperfect—has its being through and because of the other. You cannot have a perfection which is the perfection of nothing; nor a something, conditioned within a perfect system, which is perfect apart from the inclusive system that conditions it.

Thus we see the general nature and position of the finite. We see, *a*, why the finite world is one with the world of appearances; *β*, why the finite has always a double or self-transcendent nature—a reach beyond its grasp, or a content leading beyond its existence; *γ*, what is the difference between appearance and illusion; and *δ*, why we hold it a blunder to say that the existence of the finite world is an illusion, or, in other words, that the finite world does not exist.[1] As regards this last point, it should be observed that it is just the finite world which does exist. Successive appearance in space and time is what existence means. Reality, indeed, that is to say, the total of stability or satisfactoriness, is not merely existence, though it includes the existing world, and without it would not be itself.

3. Now we are able to explain the general course of our consideration of finite self-conscious beings. The three main characters of Finite Mind.

[1] On this question I am following Bradley, *Appearance*, 377 ff.

Division of the lectures.

From what has been said above there follow three main characteristics of finite mind, which cover, as I believe, the central paradox and interest attaching to the problem of their value and destiny. And the present course of lectures will be subdivided in accordance with these three main considerations.

Finite Mind shaped by Universe, and yet shapes itself.

i. After an introductory discussion of the conditions of finite personality, I shall speak of the moulding—the temporal genesis—of finite mind, and the method of its formation into a representative member of the world. Soul-making, it will be suggested, is the leading function of the finite universe. Souls are cast and moulded by the externality of nature, and of other finite souls. But again, the soul which is being moulded contains an active principle, the spirit of the whole, and what we call its being moulded is but one side of the self-determination by which it transforms its partial world, eliciting the significance of externality. Under the heading of Soul-formation we must in the end consider the miracle of will. And both sides of the process will be portrayed as, in principle, severe. To recast yourself, or to be recast by circumstances, must alike involve pain and conflict. Even the search for pleasures is a search for burdens.[1]

The Life of Finite Mind an Adventure.

ii. Secondly, it will be necessary to deal at some length with what may be summed up in one word as the adventurousness of finite mind—the hazards and hardships which attend upon it, not incidentally, but inherently. This essential character of its life is rooted in the double nature of the finite, and reveals itself in its self-maintenance as in its formation. Being double-natured, it is torn between its

[1] George Meredith.

existence and its self-transcendence. For no finite existence as such can maintain itself in the whole without incurring contradiction, and the spirit of the whole, present in the finite mind, is bound in its intolerance of all contradiction to contradict its own existence. Thus the self, in the striving to complete itself, will break in pieces every partial form of its own crystallised being, will welcome the chapter of accidents, and clothe itself in conflict and adventure. It will shatter the world of legal or relational morality, and find its path beset by the chances of pleasure and pain, and haunted by the inherent conflict between good and evil. Now these conflicting terms and correlatives, and their opposition, are essential to finiteness, and unending. But being imputed to ultimate reality they give rise to the illusory demand for a real advance and temporal victory of the good, in which it shall annihilate the opposite which is necessary to its own being.

iii. Thirdly, then, it will be our endeavour to explain the true lesson of finiteness, in the genuine stability and security of the finite self by which alone the vice of finiteness can be cured. This will be identified with the self-recognition of the self in the religious consciousness, through which the only genuine transcendence of the finite is accepted by the finite, with a less or greater degree of reflective awareness. This recognition will be represented as arising and maintaining itself throughout, and actually by means of, the pangs of self-formation and the adventurousness of finite living, and as apprehending the security of the self by union with the whole actually in proportion to the reach of self-transcendence which, while amplifying it in the

*Stability and security of the self.*

C

direction of the whole, still shows it the weakness and worthlessness of finite existence *per se*. We shall reject all ideas of a future happiness and compensation, here or hereafter, by mere overbalancing of pain with pleasure; but we shall endeavour to show, as a theoretical truth, which also to some minds may be an aid and inspiration, that the troubles and adventures of the finite arise from one and the same source as its value; that is, from the impossibility of its finding peace otherwise than as offering itself to the whole.

From and throughout these three characteristics, which amount simply to a theoretical expansion of the nature of finiteness, we shall be able to read off in general terms what it most interests us to know of the finite individual in his worth and destiny. Strictly speaking, these two are one, and one also with his genesis, his adventure, and his security. For his value lies in his contribution as offered to the absolute, and his destiny, in its essential features, must be the detail of the self-recognition on which this offering depends. Self-recognition, as we shall see, is another phrase for the religious consciousness, and to feel where his value lies is the same thing with offering up his attainment to the whole by faith and worship, supported by and included within an ultimate sense of inviolable unity,[1] on which all sanity and coherence, say, in the religious consciousness, ultimately reposes.

Now it is plain that the essence of the self-recognition lies in grasping the nature of that self-trans-

---

[1] The sense of the absolute, as permeating and holding together opposites like good and evil, or human and divine. See p. 310, below.

cendence which is the source at once of all relative
attainment, and of the perpetual dissatisfaction which
shatters the given ; and lives in self-genesis, in progress, and in trouble and adventure.   Thus, as we
shall attempt to make clear throughout our discussion, the troubles and adventures of the finite
creature have the same root as its value, for both
are inherent in the spirit that seeks the whole.
And, moreover, these very troubles and adventures
are instrumental, through shattering the given, to
that very awareness or self-recognition in which the
nature of the self-transcendence stands revealed.
Therefore, while maintaining that positive attainment in the structure and coherence of finite life is
not by any means indifferent, as a symbol and embodiment of perfection, we find it hard to suppose that,
as appears to be the general view even among serious
thinkers, the destiny of the finite being holds for
him, as finite, here or hereafter, a release, complete
in principle, from all such trouble and adventure.
His value lies in the destiny through which he
recognises his true being.

What, then, are we to say of actual finite attainment and achievement in so far as it implies no
such self-recognition as we have spoken of, but is
claimed by the finite being for itself in a mood of
false absoluteness and self-satisfaction ?   We must
make allowance for the ـ naïve mood of implicit
religion ; that is, of sincere and unselfish self-transcendence in the work of life, in devotion to aims and
causes beyond our immediate selves.   And it may
well be doubted whether there can be genuine
attainment in which a religious consciousness, of this
kind at least, is not operative.   But, in principle,

and to make provision for the case as stated, we must say, I think, that the mood of false absoluteness and self-satisfaction in finite attainment is of sin, and the value of what is so attained, though contributory to the Absolute, is not offered to it, and therefore does not attach to its author, just in so far as he claims it for his own.   The mood in question corresponds especially to-day to the aberrations of a mechanical civilisation, which has lost in the accumulation of means that recognition of the end which is one with the true sense of the nature of the finite.   And it seems a view in accordance with the essential demand of finite destiny that the main condition and result of progress will be more and more thoroughly to learn the lesson of the vanity of such accumulations ; except under the condition of that very controlling appreciation of their vanity in and for themselves, which the evils of civilisation will—as part of the adventure of the finite—continue to teach.   And it is obvious that such a sense of the vanity of instruments in themselves must become the condition of their better direction and of a higher spirit permeating society—in a word, of the very self-recognition which at first sight the labyrinth of civilisation seems calculated to destroy,[1] but which in truth, perhaps, it alone can ultimately teach.

Does self-recognition demand reflective theory?

4. What we have thus arrived at as the essence of the religious consciousness, and the open secret of stability and security in the finite self, we have called by the intentionally general name of self-

---

[1] " L'homme sociable, toujours hors de lui, ne sait que vivre dans l'opinion des autres," Rousseau, *Discours sur l'origine de l'inégalité parmi les hommes.*   Cf. Tarde, *Les Lois de l'Imitation,* 83, " L'état social, comme l'état hypnotique, n'est qu'une forme de rêve."

recognition.   For recognition is a word which does not prejudge the question whether reflective theory need or need not be present.   And here there are two considerations to be very emphatically insisted on.

i. The first is that the peculiar nature of self-recognition as we have here arrived at it, and shall expand it in the later lectures, certainly helps us to appreciate the fundamental importance which many of the greatest minds have attached to what they have considered as the highest kind of knowledge. It is true, of course, that in everyday moods what we call knowledge may fall apart from what we call practice.   You may think of a thing without doing it, and you may do it without thinking about it.   To think about paying your debts is not the same thing as to pay them.[1]   But all this becomes comparatively unimportant when you touch the higher grades of knowledge, when deeper experience has enlarged the self, with amplified intellectual vision as an element in the result.   And it is an experience of this kind, however feebly I may succeed in expressing it, which one must bring with him if he is to understand Spinoza's third genus of cognition, or Plato's knowledge of the good, or Hegel's notion of philosophy as religion in a higher form.[2]   Let us consider for a moment the first of these three doctrines, which is probably, when taken literally in its author's phraseology, the hardest to appreciate.   When we are told that there is a mode of knowledge named "intuitive," by which we immediately perceive the

*It is akin to the subject-matter of philosophy. Compare Spinoza's third kind of cognition.*

---

[1] Green's *Prolegomena*, sect. 150.
[2] I am not assenting to Hegel's expressions in this sense.   But I think that their meaning is more easy to see and to justify than some good critics have admitted.

essential dependence of all things, and especially of our own minds, upon God, in the same way as we immediately perceive that 6 is the fourth proportional to 1, 2, 3, all sorts of logical criticisms spring into our thoughts. The notion suggested is unfamiliar, and may even appear uninteresting. It brings to mind demonstrations which we have read of, to the effect that God must exist as a Creator and First Cause. We have probably thought them unconvincing, and more than that, in no way directed to anything that would interest us if it were established by a line of proof. No doubt proofs of that description might endow us with a fine orthodoxy if we wanted to theorise about a Creator, or moral governor of the world by rewards and punishments, or guarantor of poetic justice by his treatment of Dives and Lazarus in a future life. But for our straightforward reason and humanity to-day, the sheer existence of this external person has but little interest. What we care for is the religious consciousness, and such a proof has but little to do with it. And a metaphysical theory which warrants us in an intuition of his existence we take to mean some kind of unreasonable appeal to an uncritical conviction. It seems clear that we cannot assert external fact conformable to an idea in our minds, and on the ground of that idea, just as that idea stands.[1] And the suggestion is *prima facie* an intellectual offence to us.

But when any one has entered even a little into

---

[1] See Bradley, *Appearance*, ed. 2, p. 394 ff. We have to remember that every idea qualifies reality in some way. But to know *how* it qualifies it, we must criticise the idea, *i.e.* subject it to the demand of the whole system. And that is fatal to asserting particular external existence merely because we think of it.

Spinoza's mind,[1] he sees that here such criticism does not apply. And this is all the plainer, I hope, if we bring with us some such considerations as we are pursuing and mean to pursue.

Because what we then find is, that what he tells us in his curious formal idiom, which to my mind recalls always Dante in its union of austerity and passion—what he is telling us is what we shall have been brought to see when we have made the most complete analysis of experience in our power. And perhaps it might be said on the whole that we can never understand great writers at all, unless to some extent we thus go to meet them with relevant demands which we have seriously felt. Spinoza is telling us, then, what we in our inarticulate fashion have tried, and shall further try to exhibit, that if we carefully consider our experience at its fullest, with our relation to nature and society (or rather *in* them), we must come in essence to what we have set out under the name of self-recognition. The reason is that this amounts to nothing but a logical account of what we find that we have actually done and relied on, not by any means in superstition and inward fantasy, but, on the contrary, in as far as we have made our own any strenuous endeavour in knowledge or practice, and any serious experience of life and love. I am not to argue the matter here by anticipation, but that is what I hope to exhibit through the whole scheme of our present course. It is with that object that I shall draw out, as I have outlined our plan, the conditions of finite self-

---

[1] Fortunately there is now excellent help available for the English student in the works of Joachim, Duff, and Hales White (translation), and Sir F. Pollock's well-known volume.

conscious being, first in its temporal formation, next in the whole adventure of its life, and, lastly, in the security which pervades them all—what in Spinoza's language is "peace." It is true, no doubt, as we are told on good authority,[1] that "the intuitive knowledge of the human mind in its essence and in its individual dependence on God, if it is to answer to the ideal of intuitive science (*i.e.* Spinoza's third kind of cognition), presupposes a complete apprehension of the total nature of the universe, and a complete scientific demonstration of the coherence and inner articulation of all its properties." But this need not alarm us. We should see the truth better if we had fuller experience, but the perception in question, if we have eyes to see it, is in all the experience we possess. And to learn to see it there is not dispensing with logical proof, but presupposes, as Spinoza profoundly implies, the method of science throughout. And logic fully recognises that this is so,[2] and therefore we can understand how our experience of self-recognition is really what the greatest men appeal to when they say that the best of all knowledge is a higher form of the religious consciousness. It has been well shown [3] that, in the demonstrations which I referred to, the underlying consideration is the experience in which the soul becomes aware of its own full nature, an experience to which the formal shape of the argument does less than justice. It is not a proof of something external, as that Cæsar was murdered on the Ides of March. It is

---

[1] Joachim, *A Study of the Ethics of Spinoza*, p. 185.

[2] For the conclusion of inference is always the premises seen in a new light as a new whole. See especially E. Caird on Anselm's argument for the being of God. Cf. also my *Essentials*, p. 137, and *Logic*, ii. 1 ff.      [3] Caird, *op. cit.*

a recognition of what we are, and the fullest nature of proof—of systematic necessity—is present in it.

ii. On the other hand, we shall maintain with equal emphasis that the religious consciousness, at least in an implicit form, is necessarily present throughout finite self-conscious life, if not even more widely. By an "implicit" form I mean a form in which the characteristic structure can be recognised by the observer and identified by theory, though the subject of the consciousness in question might never think of himself as religious. The general structure of finite mind is, as we have maintained throughout,[1] that of an element which finds itself in its other. We take as an obvious instance the satisfaction of desire. The finite being transcends itself in the endeavour to fulfil itself, and, in transcending itself, relatively, and in some degree, reaches out towards the whole. This general structure gives us the outline of all finite consciousness in respect of its attitude to its world, and we want nothing more to furnish the general and abstract clue to what we mean by the religious consciousness.

*[margin: But religious consciousness is co-extensive with finite self-consciousness.]*

For it will appear that we have the essence of religion wherever certain characteristics are ascribed with a certain intensity by the finite subject to the object with which in his self-transcendence—in thought and will—he unites himself.[2] Wherever, in a word, we have devoutness, devotedness, devotion, we have the primary feature of religion. When we are told of Sir Andrew Aguecheek, "He is a

---

[1] See *Principle*, Lect. VI.
[2] Is it necessary to quote the famous lines ?—

> Who sweeps a room as to thy laws
> Makes that, and the action, fine.
> GEORGE HERBERT.

coward, a devout coward, religious in it," it is, I suppose, the bitterest of bitter jests. His comfortable self, we are to understand, safe and unharmed, is the object before which his whole being is prostrate, identified with it in will and hope. The same bitter irony has been more seriously used,[1] and if we made a catena of the language of teachers and preachers in dealing with the whole subject of "idols," we should find it hard to draw the line between what was not religion at all and false religion, or between false and undeveloped religion. But these matters of nomenclature belong rather to curiosity than to theory. When you come to a serious and complete devoutness or devotion, in which the whole man feels himself worthless apart from the object to which he goes out in will and conviction, it must be something at least capable of being regarded as good, and the attitude towards it cannot be denied to be religious. Even Sir Andrew must have had adoration for other things than his own safety; that is, I suppose, why the bitter jest is only a jest after all.

Here, then, we find the primary principle of religion, in devotion and worship, such that in them the self not merely as in all action passes beyond itself, but consciously and intentionally rejects itself as worthless, because of the supreme value which it attaches to the object with which it desires and affirms its union.

The point I am desirous to insist on at the

---

[1] "Whose god is their belly, whose glory is in their shame, who mind earthly things." So we hear of people making money, ambition, a human being, the "world," their god or "idol." Idol implies, I suppose, false god. But the difference is hardly one of kind.

present stage amounts then to this. In religion in the widest sense, at whatever point of intensity and conviction we hold that the name may properly begin to be applied, what we have is just a glowing intensification of the ordinary attitude of the finite being in inherent and normal self-transcendence. It now not merely wants, as in desire, an object which will give it satisfaction, but it sees the essence of things so entirely in this object as to prostrate itself before its excellence and power — spiritual power or lovableness it may well be, for nothing is commoner than such prostration before what are the weak things of the world according to any standard of secular force.

Therefore I shall uphold the general position that religion, so far from being confined to or dependent on the insight considered in the previous section, is, as one might say, the normal attitude of the healthy finite mind, and exists whenever its always present structure is operative with a certain degree of emphasis or intensity—that is, when the mind cares for anything else very much more than for its given self. And this I believe that it usually does. And it is even difficult to think that something like the religious attitude may not be predicated of some among the lower animals in a restricted but fairly genuine sense.[1]

It follows from this general view, as we have anticipated, and as I shall maintain throughout, that the stability and security of the finite self is not restricted to the higher orders of consciousness, or to the explicit apprehension of what is traditionally called religious truth. But it extends wherever and

[1] See p. 236, below.

however a genuine devoutness and loyalty, before which the given self seems a little thing and lightly to be sacrificed for the chosen transcendent good, is found to be the ruling passion of a finite mind. The adventurousness and trouble of the finite self, so far from being hostile to this principle, are, as will be observed, its actual proof and embodiment. It is the very fire of self-transcendence for a good whole-heartedly believed in that in the main brings these pains and adventures to pass. Stability and security are begotten in the very torrent and whirlwind of passion. It is not necessary that a mind so partici-pant in the greatness of life should know the meaning of such terms and formulæ as we are using. It is a question of faith and conduct, not of theory and explanation. And we should find if we examined the detail that the stability and security here in question belong, at the very least, as frequently and as genuinely to the humble as to those whose opportunities might entitle them to share the aspirations of Dante himself. And such an attitude, we shall further argue, must have an immense reaction on society the more it is realised, and the winning of such an attitude through the negative experiences of mechanical progress seems likely to be our main hope for advance in the future.

Conclu-sion ; Spinoza cited on behalf of this universality of religion.

5. To express the simplicity and potential universality of the attitude in question, which con-sists in the sincere devotedness of ordinary people to the aims and affections which make the world go round, I will close this introductory lecture by quoting a passage from Spinoza, the manliness of which is always a refreshment to my mind. Yet, before reading it, I would say that in part it has a

certain malice of expression with which I do not sympathise; in other words, it neglects, as I think, the fact that utterances of popular religion, which appear to identify it with very material hopes and fears, are largely due to mere inarticulateness, and fail to express the spiritual meaning which really underlies them. Though, on the other hand, I feel sure that the materialism is not without an evil reaction upon the idea which it seeks to convey. The bearing of the quotation is, that without the "third kind of cognition," and without supernatural expectations, the essence of religion is normal to finite mind, and runs through the whole of life.

"The primary and sole foundation of virtue or of the proper conduct of life is our own profit.[1] But in order to determine what reason prescribes as profitable, we had no regard to the eternity of the mind, which we did not recognise till we came to the Fifth Part. Therefore, although we were at that time ignorant that the mind is eternal, we considered as of primary importance those things which we have shown are related to strength of mind and generosity; and therefore, even if we were now ignorant of the eternity of the mind, we shall consider those commands of reason as of primary importance."

Scholium—"the creed of the multitude seems to be different from this; for most persons seem to believe that they are free in so far as it is allowed them to obey their lusts, and that they give up a portion of their rights, in so far as they are bound

---

[1] Cf. iv. 37. "The good which every one who follows after virtue seeks for himself he will desire for other men; and his desire on their behalf will be greater in proportion as he has a greater knowledge of God."

to live according to the commands of divine law.
Piety, therefore, and religion, and absolutely all
those things which are related to greatness of soul,
they believe to be burdens which they hope to be
able to lay aside after death ; hoping also to receive
some reward for their bondage, that is to say, for
their piety and religion.  It is not merely this
hope, however, but also and chiefly fear of dreadful
punishments after death, by which they are induced
to live according to the commands of divine law,
that is to say, so far as their feebleness and impotent
minds will permit, and if this hope and fear were
not present to them, but if they, on the contrary,
believed that minds perish with the body, and
that there is no prolongation of life for miserable
creatures exhausted with the burden of their own
piety, they would return to ways of their own liking ;
they would prefer to let everything be controlled
by their own passions, and to obey fortune rather
than themselves."

"This seems to me as absurd as if a man, because
he does not believe that he will be able to feed his
body with good food to all eternity, should desire
to satiate himself with poisonous and deadly drugs;
or if, because he sees that the mind is not eternal
or immortal,[1] he should therefore prefer to be made
to live without reason—absurdities so great that
they scarcely deserve to be repeated."  We may
read the thesis as the conclusion—"Even if we
did not know that our mind is eternal, we should
still consider as of primary importance Piety and

---

[1] Spinoza does not refer to a future life in our sense, but to
oneness with God.  There can be religion without the speculative
consciousness of this.

Religion, and absolutely everything which in the 4th Part we have seen to be related to strength of mind and generosity."[1]   Life, on the whole, we shall maintain, justifies Spinoza's own doctrine; what he imputes to the multitude does not represent them fairly, but is the outcome of a false tradition.

[1] *Ethics*, v. 41, Hales White's translation.

# LECTURE II

## PERSONAL FEELING AND THE DISTINCTNESS OF PERSONS

Feeling and the exclusiveness of personality.

1. THE stronghold of an irrational personalism is in the importance attached to personal feeling and to personal initiative, according to a false and minimising interpretation of these most actual experiences. In a lecture of the previous course[1] we have discussed the true nature of personal initiative, and we will now corroborate our doctrine by pointing out what personal feeling means and where its value resides, and by discussing the nature and limitations of the distinction between one person and another.

It is freely admitted that in cognition the self is universal. It goes out into a world which is beyond its own given being, and what it meets there it holds in common with other selves, and in holding it ceases to be a self-contained and repellent unit. This objective character is apt even to be proclaimed a defect and a loss of individuality,[2] owing to a vicious logic of the abstract, and a failure to apprehend the relation of immediate to mediate experience. In conation and initiative the

---

[1] *Principle*, Lect. IX.

[2] Ward, *Naturalism*, ii. 134, 163, and elsewhere.

same universal character, though its presence is not
to be denied, is more apt to be disregarded ; and
though the social and rational character of the
world of purpose is constantly insisted on, yet we
find that spontaneity and activity are emphasised
as special features which are needed to vindicate
the personal self as an exclusive entity, simply living
out a nature of its own.   Our criticism of this attitude was offered in the chapter just referred to, and
what we now propose to discuss is the strongest
support of exclusive personality, the experience of
personal feeling.

But how, it may be asked at starting, can such
an experience conceivably be exploited in the sense
we deprecate ?   Is it not clear, according to the old
Idealist doctrine, that there are two principal manifestations of self-consciousness or the self in the
other, love and thinking, and that the essence of
what makes a finite being participate in the universal
is as evident in either of these forms as in the other ?

In the end this question will prove unanswerable.   Personal feeling is the last thing really to
furnish an argument in favour of an exclusive and
repellent personality.   But it is currently held to
do so, and there are reasons for the opinion.

i. The main point, which might be held to settle The dis-
the question in a sense adverse to our view, is the tinctness of
*de facto* distinctness of immediate experience in experience.
different finite centres.   I can have your knowledge;
I can take a share in your act or purpose ; but your
sensation [1] or your pain, or your love and hate, as

---

[1] I will grant that this is here to mean the act of apprehension,
in order to avoid the controversy about the psychical character of
sense-data, which is here irrelevant.

D

the directly experienced quality of your mind, that
I can never possess in my own.    And it is precisely
this impossibility, we are told, in which individuality
consists.[1]    We shall have to return to the value of
this distinctness below.    But we are concerned at
present with the *prima facie* suggestion which it
furnishes to the effect that feeling, which is in form
immediate, must be of the nature of an inner unity,
something in which the self is at home with itself,
and does not issue out into a content uniting it with
others and with the world.

The "bodily" nature of the cœnæsthesia.

ii. This conception is confirmed by the well-
known analysis of the sense of self-identity into a
mass of feeling continuous in quality, and changing
more slowly than the succession of ideas and perceptions.    Here, it may be said, we have our particular and distinctive self actually constituted by the
peculiar quality of our feeling.    It is this which is
essentially private to us, and it is its privateness
which keeps us ourselves and prevents us from
becoming somebody else.    Whether or no we
accept the somatic theory of emotion, it is plain
that much of the strength of feeling is closely connected with bodily "resonance"; and in this way
the distinctness of the body, as one natural object
among others, is prayed in aid of the distinctness
of the soul or self, through the medium of feeling
as essentially bodily.    It is our feeling, it would
seem, that makes and keeps us what we are.    As
purely cognitive or as effectively conative, apart
from the peculiar quality of our conative interest
which depends on the privacy of feeling, we might
be anybody.

[1] Ward, *op. cit.* ii. 167.

iii. And against the argument from the *de facto*  The alleged non-distinctness of pleasure.
community of feeling and interest, as *e.g.* from the
alleged acceptance of pleasure and pain as common
possessions,[1] it would be pointed out that in feeling
as such there can at any rate be no sense of this
community. There has been no dissociation, and
there can be no sense of union. Granting for the
sake of argument that a child is pleased with pleasure,[2] wherever and however it is suggested to him,
yet it cannot be said that what he is pleased with
is the pleasure of others. The whole point is that
he is at a stage in which "self and others" have
as yet acquired no meaning for him. It is one thing
to say that the soul may in a certain phase be in a
oneness of feeling with what surrounds it—may not
distinguish the love and brightness or the anger
and gloom of its surroundings from what it feels
within itself—and another to say that when the self
is fully formed it can recognise a unity with the
world and with other selves, and yet not transcend
the limits of immediate feeling. When the unity
of feeling is unbroken and continuous, there is,
properly speaking, no distinction of selves. The
other person's love or pleasure, pain or anger, would
be one's own, just as a brightening of the sunshine
seems an immediate change within one's private
mood. I suppose a dog's anger when his master
is threatened might be something of this kind. He
does not know that he is unselfish.

This is what would be urged against denying
the privateness and intimacy of feeling on the

---

[1] Professor Taylor on Cornelius, *Problem of Conduct*, p. 118;
Bradley on Sidgwick, *Ethical Studies*, p. 117.
[2] Professor Taylor, *l.c.*

ground of its undistinguishing unity in undeveloped phases of the self, or previous to the self's emergence.[1]

Sentiment-<br>alism of<br>the inner<br>life.

iv. And thus the door is opened to the full pathos and bathos of sentimentalism. When the self is most itself it is most alone. " Not e'en the dearest heart and next our own——" To realise our individuality is to absorb ourselves in our exclusiveness. The dim recesses of incommunicable feeling are the true shrine of our selfhood. What really matter are our conscious states as states of a conscious being,[2] our inner life as a series of moods and emotions ; the heightened self-awareness, the transparency of the warp and woof of our psychophysical being, which accompanies the sensitiveness of a disintegrating body and mind.[3] Death is for every man a lonely agony, and life, it would appear, is not much better.[4]

The<br>fallacies<br>involved<br>in the<br>above<br>contention.

2. All this sentimental commonplace, as summed up in the last paragraph, is being utilised to-day in favour of a very common type of error, the confusion of form with content, aggravated by a certain special type of fallacy.

---

[1] For illustrations of such a condition as a fact, cf. Cornford, *From Religion to Philosophy*, p. 77.

[2] I do not suggest that this conception as employed by Dr. McTaggart has the implication of absorption in the exclusive self which I here ascribe to it. On the other hand, I am strongly of opinion that the stress laid on states of consciousness as such (cf. *Principle*, p. 302) must logically go to reinforce a vicious individualism or even an infra-individualism.

[3] Amiel's *Journal Intime*, April 28, 1871.

[4] James, *Varieties of Religious Experience*, p. 163 : " Every individual existence goes out in a lonely spasm of helpless agony " ; and see *Pragmatism*, p. 28 ff. : " A fine example of revolt against the very shallow optimism," etc. Contrast Haldane, *Pathway to Reality*, ii. 214, and R. L. Nettleship, *Remains*, lvi. : " Don't bother about death ; it doesn't count."

We will say a word on each of these two points, and then consider the true nature of personal feeling at its worst and best.

i. It is an old story that feeling is immediate experience, and, simply as such, does not admit of being shared or communicated, or of referring to an object beyond it. This is the formal character of feeling. It is what a being capable of experience simply *is* in his experience, and *prima facie* it has no meaning or reference or suggestion beyond itself. Such, for example, is a very simple pleasure or pain or organic sensation. Pleasure may no doubt produce persistence in a behaviour, and pain an effort after relief; but these already imply contents closely united with the feeling, while exhibiting the tendency of all contents to go beyond themselves. As feeling, however, the pleasure or pain simply are ; they tell us nothing beyond themselves, have no meaning, and suggest no object or idea.

The confusion of form and content in interpretation of feeling.

This is the characteristic of feeling which the votary of exclusive personality transforms into ultimate privateness and incommunicability. It is in principle the old story of subjectivism. Because a state is my state, therefore it is nothing more. And with feeling the conclusion is more plausible than with action or perception. For, as we have seen, feeling may be very blank, very empty of content. It may approach very nearly to "pure being."

But it has to be remembered that all the wealth of our world has an immediate aspect, and both can and must pass through the form of feeling. We feel all that makes a difference to us ; and in principle, as we have seen, there is nothing that

does not.[1]   Thus the pure privacy and incommunicability of feeling as such is superseded in all
possible degrees by the self - transcendence and
universality of the contents with which it is unified.
And as these contents[2] are constituents of our
individuality, the conception that individuality or
personality has its centre in the exclusiveness of
feeling neglects the essential feature of individuality
or personality itself.   It has an aspect of distinct
unsharable immediacy ; but in substance, in stuff
and content, it is universal, communicable, expansive.

The con-<br>fusion of<br>impersonal<br>feeling with<br>exclusive<br>feeling.   ii. The special fallacy, which draws in an important truth to aid the prejudice of exclusiveness,
lies in a confusion between the impersonal and
therefore non - altruistic interest and that which
seems to be exclusive or particular ; between the
non-social which is supra-social (in the literal sense
of the term social in which it implies direct belonging to a plurality) and the repellently self-centred
or particular.[3]

It is true that very much of the content which
makes the stuff and solidity of our individual and
personal being is not directly social in its reference.
It has nothing immediately to do with social grouping, social welfare, the moulding of social relations,
or the enjoyment arising from them.   In religion[4]
many have held themselves to be alone with God ;
and in the same way the love of solitude, and the

---

[1] *Principle*, p. 300.

[2] Cf. Stout, *Fundamental Points in Theory of Knowledge* (St.
Andrews Publications), p. 7.   He speaks of "objects as meant," in
term of the distinction of Inhalt and Gegenstand.   I had not this in
view.   It is the content of the objects that determines their identity.

[3] See the author's *Philosophical Theory of the State*, Introduction
to ed. 2.

[4] As Dr. McTaggart rightly insists. .

strongest repulsion to given social pluralities and arrangements, often accompanies the deepest experience in the life of nature, in science, art, speculation.

Now the point is that all these contents, *prima facie* non-social, are nevertheless universal, and organs of self-transcendence. They are more universal, that is, they are more deeply intertwined and interfused with the affairs of man and the laws and meanings of nature, than the social plurality itself, so far as it merely claims consideration on the score of the number of human beings it includes. Hence, as is continually the case, there is apt to be a confusion between the maximum and the minimum of experience. The man who has merged his world in God is mistaken, and perhaps mistakes himself, for one who has never risen out of himself to communicate with the world at all. The artist and the philosopher, whose enthusiasm goes out to all order and intelligence, may, as against a given social group, rank as types of the unsocial and the recluse.

If we were able to analyse the grounds on which individuality is equated with exclusive and incommunicable feeling, we should find that nearly all which are plausible rest on this error of identification. All feeling that is not explicitly altruistic is set down to the credit of exclusive and unsharable immediacy. And it is rightly seen that the deepest phases of individuality—those in which the man is most of what he has the capacity for being—may fall in different degrees under this category. And therefore it seems plausible to say that the shrine and centre of personality lies in self-contained unsharable feeling. And the misapprehension thus engendered reacts detrimentally on the conceptions of speculative thought, of beauty,[1] and of religion.

Personal feeling at its worst and best.

3. Having spoken thus generally of the sources of error, we will go on to consider some cases of personal feeling at its worst and at its best.

In the bad sense as negative.

i. In ordinary parlance, " personal " feelings, "personal" interests, "personalities," like "self-consciousness," indicate something bad. Why is this? The controversialist in contrast with the thinker,[2] Plato tells us, is always talking about persons (περὶ ἀνθρώπων). He argues for victory and not for truth. Thus truth would commonly be called an "impersonal" end, and "personality" would be taken in a sense opposed to such "impersonal" ends. This is the root of the feature we are observing. A person is his own object; but what he is worth depends on what there is in him. At his minimum he is almost mere exclusiveness and antagonism. At his maximum he is one with the greatest and widest forms of life.[3] " Personal feeling " and "personalities," in the bad sense, belong to the person at his minimum, when he is for himself mainly a feeling of repulsion against others—when his distinctness, so valued to-day, may seem to be at its highest point. The same is true, of course, about self-consciousness in the colloquial sense. In order to be thus negative, one must no doubt be identified with something positive, and we have seen the nature of the self-feeling which is the condition *sine qua non* of the awareness of a self. It may be that persons normally

---

[1] Cf. Tennyson's " Palace of Art." Perhaps its conclusion is intended to point this moral.          [2] *Rep.* 500 B.

[3] Hegel, *Philosophie des Rechts*, sect. 34 ff.

attain to the wider self through the experience of antagonism, like Benedick and Beatrice, or master and slave in Hegel's account of recognitive self-consciousness.[1]     But to remain at this phase, or to revive it in contrast with the wider self when achieved in principle, is to remain at or return to a lower level.   That is why "mere personal feeling" and "mere personalities" are terms of censure, though personal affection, personal loyalty, the influence of personality, may indicate some of the best things in life.   The criterion is our old one, individuality or participation in the real.   We instinctively judge by the comprehensiveness and harmony of the experience which, in making himself his object, the person takes as his object.   This helps us to understand how the value of personal feeling, though it may rightly be found in features contrasted with what passes as altruism, is never-theless opposed in principle to absorption in the private self.   The typical forms of the sense of isolation, it has been said,[2] are fear and desire, that is, as I understand, unsatisfied desire or discontent. The character of personal feeling in its discon-nectedness or exclusiveness inevitably gravitates towards such negative attitudes.   This is in principle the nature of self-absorbed personality.

ii. We can throw light on the transformation which personal feeling undergoes as its content becomes objective by considering the nature of objective emotion, or, in other words, the relation of feeling to expression.

*As transformed by a universal content; objective emotion; tragic fear.*

The essential point is that feeling, being the

---

[1] *Encycl.* sect. 430 ff.
[2] Nettleship, *Remains*, i. 82.

difference which experiences make to us, is not separable from and prior to the ideal content which as we say is its expression. Though formal and immediate on one side, yet, through the matter of which it is the reaction upon our life, it obtains a meaning and a vehicle. And with this meaning and vehicle it, the feeling, the difference made to us by the content, the emotion towards or from an object, the pleasure or pain, necessarily takes on new characteristics. The pleasure in the contemplation or creation of beauty, for instance, we are told, so far from being like everyday pleasures, private, casual, incommunicable, is essentially social,[1] necessary, communicable. A feeling which is to be objectified in art must take on a certain permanence and determinateness. You cannot embody in objective form what has no detail, no organisation or articulation, in a word, no universality. I have illustrated this in a previous writing [2] by the dignity of utterance which a great passion or a great sorrow will sometimes confer upon a common man, raising him for the moment to the level of words and actions which no one who has witnessed them can forget, and from which all that is trivial has been refined away as by fire. The greatest of great feeling can only be embodied in great constructive works; it is not antagonistic but proportional to rationality of expression. " In any art, the more artistic the work is, the more form is there, *i.e.* the more measurable, definable, calculable, is it—the

---

[1] It must be remembered that the attitudes which are supra-social are by that fact social, and more. Beauty certainly addresses the universal mind ; but it is not every man or every group that has enough of the universal mind to care about it.

[2] *Mind,* 9, N.S. p. 153.

more rational or intellectual.  Yet, on the other hand, everybody since the world began has associated with art strength of feeling and unconsciousness of effort. A great piece of music can be taken to pieces like a clock ; a great poem, compared with any other piece of language, is intensely artificial ; yet the amount of feeling which they represent is stupendous when compared with the song of a bird or a simple story. And this relation of feeling and intellect seems to hold good both of the artist and of his public.  Nobody doubts that artists are more emotional than ordinary men ; nobody ought to doubt that they apply more intellect than ordinary men.  And as to the audience . . . if you go to art to get your own feeling reproduced, you find it useless and flat, just because mere feeling cannot find expression, and your feeling must be at any rate potentially endowed with form before you can be emotionally receptive of real form." [1]

The idea that for truth and depth of emotion you must go to the naïve and undeveloped soul is a fallacy of the type which opposes spiritual depth to spiritual expansion.  Or it is like thinking that for originality you must go to the ignorant ; like the mother who, believing her boy to have musical genius, forbade him to study the great masters, for fear his originality should be impaired.

Feeling, then, in order to be capable of utterance in determinate form, must take on an objective character.  It must cease to be a blank intensity ; it must gather substance from ideas. [2]

And in thus acquiring objectivity it must change

---

[1] Nettleship, *Remains*, i. 61.
[2] Including, of course, for this purpose, perceptions.

its reference to self, or modify the self to which it refers.   An instance that has often been worked out is the relation of tragic fear to actual and selfish terror.   Tragic fear is mediated by a representation which appeals to humanity in its heights and depths. It is no longer personal terror, though akin to it. It has become impersonal, or if we like super-personal, from the sheer necessity of being uttered in a shape which can make determinate and persist-ent appeal to the general mind.[1]   It has passed from a shrinking before personal disaster to a sense of what is inevitable but triumphant in the contradic-tions of human destiny.   And in all this, as we have seen, the personal emotion is not minimised but maximised.   The attainment of individuality is not less, but greater.   The self-absorbed personality, determined mainly by negations, is not the true nor self-evident, but is only the lower obvious personality.

"Active" emotion more than "passive" emotion.

iii. It is all-important for a right estimate of personal feeling to grasp the full bearing of Spinoza's teaching, that nothing can be done as a consequence of a "passive" emotion which cannot be done, and better done, from a desire arising out of reason, an emotion in which we are "active." The point is this.   It is the common prejudice to conceive that we are in a moral and emotional loss if we succeed in determining our personal feeling and desires by distinct and comprehensive ideas, instead of by stimuli impinging upon us casually and *ab extra*.   In Spinoza's language this is to become active instead of passive ; because to be passive is to react to stimuli, the nature and conditions of

---

[1] Author's *History of Aesthetic*, p. 236 ff.

which are for the most part unknown and so external to us ; to act, or to be guided by reason, is to follow an idea in which the occasion of our desire is distinctly exhibited in its total nature and conditions as a fulfilment of our being. And what Spinoza desires to affirm is that in the latter mode of our nature, contrary to popular prejudice, we have gain without loss. In such action, the only " action " proper, our temper is that of high courage (*fortitudo*), which takes the shape of lofty-minded-ness (*animositas*) in our own affairs, and nobility (*generositas*) in those of others. In this " active " mood we are simply living at a higher pitch ; and nothing that is positive in our nature is there omitted or fails to find its completion.[1] Spinoza purposely insists on the strong instance of pity or commiseration, obviously in order to challenge commonplace ideas at a decisive point. Pity he takes as a passive emotion, that is to say, as arising from an external stimulus little understood. To be guided by it is not to act, that is, not to let our full being exercise its powers, but to suffer—we may say, to react in contrast to acting. In such reaction we do things of which we subsequently repent, and everything good or positive in such a feeling, everything that it can do, which we should seriously wish to be done, survives in the mood of " nobility " ; that is to say, in the truly active emotion in which we follow an adequate idea of the whole occasion which solicits our efforts, and therefore may be said to exert our*selves*.[2]

[1] *Ethics*, iii. 1, 59 S. iv. 59.

[2] *Ethics*, iv. 50. It follows from Spinoza's doctrine of activity that every emotion is bad so far as painful. Considering what he means by activity, I cannot but think that this view requires modifica-

Thus by the escape from negative self-absorption — from the mood of fear and discontented desire — nothing is lost to personality; and it becomes a verbal question whether personality is considered the most appropriate expression for what survives. All that we contemplated was to make it clear that the nature of feeling, though it gives a *prima facie* support to the exclusive and repellent idea of personality, does not in the end sustain it. In feeling, as in all else, the increase and deepening of individuality is a progress towards unity with the whole. Self-distinction, no doubt, becomes more marked; but true self-distinction is hostile to self-absorption. It is a distinction in identity, and is the reverse of exclusiveness, or of brooding over a blank indeterminate content.

The distinctness of persons. 4. I will push this argument further by offering some suggestions on the nature of the distinction between finite selves or persons, with the view of helping to break down the unreflecting attitude which accepts them as fundamentally isolated self-subsistent beings, externally connected, but not in any genuine sense parts of the same stuff, or elements in the same spirit. The question is a difficult one, and I only aim at paving the way for a freer consideration of it than appears to be currently held permissible. I am not suggesting that our ordinary way of distinguishing between persons and between their respective responsibilities is practically wrong. I am suggesting that we are too little alive to diversity within one soul (or if we

tion. I feel sure that in the highest activity there is a meeting-point of what we call pain and pleasure. The reason is that this activity of the whole involves a degree of immediate apparent loss by transmutation of inferior states. See *Principle*, p. 389.

prefer another form of speech, to diversity of souls within one body), and to unity between more than one.   We construe their nature, as it seems to me, far too much on the analogy of hard nuclei, impenetrable by one another.[1]

i. No one would attempt to overthrow what we have called the formal distinctness of selves or souls.   This consists in the impossibility that one finite centre of experience should possess, as its own immediate experience, the immediate experience of another.   The rule seems to be that one self cannot get to the experience of another self except by communication through the external world.   And if it could experience directly the inner states of another, still I suppose they would come to it either as its own states, or as states of the other; but, *ex hypothesi*, not immediately as both.[2]

It may be that this formal distinctness depends on what are at bottom unessential limitations—limitations, I mean, not grounded on the nature of mind, such as the fact of differences of vital feeling, depending as a rule on the belonging of different selves to different bodies.   But none the less, if the hindrance against two selves having the same immediate experience could be removed, the result involved would be the coalescence of the two selves into one.[3]

Formal distinctness a difference of quality of content.

---

[1] Cf. Hegel, *Wiss. der Logik*, iii. 318.  "Atomic subjectivity" in its highest form at the same time finds its own objectivity in another.

[2] Of course when we come to speak of the organised content of a common self, all this is different.   But then the experiences are primarily mediate, though they may have become practically immediate.   Take, *e.g.*, the common feeling between people who sing together.

[3] We see this, I suppose, when what keeps selves apart is not difference of bodies but bodily difference, *i.e.* in cases of multiple

This inevitable distinctness in immediate experience has been appealed to as containing the essence of individuality. And it is, no doubt, inevitable on the assumption that there are to be finite individuals, because, if the centres ceased to have the different bases of feeling that keep them from merging, they would be one without distinction even if in different bodies, and there would be no two experiences to blend ; while if the bases persist, the experiences will be formed round different centres even if in the same body, and therefore the experience of the one centre could not be experienced as that of the other. But this ground of distinction, though, as I say, inevitable, is a very different thing from the inexplicable and fundamental foreignness which common opinion postulates as between different persons. It merely comes to this, that they are organisations of content, which a difference of quality, generally though not strictly[1] dependent on belonging to different bodies, prevents from being wholly blended.

Type of material distinctness —selves in a social whole.

ii. This formal distinctness of selves, then, I agree that no one would attempt to overthrow, although in the light of the considerations just advanced its nature seems not wholly fundamental nor irreducible. But when we come to consider the principle of identity and diversity of content, the inevitable results very seriously modify the view of distinctness which we have founded on the form of experience. We may analyse the cases of

personality. The one self, it would seem, may possess immediately the experiences of the other (*Dissociation of a Personality*), but if it ceased to possess them differently, I presume the selves in question could not but coalesce.

[1] Because it can exist within the same body.

individuals who are members of the same social
whole.   The results would apply to individuals
having any kind of identical content, which must be
the case with all finite beings as far as in the same
world.

*a.* It is natural to assume for theoretical purposes
that diversity of content coincides with diversity of
form, and therefore that every finite mind is distinguished by the matter with which it is occupied,
as well as possessed of an experience formally
incommunicable.   This simplification was strongly
insisted on by Plato in the *Republic*, and as an
ideal may perhaps be justified by the ultimate
theory of membership in the universe.   Every
separate mind was to be distinguished by unique-
ness of function or service no less than by formal
selfhood ; the ideal was for the individual to render
a contribution to the whole, the content of which
could not be precisely repeated in any other individual.   And this ideal seems naturally to follow
from the very conception of diversity in an orderly
universe ; but the application of it in the case of
given finite minds must be much less simple than
Plato's State suggested.

Taking it, however, as if it were *prima facie*
roughly true, that every different finite individual
has a single and separate work or function in
society, which corroborates, so to speak, the distinctness of his formal selfhood, we are still in
presence of a thorough-going identity in diversity.
The nature of a whole in which an identity is
subserved by differences is a familiar topic ; and
the present writer has often pointed out that in
membership of such a whole a thorough-going

*Supposing distinct contents, still, identity in difference.*

E

connection and adaptation of different minds is presupposed, which is wholly hidden from us by our tendency to construe minds as similar things, repeating one another like human bodies. If minds were visible, as bodies are, the writer has argued elsewhere, they would not look like similar repeated units, but rather each would appear as a member of a mechanism pointing beyond itself and unintelligible apart from others—one like a wheel, another like a piston, and a third, perhaps, like steam. Here, then, in the simplest conceivable case of coincidence between the material and the formal limitation of the self, we find thorough-going identity of diverse selves as parts of a single whole; and that in rational beings, with more or less thinking awareness of the whole to which they contribute. The extreme case of matter coincident with form would have been in the mechanical instinct which we may perhaps ascribe to a working ant or bee, sufficing for its function, but devoid of all awareness of the whole to which its function is adapted, in short, of all self-transcendence.[1] This we must not ascribe to any rational being, but obviously there are all grades of self-transcendence, from something analogous to blind instinct, up to a higher limit which we can hardly venture to fix.

β. But when we look at the facts of individual range and endowment, we find a more puzzling and

---

[1] Some such limitation of the self to a single function, on the analogy of the insect, Mr. Wells seems to ascribe to his inhabitants of the moon, although he manages to make a highly organised intelligence instrumental to it. One is led to suspect him of a pessimistic view of progress, due to a failure in appreciating the relation of individual to universal for an intelligent being—to treating it, that is, as if the two terms varied inversely and not directly as each other.

complex state of things.   Compared with the logical The suppo-
and certain lines of the social structure—and the sition un-<br>true; self-
same is true with any of the fabrics constituted by contents do<br>not corro-
achievements of the human mind—the content borate<br>formal dis-
possessed by individuals is in the highest degree tinctness.
arbitrary and contingent.   As we said at the close
of the preceding paragraph, so far from being
coincident with a logically distinguishable function
or factor of any structure, a finite mind may conjoin
in itself an indefinite number of capacities, and may
overlap, repeat, or comprehend, in any degree, the
material experiences of other minds.[1]   Assuming
that a single experience cannot have as its organ
more than a single body—it is impossible to assume
conversely that a single body cannot be organic to
more than a single experience—there are certain
practical or *de facto* limitations on the material
range of that experience.   Such is the fact that a
single body cannot be in two places at once, or
the difference of the sexes, or fluctuating physical
disabilities like liability to fatigue or the shortness
of life.   But all this is not, so to speak, a matter of
principle, but rather a variable fact.   And within
these limitations the comprehensiveness of content
which goes to form a single mind may vary from
what just suffices for a function like that of an ant,
to a self which possesses the framework and very
much of the detail of an entire society; which
could, that is to say, but for bodily limitations, do
the whole work of a large proportion of the social
whole, and indeed, in spite of bodily limitations, in
many cases does a very large share of it.   There can
be no doubt that it is often literally true that one man

[1] Cf. *Principle*, p. 116, note.

does the work which it would take a dozen other men to do.  His range overlaps and comprehends that of a possible dozen others, not merely in general awareness of the common plan and purpose, but in actual possession of the stuff of detailed capacity and activity.

And at our present standpoint, on the ground of identical content and not of formal exclusiveness, the proposition admitted above, that two or more bodies cannot be organic to a single centre of experience, again seems only to state a matter of fact and of degree.  A single thought and purpose, it is obvious, constantly is seen to animate a plurality of bodies, and although communication of experience, it would seem, is always indirect, yet how far in practice and by habituation the very quality of the experience in our body may be identified with that in another, so that a self may learn to rely on both experiences as equally its own, seems again a matter of degree.  We learn to rely on others as on ourselves,[1] not merely in faith and judgment, but in perception of sound and colour, of heat and cold, of what is right and necessary in morals, of what is pleasant or unpleasant in society, in houses and furniture, in food and drink.  I believe that there is no limit of principle, but only a fluctuating practical limit, to the unity of experience in different bodies,[2]

---

[1] Cf. Bradley, *Presuppositions of Critical History.*

[2] It may be said, " You are confusing reliance on judgment with identical quality of feeling."  But surely the quality of feeling is an important factor in the basis of judgment, and can therefore in some degree be inferred from it.  If A and B not only like and dislike the same things, but apply the same critical epithets to them in all scales and combinations, surely it is a fair inference that the special tune or flavour of their selves is much the same.  A great deal of the paradox about reliance on authority as opposed to reason vanishes

as there seems to be hardly any to the diversity of experience in one.

If this is so, we have made an important point. The immediate or formal diversity of finite centres is not at all thoroughly sustained and reinforced by a coincident diversity of the matter of their experience, but, on the contrary, is in some degree reacted on and impaired by its identity. The convenience of the decentralisation of finite experience, as it actually exists, will be touched upon below.

γ. What we find, then, in the social fabric or, as was said above, in any of the great structures in which spiritual achievement takes shape, *e.g.* knowledge, fine art, historical continuity of the constitutional system of a country, forms a very curious commentary on our ordinary conception of the isolated and exclusive self. We find a building, whose lines and masses are plainly, though defectively, continuous and coherent; a solid erection, or, if we prefer another metaphor, a determinate organic structure. Now this structure is composed of, or, if we prefer it, is the conjoint self-expression of, finite selves or minds, but the range of these several components respectively does not, as we are apt to assume, coincide with that of any objectively distinguishable features of the fabric. Their contents overlap in the most irregular and fluctuating way ; the welds between them are everywhere, as their contributions fade indistinguishably into one another, and some of the beams, or branches, may be composed of thousands of coincident, or partially coin-

*Selves comprehend the continuous content of their worlds in different degrees.*

---

in sight of this principle. I accept another person's testimony or opinion, because I have, on the whole, seen reason to accept the unity of his mind with mine.

cident, self-contents; some, and these perhaps more important, of only one or two.   Thus the limitations of every self bear no relation to anything but its power; there is nothing, except the practical conditions of disability, to prevent any one self from expanding indefinitely over this content; nothing, again, to guarantee its self-maintenance at the range it has acquired.   The continuous lines and articulated framework of the solid fabric—if Science is suspected of wilful impersonality, take the growth of the Christian religion, or the development of Greek Tragedy to its maturity[1]—are the certain, intelligible, and necessary thing; how far this or that finite self may extend along them is not a matter of principle,[2] except that it is by this extension that the self enters upon the general life and its own individuality.

δ.  We may venture to say then that we see a use and convenience in this system of finite experiences, arbitrarily, to our thinking, bounded and discriminated, which the facts exhibit as our world.   But also we are aware of its precarious and superficial nature; and indications are not wanting of something deeper and more real which underlies it.

As regards the first point, two extreme cases will illustrate our meaning.  Suppose that in any social whole, or in any continuous structure such as

---

[1] Which Aristotle speaks of, and no one surely has doubted the appropriateness of his language, as if it were a living being following its law, "it reached its maturity, and then stopped growing.

[2] And is, *de facto*, almost always a matter of extreme uncertainty. How easy it is to place a writing or a picture in its "school"; how hard to determine its authorship!   Suppose, what is quite arguable, that the parable of the good Samaritan is not an utterance of Christ. What does it matter so long as it is a part of Christianity?

knowledge, or national development, or morality, every single mind that contributed to it was equally conversant with, and capable in, all parts of its content; just as, in any actual group, there will be some men who could easily take the place of some others as well as their own, covering and comprehending their entire capacity.[1]   In this we should see, I suppose, a certain waste of power, as we are inclined to see it in the case taken as an illustration. For it would mean that there were large numbers of consciousnesses completely coincident for the greater proportion of their range, and although the difference of centering might convey a slight degree of diversity to the common stuff as apprehended by each, we should hardly see what was to be gained by so immense a multiplication of contents all but identical.   We should be inclined to say, " If it is to be possible for single minds to cover practically the whole world of experience, it would seem more natural to strike out their formal differences, and let them fall together into one,[2] one single mind ranging through and comprising all those varieties of bodily and mental experience."   How far such a single mind would have to include contradictions wholly unparalleled by anything which happens in finite minds as we know them would be an instructive subject of speculation.[3]   How far can a single finite mind as we know it include differences of

[1] Perhaps I ought to say that I cannot suppose this to be truly and ultimately so, or even quite precisely so in our experience.   But it is near enough to the fact to make a sound illustration.

[2] If we suppose them perfected without tending to fall into one, the argument would point to a plurality of absolutes of identical content, which seems absurd.

[3] It has been suggested above that it is not certain that plurality of bodies is an *absolute* bar to oneness of mind.

cœnæsthesia, simultaneous contrasts of pleasure and pain, and incompatible sensations in different bodies, antagonistic views and interests, without ruin to its unity?

All these obstacles to unity the single mind which we have imagined would have to include or to transform ; and whatever may be the suggestions of speculation, the fact that under these conditions no such single mind is found to come into being, seems to show that in these difficulties, without further ultimate hypothesis, we have a sufficient account of the existence of finite centres ; the account, namely, that finiteness lies in powerless- ness,[1] and that minds as we know them, though they vary extraordinarily in the range of diversity they can hold together, yet all find their limits at some point or other within our world.

Or we may think of the opposite case which seems, as we saw, to be realised in some animal minds. Suppose our intelligence were adequate to certain functions necessary to the whole, but were limited by them, and in no degree transcended them, nor overlapped the content of other minds. In that case it is plain that the total groups would exist *de facto* as working systems, identities in difference, just as a commonwealth of bees or ants exists, but we, as finite beings, should not possess the spiritual unity which comes from the overlapping of intelligences ; that is, from their apprehending

[1] Why powerlessness, it may be asked ? We only try to suggest that the finiteness of mind goes very simply with all the facts of its apparent conditions of manifestation, of which the expanding variety of its degree of finiteness is one. We thus need no hypothesis about the ultimate self-existence of minds, but only to suppose that mind comes in degrees according to some conditions.

a common purpose and extending[1] over the range
of a continuous content in all possible varieties of
degree.    In fact, the hypothesis seems, strictly
speaking, self-contradictory for an intelligent being,
though its conditions are fulfilled under the reign
of instinct.    You cannot have, it would seem, an
intelligence adequate to a function, which does not
in some degree transcend it.    Every function needs
variation and adaptation, and you cannot vary and
adapt it, by intelligence as opposed to instinct,
unless in some degree you have an idea of the lives
you impinge upon and the needs you have to
supply.[2]

So then, in the condition of our finite experience as determined by our diversity and powerlessness, we seem to have what is natural and necessary
for a world at once varied and continuous.    We
have experiences differently centred and variously
overlapping, but not completely repeating each
other, kept apart by distinctions of quality, but contributing, and knowing that they contribute, to the
same great structures and progressions.    These are
built up out of them, and live in their life, but do
not coincide, each to each, in the importance and
articulation of their distinct components, with the

[1] It may be objected that in thus harping on the extent of the
self we are confusing direct and indirect experience—what we are
and what we know.    But if the objects of thought and action determine our identity (see above, p. 38), the determination of many selves
by the same objects, involving kinship of direct experience, is enough
to constitute the range and overlapping which we describe.

[2] Every one must have noted the extraordinary acuteness with
which a good railway porter or cabman, or indeed any capable
tradesman, divines the sort of person you are and the sort of thing
you want him to do for you.    I do not take instances from the
great professions, because these are intellectual *ab initio*.

importance and articulation of the minds which are their constituents. Minds have different centres, and each extends to limits round its own centre fixed apparently by chance, *i.e.* by its measure of power. And this is all we want for everyday life, and a completer unity of finite minds in one would bring us at once to a partial Absolute, and necessitate the transformation of the differences which now suffice to keep finite minds distinct.

But again we are aware of the precarious and superficial nature of their distinctnesses; and at every point we meet with indications that something deeper and more real underlies them. Let us think again of Hume's argument as applied by Sidgwick.[1] If we are not one with others, why should we be one with ourselves? Why, for example, if "conscious states as such" are what have ultimate value, should what we call my past and future self have an interest for my present self which the other selves have not? No doubt, so far as my self is recognised as a unity, it is held together at least by a continuous cœnæsthesia, which does not however exclude, at remote periods in the course of its continuity, enormous contrasts of quality, fully as great as those which at any moment separate me from others. *De facto* bodily identity, as we have seen, is not enough to guarantee the unity of a self, and the continuity of feeling, which is its basis, may be strained to any extent, and may break down altogether. There is no doubt that my past self, even when recognised as continuous with my present, may be alien and hostile to me, a part of the not self;[2] while the self

[1] *Principle*, p. 308.
[2] *Appearance and Reality*, p. 256.

of another may be in all respects but that of immediate experience, a part of myself.

If now we reverse this argument, as Sidgwick's application of it suggests,[1] and make our interest in ourself as a whole the premiss and datum, we shall find ourselves carried not merely up to but beyond our distinct personality. With the one exception, of the thread of cœnæsthesia, compatible with any degree of hostility and foreignness, there is no ground of unity with our past and future selves which would not equally carry us to unity and fellowship with others and with the world. Our certainty of their existence is in both cases inferential, and on the same line of inference ; both are alike distinct from and incompatible with my present self; both are cemented to it by the same stuff and material of unity, language, ideas, purposes, contents of communicable feeling ; and, as we have seen, the other may in these ways be far more closely knit with me than is my previous self.

What it comes to, then, is this—what we call individual finite beings are kept apart by differences of quality of feeling, and also by the reciprocal shortcomings of the content of which they are composed. These differences of quality, and these shortcomings, are often held to be the secret of individuality, the secret by which I am myself and not another, because I have not his immediate feeling, and do not comprehend his capacities within mine. But this is plainly not so. On the contrary, when I most fall short of others, and am most in discord of feeling quality with them, I am also least

---

[1] *Principle, l.c.* Cf. *Appearance and Reality* on solipsism, p. 254.

myself. Yet, on the other hand, we have seen, I cannot be fused with them, as they are, in a single mind. Our discrepant bodily existences are seemingly enough to prevent it. It would seem futile that a plurality of minds should cover the same ground ; and impossible for a single mind to include all the differences of a multitude of bodies— centres of pleasure and pain—scattered in time and space.

And yet my unity with myself, and with other selves and the world, is unmistakably indicated. Wherever we are strong, we come together. Our distinctnesses are indifferent to the real spiritual unities, which transcend us at every point.

The solution is obvious. We do not experience ourselves as we really are. So far from being an inaccurate assumption, this principle is inevitable, and is accepted and applied throughout life. No one ever dreams of acting on the assumption that a mind is for itself, especially at a given moment of time, all that it is in itself. If this were the truth, we should never argue nor persuade. For to argue or to persuade is to rely on factors of the mind which are at the moment not explicit, and which we desire to evoke into explicitness. We could never appeal from Philip drunk to Philip sober, nor even point out that there and then the man was " not himself." It is wholly irrelevant to urge [1] that the being of a mind is not affected by others' experience of it. The point lies, as we said to begin with, in the difference between it and itself; between what

[1] With Mr. Rashdall, *Personal Idealism*, p. 382. We always recognise that others know us in some ways better than we do ourselves.

it is for it, and what it is for itself. A finite mind that should possess itself completely is something to which no experience of ours at all approaches, and which is ultimately a contradiction in terms.

Why we are finite, or, as Plato would phrase it, in a great measure asleep, is the same question as why the finite world exists. And we cannot expect to give a reason for the scheme of the universe. But we can dimly see, perhaps, that the arrangement is connected with the representative character which we ascribed to our finite being. Our imperfection enables us better to stand for something which is to have its due stress and emphasis in the whole, but no more than its due.

Is our perfection, the self-consistent individuality which we set before us, at an opposite pole, then, from the function we discharge in the universe? If imperfection is our function, that we may stand for the parts, is it consistent to say that our true nature is in the coherence and perfection of the whole? Are we not then saying, with vulgar mysticism, that our actual being is a vice, and our perfection is, not to be? The only sense in which we can assent to this will appear when we come to speak of the religious consciousness. Our grasp of perfection involves that as finite we are nothing in our own right. But we hold to the conviction, which we too rarely, if at all, find suggested in Plato, that the soul's earthly investiture contributes to its perfection, and is not a sheer loss and evil. We want him to maintain, what he unquestionably hints, that to a full experience of the "Forms" the terrestrial world is indispensable no less than the pre-natal vision.

Our answer, then, in general seems to lie in

the direction of regarding finite mind as the embodied tension between imperfection and perfection ; the effort by which a complex or content finds its place in the Absolute, and the Absolute transfigures, in embodying, a content. Finite mind, we might argue, does for the externality of the universe what the absolute does for finite mind. If we ask again, " But why this gradation ? " we could only appeal to something like Leibniz's principle of continuity. It would seem as if the greatest variety or richness of being—the giving everything a chance—might result in this way. But at least we see that separateness is not an ultimate character of the individual, but is a phase of being akin to externality, and tending to disappear in so far as true individuality prevails.

# *A.* THE MOULDING OF SOULS

## LECTURE III

### NATURAL AND SOCIAL SELECTION

1. I will begin with a passage [1] from one of Keats's The "Vale of Soul-making." letters, as a suitable introduction to the five following lectures, which deal with the "Moulding of Souls" and the consequent "Hazards and Hardships of Finite Selfhood."

"The whole appears to resolve into this—that man is originally a poor forked creature, subject to the same mischances as the beasts of the forest, destined to hardships and disquietude of some kind or other. If he improves by degrees his bodily accommodations and comforts, at each stage, at each ascent, there are waiting for him a fresh set of annoyances—he is mortal, and there is still a heaven with its stars above his head. The most interesting question that can come before us is, how far by the persevering endeavours of a seldom-appearing Socrates mankind may be made happy? I can imagine such happiness carried to an extreme, but what must it end in? Death—and who could in such a case bear with death? The whole troubles of life, which are now frittered away

---

[1] Cited from Professor A. C. Bradley, *Oxford Lectures*, p. 222.

in a series of years, would then be accumulated for the last days of a being who, instead of hailing its approach, would leave this world as Eve left Paradise. But in truth I do not at all believe in this sort of perfectibility. The nature of the world will not admit of it—the inhabitants of the world will correspond to itself. Let the fish philosophise the ice away from the rivers in winter-time, and they shall be at continual play in the tepid delight of summer. Look at the Poles, and at the sands of Africa—whirlpools and volcanoes. Let men exterminate them, and I will say that they may arrive at earthly happiness. The point at which man may arrive is as far as the parallel state in inanimate nature, and no further. For instance, suppose a rose to have sensation ; it blooms one beautiful morning ; it enjoys itself; but then comes a cold wind, a hot sun. It cannot escape it, it cannot destroy its annoyances—they are as native to the world as itself. No more can man be happy in spite [of] the worldly elements which will prey upon his nature."

" The common cognomen of this world among the misguided and superstitious is 'a vale of tears,' from which we are to be redeemed by a certain arbitrary interposition of God and taken to Heaven. What a little circumscribed straitened notion ! Call the world if you please ' The vale of Soul-making.' Then you will find out the use of the world (I am now speaking in the highest terms for human nature, admitting it to be immortal, which I will here take for granted for the purpose of showing a thought which has struck me concerning it). I say ' Soul - making ' — Soul as distinguished from an

Intelligence.[1]    There may be intelligences or sparks of the divinity in millions, but they are not Souls till they acquire identities, till each one is personally itself.    Intelligences are atoms of perception—they know and they see and they are pure; in short, they are God.    How then are Souls to be made? How then are these sparks which are God to have identity given them—so as even to possess a bliss peculiar to each one by individual existence? How but by the medium of a world like this? This point I sincerely wish to consider, because I think it a grander system of salvation than the Christian religion—or rather it is a system of Spirit-creation.    This is effected by three grand materials acting thus one upon the other for a series of years. These three materials are the *Intelligence*, the *human heart* (as distinguished from intelligence or mind), and the World or elemental space suited for the proper action of *Mind* and *Heart* on each other for the purpose of forming the *Soul* or *Intelligence destined to possess the sense of Identity*.    I can scarcely express what I but dimly perceive—and yet I think I perceive it.    That you may judge the more clearly I will put it in the most homely form possible.    I will call the world a School instituted for the purpose of teaching little children to read.    I will call the *human heart* the horn-book read in that school, and I will call the *Child able to read* the *Soul* made from that School and its horn-book.    Do you not see how necessary a world of pains and troubles is to school an Intelligence and make it a Soul?    A place where the heart must

[1] Keats's use of the word is suggested, probably, by Milton's "pure intelligence of heaven" [Professor Bradley's note].

F

feel and suffer in a thousand diverse ways.    Not merely is the Heart a horn-book, it is the Mind's Bible, it is the Mind's experience, it is the text from which the Mind or Intelligence sucks its identity. As various as the lives of men are, so various become their Souls ; and thus does God make individual beings, Souls, identical Souls, of the sparks of his own essence.    This appears to me a faint sketch of a system of salvation which does not offend our reason and humanity."

2. It is only on the general spirit of this remarkable passage that I desire to insist.    The idea of antecedent "sparks of intelligence" appears superfluous.    We gain nothing, it seems to us, by antedating results which are found to depend for their revelation on conditions heterogeneous to them. Their manifestation in connection with certain arrangements of the Universe can be understood just as well apart from pre-existence as presupposing it.    If we admit change and difference at all, there is no reason for cutting down their continuity into similarity.

This is one point in Keats's idea which we need not emphasise.    And a second is the implication that terrestrial life is at any rate best regarded as a state of preparation for something quite different in the future.[1]    The only ground for rejecting this view appears to me to be that there is no cogent reason for accepting it.    If it is urged as a matter of principle or necessity (which I do not gather to be Keats's position), that implies something false.

---

[1] Dr. McTaggart strongly suggests an analogous idea in arguing for his contention that not society but the individual is the end of social life.    He also uses the comparison of a school (*Hegelian Cosmology*, sect. 195).

If not, it merely amounts to an attractive imagination of something larger and happier than what we have; something of the same kind, but arbitrarily supposed as extended.

It is important to avoid the false implication of the former view, viz. that the moulding of a soul or self or centre of experience which is to pass away and give place to centres discontinuous with it, cannot be conceived as worth while, as contributing to a whole of value.[1] Suppose that the souls or centres are the energies or elements of self-expression in which the Absolute consists, and which are dissociated from themselves and from each other by the condition of finiteness; by the fact, that is, that in and for finite experience they are all, as Plato would say, more than half asleep, and unable to grasp their unity with themselves or with others. How can the precise degree of their apparent completeness and duration be a matter of principle not merely affecting, but at a certain point destroying, their relation to the value of the whole?

At best, it is admitted and maintained, they are finite and imperfect, and we have seen reason to think that it is through their imperfection, through the emphasis and tension which it confers, that the Absolute is enabled to affirm itself in all its thorough-going self-utterance. It is plainly false to say that we must at least be real and enduring in the light in which we are aware of ourselves. We know ourselves, one is tempted to say, much less than others know us. The indi-

[1] Cf. Varisco's interpretation of the conservation of values. *Principle*, p. 21.

viduality which we divine falls outside our actual experienced being.[1]

And what about minds obviously so imperfect that few, though these few great philosophers, have claimed survival for them, and, applying a method of degrees, it seems hardly possible to claim it throughout—the minds, for example, of the lower animals?[2] We have already denied that their transitoriness, if admitted, destroys their contribution to value ; and we insist on this denial.

There is no reason for denying value to minds or spirits, such as cannot, as they stand, reasonably claim survival. Perhaps, indeed, as they stand, no spirits can.[3] It is enough that in them, in their power and impotence, their achievements and limitations, the absolute which acts in them sustains and expresses its being like the poet's mind in a drama.

Perhaps it is just in the making that souls have

---

[1] This doctrine, familiar in Idealism, has also the empirical support of M. Bergson. " Nous ne nous tenons jamais tout entiers. Notre sentiment de la durée, je veux dire la coïncidence de notre moi avec lui-même, admit des degrés." *E.C.* p. 218. How else should the aspiration have become a commonplace ?—

> " Oh, wad some power the giftie gie us
> To see ourselves as others see us."

[2] The question of the Feeble-minded, not to speak of the deaths of infants, offers a difficulty to the metaphysic of orthodoxy. We all wish them well, so to speak ; we would welcome a justified theory which should promise them a perfected soul in the future (see Mr. Feeble-Mind in the *Pilgrim's Progress*, and Jeremy Taylor's beautiful prayer "to be used on behalf of Fools or Changelings "). But can we justify it ? Must we not rather believe that, having contributed their spark of conflict and struggle and dim feeling to the Absolute, they survive only in the whole, and are not connected, each to each, with any special continuance of centres of experience ?

[3] We must understand clearly what we are speaking of. We must not confuse the supposed future life—a survival in time of a finite being—with "absorption " into the Absolute. We are in the Absolute now and always. The question of survival is merely one of a certain mode of appearance.

their value. What would be the interest of a drama in which the characters had ceased to develop? The Absolute, we believe, is a tension. And we have seen how easy and natural it is, only pre-supposing the dissociation in which finiteness con-sists, for its elements to be shown in the most various and many-sided dispersion, isolated in appearance by way of subjective centering, by way of extension and of succession.[1]

3. We are then to make the attempt to show in Sketch of outline how the Absolute, seen from our side as a remaining world of appearances, keeps throwing its content into living focuses, vortices, worlds ; and how these again, each transmuting towards unity its realm of externality and eliciting its values, initiate and sustain the character in which, under the special emphasis lent by the special dissociation operative at that point, the absolute appears.

We are to speak of the Moulding of souls and selves. First, under the present heading of Natural and Social Selection, we shall discuss the genesis and evolution of Life and Mind in its general and, so to speak, logical aspect. Secondly, we shall describe the transmutation of environment through the focussing of its total significance, which is actually the same genesis considered as embodying the activity of the spiritual being in which a sphere of externality "comes alive." This discussion we shall conduct under the title of "The miracle of Will," insisting on the true inwardness of circum-stance and character.

---

[1] In the question of the reality of time, much hinges on the popular prejudice that the mind is not dissociated in succession. But, as we have seen, the fact is quite undoubtedly otherwise. Plainly the mind as given in time is not itself.

After this, it will be natural and necessary to speak of the incidents of finiteness which may be called the "Hazards and Hardships of Selfhood," comprehending the subjects of evil and failure, from physical pain and apparent waste in the lower creation, to the sense of wrong and of despair which finds its climax in the provinces of morality and justice. Our general view will breathe the spirit of the saying χαλεπὰ τὰ καλά.[1] Judging from our highest experience, the whole itself, if it is to command our reverence, must possess, though in due subordination, a quality analogous to what we mean by austerity or sublimity. It is not then to be supposed that its spirit, as it perceives and feels itself in the detail of partial worlds, should be free from pain and conflict and the sense of an overwhelming burden. If it were so free, we know very well that the heights and depths of the spiritual nature would remain unscaled and unsounded, and the Absolute would fall short of what in fact the humblest Christian habitually achieves.[2] But here we are anticipating, and must not be led on to deal with the subject.

When we have done our best with these incidents of selfhood—in limiting cases perhaps insuperably difficult, but in principle, as we hold, not beyond being grasped as conditions of value by the sense and courage of men of goodwill—we shall begin to draw to a conclusion. It will remain to gather

---

[1] Schrecklich ist es, deiner Wahrheit
Sterbliches Gefäss zu seyn.—SCHILLER'S *Cassandra.*

[2] I may appeal to Mr. Bertrand Russell's splendid estimate of Tragedy in *The Free Man's Worship*, which coincides in some degree with what I am attempting to express. Mr. Russell's ultimate position is, of course, as far removed from mine as possible.

together the results of our argument as bearing upon the stability and security of the finite self, in a discussion of the religious consciousness by which the finite recognises its own full nature, and of the desire for survival after death.

And in a closing lecture, under the same general heading, it will seem appropriate to consider in what sense it is true that "the gates of the future are wide open." What, we shall ask, does a sober philosophy really expect from the future, rejecting as it must both a progress in ultimate reality and a final cessation of time? How can progress be all included in, and belong to, a timeless reality?

4. The genesis of life, if not the first step, is at least a characteristic phase in the appearances which belong to soul-making. It has often been treated as a question of ultimate importance whether life has a primacy over the environment in the determination of the trend of evolution, or whether it is rather of the nature of an omnipotential system, which accepts its development from beginning to end as dictated by its surroundings through reaction and natural selection. It must be borne in mind that the nature of life cannot be found in fact separate from the nature of some particular substance, and therefore is attached from the beginning to a piece of externality ; and its very first reaction —the first move in the game of evolution—may be taken as a special response in the interplay of environing substances, no less than as a primary exhibition of the inherent trend of life.

To answer the question is not within the author's competence. But it is worth while to reflect on it for a moment, precisely in order to deny that any

The genesis of life. Its line of evolution a summary of its world.

result of philosophical importance attaches to its solution in either sense; or rather to point out that what is known of the general character of evolution is sufficient to determine our general attitude, whatever may be the answer to the special question as stated above.

For all views agree that, negatively at least, the course of evolution is shaped by the environment. Nothing can persist which does not satisfy the conditions that form its world. . This, at any rate, is a truism.    And by its positive development under this condition life shows itself so nearly omnipotential, so capable of positively producing the characteristics demanded by any form of environment, that to suppose it in possession *ab initio* of a further independent and inherent direction of development, even if in fact it should prove true, throws no light on evolution and has no significance of general principle.    If it were true, it would only indicate an additional condition dictated by some prior environment, or present *de facto* in the earliest matter in which life may have been embodied.    The value and importance of life in evolution depend on its correspondence with the whole, and this is achieved in principle by the sculpturing process of natural selection.    Whatever properties are indispensable to make this process possible we must undoubtedly attribute to living matter.    We must think of it as capable of being the vehicle of an omnipotential principle—of a principle, that is to say, equal *ab initio* to every situation, and capable of forming a whole adequate to every environment; but in every given embodiment particularised by its given surroundings, in which must be included the special characteristics of the substance to which in that case it is attached. It is quite a different thing to be capable of adaptation which resumes in itself the significance of a world, and to be equipped *ab initio* with an independent character which imposes a special course and a special particularisation upon the world *ab extra*. The former idea is analogous to the true conception of an organism of experience ; the latter to a rigid formation of *a priori* knowledge.

Our attitude, then, is that for the theory of individuality there is no advantage, but rather the reverse, in a hypothesis of the primary or independent self-direction of living matter, such as Bergson has postulated in his doctrine of an *élan vital*, or such as Ward has advocated in his conception of a primary directive capacity inherent in the living being. If it is capable of responding and reacting to a world of surroundings, and, by accepting correction from it, of adjusting itself to that world's requirements, this is the essence of what, philosophically speaking, we demand for the genesis of individuality. We do not want an independent directive power or a special set of organic characters brought in from out-of-doors. If they are there in fact—*e.g.* a tendency to develop in the direction of the vertebrate kingdom—they are a simple fact like another ; a circumstance to be utilised in that response to circumstances which is the essence of an individual centre, whether of life or of conscious experience. What is needed in terms of the logical postulate implied in the essence of life is a centre sensitive to a more concrete environment than that to which physical matter reacts, and capable of maintaining, combining, and transmitting adaptations so as to build up a series of adapted creatures. In a word, what is needed is a centre of unification, differentiated by the externality which it unifies; nothing more, in principle, than this. The rest depends on the nature of the environment.

5. It has been urged against such views as these that to depend on the environment is no guarantee of advance, even in the mere sense of change. For in fact, we are told, there are certain organisms which during ages of geological time have not advanced. And it is suggested that apart from the inherent forward impulse of life as such, the whole organic evolution might at any point have been similarly arrested. But, I imagine, we are here in presence of a proof that, though parts of the environment may acquiesce in the partial arrest of evolution, yet on the whole the changing environment will not accept a stationary organic world. If evolution depended on private properties of life, it might, to speak brutally, go on or stop as living matter chose, and nothing else would have any say in the decision. But if it depends on a power of response and adaptation which makes a living being the quintessence and summary of an externality, then its arrest or advance is no private concern of the living being, but a characteristic of the whole world which is its circumference. If that is a world of change, the change must reflect itself in life; as, on the whole, we see that it has done.

A similar difficulty is propounded when we are told that to depend on adaptation to the environment is no guarantee of progress in desirable qualities. The fittest need not be the best; evolution may mean deterioration. But here again, when we look straight at the facts, the case supposed leads up to a proof of its contrary. If our attitude had been to hold that life draws its progress and its value from characters internal to itself, conditioned by an arbitrary environment, we should have nothing to say against the hypothesis that the harmony of the two was accidental, and might at any point fatally break down. But if, in the character of life, we see the abstract and brief chronicle of the external world, then the fact of all the significance and value which it has brought into existence mean not merely a precarious success of living organisms within possibly hostile surroundings, but a revelation of the inner nature of the co-operating circumstances themselves. The inference seems inevitable. The objection was, "If the environment is hostile or indifferent, evolution by adaptation to it need imply no excellence." And the obvious answer is, "Evolution by adaptation to environment has presented us with a world of immeasurable values, and therefore it is not true that the environment is hostile or indifferent." It is a serious fault in the miraculous or self-directive view of life that it deprives us of this argument, which on any reasonably critical conception of the nature of vital adaptation is wholly irrefragable.

6. Thus it was not without a philosophical significance that we insisted, in our own sense of the terms, upon the all-sufficingness of natural selection. For us natural selection means the operation of a realm of externality in modelling its responsive centre, and thereby coming alive itself in a partial individuality which represents it. In this centrality

*Life passing into soul.*

or representation we have the clue to the work of
soul-making, which begins—belonging, of course, to
the world of appearance and succession—with the
genesis of life.   In all life we find, as we have seen,
a certain relative individuality—that is to say, a self-
maintaining system, consistent and coherent in the
main when taken together with the environment
to which it is adapted, and which, taking present
and past as a single system, has dictated its form.
The creation of such a system is due to the operation of the positive principle of non-contradiction
in a definite embodiment and environment.   The
self-maintaining system of Life, under the guidance
of its surroundings, has rejected whatever variation
was, under all the conditions, out of harmony with
its end of self-maintenance.   Non-contradiction, as
we saw, is the principle of individuality ; and here
we observe it at work in the initial formation of the
finite centre of experience.

It is impossible to determine, I suppose, at what
point in evolution we are first justified in speaking
of a *soul.*   But the gradual concentration of forms
of sensitiveness[1] in a living being is obviously its
foundation.   The concentration in question has been
represented, with striking verisimilitude, as beginning from susceptibility to the most general characteristics under which life has to be carried on
within the solar system.   "While still a substance,
*i.e.* a physical soul, the mind (1) takes part in the
general planetary life, feels the difference of climates,
the character of the seasons, and the periods of the

---

[1] I purposely use the term sensitiveness to indicate a susceptibility, evident through movement and tissue change, of which we
really cannot tell at what point it comes to be accompanied by
sentience.

day, etc. . . . In recent times a good deal has been said of the cosmical, sidereal, and telluric life of man.[1] In such a sympathy with nature the animals essentially live."[2] In man, the writer goes on, these influences survive only in faint changes of mood, and are evident mainly in periods of illness or depression. Then further he refers to the general planetary life of the nature-governed minds which on the whole give expression to the nature of the geographical continents, and constitute the diversities of races. " This diversity descends into specialities that may be termed *local* minds—shown in the outward modes of life and occupation, bodily structure, and disposition, but still more in the inner tendency and capacity of the intellectual and moral character of the life of peoples." ". . . The soul is further de-universalised into the individualised subject. But this subjectivity is here only considered as a differentiation and singling-out of the modes which nature gives ; we find it as the special temperament, talent, character, physiognomy, or other disposition or idiosyncrasy, of families or single individuals."

7. I have cited this account of the focussing of qualities into souls, not as authoritative to-day, but as an aperçu embodying on the whole a sound attitude to the problem of soul-making, and one which the subsequent theory of natural selection, in our large sense of the term, has in substance corroborated.

*Formation of intelligent centres in a way parallel to that of living centres.*

---

[1] Cf. Darwin on the significance of tidal, *i.e.* lunar periods for animal and human life, *Descent of Man*, i. 212.

[2] Hegel's *Philosophy of Mind*, sectt. 392-4. Wallace's Translation. This "de-universalising" process is curiously parallel to the genesis of the individual out of the collective soul in Mr. Cornford's *From Religion to Philosophy*.

We are prepared in this way for the parallelism
of principle between Life and Mind. Once granting
that an omnipotential principle, the active form of
totality, can attach itself in an unconscious or a conscious shape to certain arrangements of matter, the
problem of soul-making, which in our ignorance we
must accept as stretching downwards to the beginnings of life, offers no difficulty nor mystery. The
important point for us is to know where the content
of life and mind, beginning with the differentiation
of organic bodies, is derived from. And the answer
is plain; it is elicited by the bare principle of totality
or non-contradiction, according to the working
rules of the universe, from external environments
of which the substances which act as its vehicles
themselves form a part. It is all-important to
remember, as we have urged before, that in the
immense domain of organic life, reaction and response, though different in character from those of
the inorganic world, are no less absolutely "subject
to law"; or rather, relevant to specific conditions.
The restitution of an organ or of a whole organism
is something more than a mere chemical reagent
can carry out; but it is quite precisely relevant to
the place of the wound or nature of the fragment,
combined with the conditions under which the
organism is placed.[1] And—this is perhaps not sufficiently noticed—it cannot do everything; it cannot
freely contrive. All it does at most is to restore the
normal form which the organism has so far been
accustomed to develop.

There is no more probability that the growth and

[1] See, for the definition of a routine which may be called mechanical, Lloyd Morgan's forthcoming work on *Instinct and Experience.*

character of soul is unconnected with relevant conditions because it implies and is on the top of Life,
than that Life is so because it implies and is on the
top of physico-chemical reactions.

One last word at this point must be given to
Pan-psychism. Why, it will be asked of us, separate
the problem of soul-making in the organic world
from the similar problem which might be raised for
the inorganic world? The answer is plain, and has
been anticipated in the previous course.[1] What we
want and can use of the inorganic world is only its
externality. Without it we cannot grasp or in any
way approach the problem of soul-making. If it has
souls of its own, they do not help us, because we
cannot communicate with them, *except by the very
process which we are describing of eliciting our own
souls from their outsides*, by which " our own nature
is being communicated to us." And perhaps at this
point these divergent views might find some common
ground. But it is enough to say, that whereas with
conscious beings [2] we can use both their bodies and
their souls, with the *prima facie* unconscious world
we can only get at their souls, if at all, from their
bodies pure and simple, or at most, from what their
bodies contribute to our souls.

The continuity and analogy between the conditions of the formation of Life and those which rule
the formation of mind, experience, knowledge, in
short, of the conscious soul passing upwards into

---

[1] *Principle*, p. 362 ff.

[2] The lower animals might be taken as a half-way house. It
might be said that as they share no language with us (but do they
not?) we can only presume their souls, and the nature of their souls,
indirectly, much as we might the soul of a river or a mountain. But
evidently this *rapprochement*, though instructive, is exaggerated.

the self, will now be obvious. We may describe knowledge, not as the nearest, but as the clearest case. It comes before us as a definite structure, with an apparatus or skeleton of categories, laws, and principles, which looks like a determinate endowment from some highly specialised source, perhaps from a fabric inherent in the nature of reason. Its individuality, that is, the constitution which embodies its non-contradictory self-maintenance, seems so obviously dependent on formations foreign,[1] as such, to the experience out of which it grows, that we are tempted to believe them derived all of a piece and in a rigid shape from some source beyond what is given in current thought and perception.

Yet we know that this is not so. The laws, categories, and principles of knowledge recognised by logic are analogous not to a rigid pre-existing framework, but to the indispensable functions of a living body.[2] They have all been elicited by the active form of totality from the requirements of actual experience ; and the principle of non-contradiction, as we have seen, is dependent for its significance and certainty on the whole organic structure which it has been instrumental in eliciting.[3] Such a principle, for instance, as that of causality, is not a dogma which can be determined within its own four corners as fixed in a certain shape apart from the growth of the body of experience.[4] It is an indispensable function of that

---

[1] Of course a logician will try to show that a judgment, as he understands it, is a fact of experience. But he will not maintain that his technical terms and rules or laws are present as they stand in common experience.

[2] Author's *Logic*, ed. 2, vol. ii. p. 230.

[3] *Principle*, Lect. II.                    [4] *Logic, l.c.*

body; but its formulation has changed and is likely to change as knowledge grows and alters. If this simple point were rightly appreciated, we should probably hear less of a modifiable Reality. A system, such as that of knowledge, which is imperfect and only partially individual, must necessarily be imperfect and modifiable in all its parts.

Our point, however, in the comparison of the system of knowledge to the living organism was merely this—to show in this strongest case how a highly articulate individual system, equipped with all sorts of special apparatus which are not visible in its environment,[1] can be brought into existence and maintained by a mere succession of responses to surroundings in conformity with the principle of positive[2] non-contradiction. Such was the process operative in the genesis and evolution of Life; and the further process of soul-making—and the genesis of cognition is a branch of it—will correspond to this general type.

8. In the previous section the relation of knowledge to its world was analysed, not as the next case in order of evolution, but as the clearest case of a highly articulate individual whole arising out of an environment that contains no apparent trace of it, by the operation of the principle of non-contradiction in and upon such an environment.

*Formation of mind, how analogous to that of knowledge.*

---

[1] Cognition, as I understand it, is a way of experiencing reality. If we are told that there is no knowledge, but only the mind and the real objects, I say that to any one who understands what reality means, the distinction is verbal. The "environment" here referred to is reality in a primitive phase of being apprehended. Of course most people have never heard of a law of contradiction or of causation.

[2] According to the doctrine of *Principle*, Lect. II., the word positive is here superfluous. But it is retained in order to recall that doctrine to the reader.

G

What has thus been shown in the cases of Life and of Knowledge applies *a fortiori* to all the intermediate phases of Mind, and it is not necessary for our purpose to draw out these in detail ; more especially as we do not profess or propose to determine at what phase in particular it is well to speak of the emergence of soul *par excellence.* Our purpose is merely to make clear, in the case of human individuality—the completest case known to us of finite intelligence—the moulding of the soul through its surroundings, the communication, through these, of its own nature to it, the modification thus brought to these surroundings, and the results achieved through them.

Two points. What Mind inherits from Life.

i. Two preliminary points must be noted.   *a.* We saw in the first part of this course how greatly our ideas of Mind, Soul, or Self must be affected by the recognition that all of these in their developed shape grow up on the top of an immense previous acquisition of instincts, habits, and automatic arrangements, constituting an order in the nervous system and a relevancy to the world of stimuli in physical action, and implying some degree of consciousness. Thus the Mind or Soul is full, we may say, before it exists, and probably as a pre-condition of its existence. It does not first exist, and then have to be filled from experience.[1]   It takes over its household furniture, or at any rate enough to keep house with, from Life ; and is itself at first merely a better order

[1] It might be urged that this fact ought to modify the account above given of Knowledge, in so far that like all Mind it starts not from a marked point of departure but from a full though indistinct experience.   But the reason why Knowledge was a good illustration of our point lay in the very fact that though full *de facto* it has to treat itself as empty till it has justified its fulness.

and a clearer purpose in making use of the same, or of that portion of it which specially demands order and purpose.

The application of this fact to our present argument is only to make a warning necessary. Mind, then, it might be objected, is not elicited from environment by a bare principle of non-contradiction. It comes to the birth with all sorts of tendencies and predispositions and abilities—as a world in itself from the beginning. No doubt; but then all this world is due, as we have seen, to a prior operation of the same principle in and through an externality at first purely external.[1] No conclusion can be suggested on this ground to the effect that the concrete heritage of mind or minds, what they take over from the Life, so far particularised, on which they are built up, is other than a detail elicited from and through the external world by a principle which receives its entire filling from that source.

In the large sense in which we have spoken throughout, Mind (or its inseparable concomitant the nervous system) is an adaptive variation sustained by natural selection—an adaptive variation such as to be the source of untold consequential adaptations, often different in the mode of initiation from those of mere life, but falling on the whole within the same pre-eminent sense of natural selection as the communication of the soul's nature through the demands of the environment.

β. We all know that the nature which constitutes the environment of Mind is not mere external nature. It is a " second nature," and indeed, if we look for-

*The second and third " nature " contained in the environment of Mind.*

---

[1] Life itself, as we saw, must begin with some matter, by the qualities of which it is bound.

ward to the condition of the developed human intelligence, a second nature including two removes.

To begin with Mind is the environment of Mind; and further, the spatial externality itself which surrounds the developed intelligent centre is an externality which itself is twice-born; which, though still spatial and external, has been modified by passing through the mind, and has become, it may almost be said, a real though modest member of the human community. And indeed, while on this topic, we might suggest that the second nature which surrounds the civilised intelligence covers a third remove. For after the revelation of Mind to itself in the spiritual environment, and after the transformation of the spatial environment into a practical servant of mind, comes the reflection, largely due to that latter experience, which reveals in the unmodified and pristine externality itself— the first nature of all—the significance which we call æsthetic and scientific[1]; something new, and different from its actual operation in the task of natural selection.

But the main differentia of the genesis of Mind is the pre-eminence in it of Mind as an environment— not, we may insist, with reference to previous arguments,[2] Mind as a naked inwardness, but Mind differentiated and interpreted through a definite externality. In other words, Mind is in man a social characteristic, and lives in the medium of recognition.[3]

---

[1] In these kinds of significance if anywhere we get at the Soul of external Nature.    [2] On Pan-psychism.

[3] In principle we must insist that we can have with our past and future self such relations as connect us with other selves. Man is certainly a society within himself. But the main influence in eliciting this organisation within him is an actual society outside him.

Here is a paradox which leads up to an important truth. We said that the main thing in the genesis of Mind is recognition, or a mental environment. But does not this presuppose Mind prior to its own genesis? How is Mind to be generated by contact with Mind, if Mind does not exist before Mind exists? And the answer is not altogether given in the fact that Mind is a matter of degree and that in the animal world we have it in modes closely akin to those which belong to humanity. This fact makes the answer more possible, but it is not the answer, and is itself subject to something of the same difficulty for which the answer is required.

But the answer itself is that intelligent Mind is essentially reciprocal (and so probably all the Mind of the higher[1] animals in its degree) and lives in the medium of recognition ; and therefore, when a certain *de facto* continuity of centres, each with itself and with others, is attained in the correlation of organisms, the recognition of the continuity is generated *pari passu* in a plurality of centres. For, like the filling of Mind in general, the continuity exists before the consciousness of it. What has been called "consciousness of kind" indeed—an awareness of it shown in action—must run right through the animal world ; the relation of the sexes is enough to prove it. But in the social being a new variation of Mind arises from the very fact of reciprocity. As the one relies upon the other, so the other relies upon the one ; and both together, in this reliance, and in the language and other social utterances which embody it, become elements in a universal consciousness or

[1] Perhaps the mind of the quite lower organisms is conditioned by reciprocity between the parts of the organism.

social Mind within which individual centres recognise themselves and each other. The recognition and the genesis are in principle simultaneous, that is to say, while one-sided it is imperfect.[1] I cite a fine illustration from Wallace.[2]

"The mother, already enriched with reason and love, bending over her infant, does not by her glance, her smile, her touch, give it a soul, a spirit, a reason; and yet in that glance, that smile, that touch, soul, spirit, reason, are as certainly born as the physiological life of the same child is born, and so far as we know only born, in the congress of male and female. As in that case the elements of the living being, the constituents which build up structure, are older, far older than the two parents, who to popular apprehension are the authors of the being of their progeny; so in the spiritual world the child and its mother severally bring to their union of soul a store of powers and faculties prepared by, it may be, centuries of inherited tradition. Yet it is in the main true that it is the mother's and father's look and touch, charged with the fruits of life, of life both theirs and that of myriad others which have gone to make up theirs, which kindles into flame the dull materials of humanity, and begins that second birth, that spiritual parentship which, at least not less than the first, should be the peculiar glory of human father- and motherhood. And, to prevent misconception, the gift of soul and spirit, if gift it be, is not on one side only. If the parent, in a way, makes the child, it is not less true that the

---

[1] Cf. the well-known doctrine of Hegel, *Encyclopedia*, sect. 430 ff., of the recognition of master and servant.

[2] *Lectures and Essays*, p. 114, by Professor William Wallace.

child makes the parent. He kindles new lights, and pierces out new depths, in the parent soul; builds his world anew, with other features and fabrics than of old; brings him nearer heaven or nearer hell; but at any rate, if the parent ever really sees his child eye to eye and approaches him touch to touch—and unfortunately we dare not assume that this always happens, so many parents and children have never seen each other's soul-face—he is not as he was before."

*How*, more especially, it will be asked, does mind recognise mind, and, in recognising, become mind? We are not, of course, explaining the nature of consciousness; but the relevant condition of its appearance seems here tolerably clear. It must be in response; that is, through participation in the same situation, which, when recognised, becomes a mental situation common to two or more centres of experience. We are often told it is in "imitation"; but imitation is too narrow an idea for the response or relevancy of action which is really in question. I should suppose co-operation, the *de facto* combination of different acts towards what is, though not yet distinctly stated, a common purpose, to be the most usual stimulus to recognition. Conflict, which Hegel names as the essential, is for him really a world-phase, introductory to the reign of co-operation.

ii. Although the environment of intelligent Mind is thus different from that of mere Life, yet in the main and in large outline the power which moulds it is still that of natural selection. Like all embodiments of the omnipotential principle, Mind, Soul, or Self, has inevitably for its test and formative law the

*Natural Selection the method by which intelligent centres are formed.*

need of being equal to the situation. Still, as always, it is true that the centre which is not equal to the situation cannot persist ; and that the values developed in and through the several centres are a safe indication of the significance of their whole environment. Only it is true that in two main points the working of natural selection is modified when it deals with an intelligent centre.

First, the province of positive suggestion is greatly enlarged. There is already what might be called suggestion in the relation of an external environment to an organism ; that is to say, there are variations directly produced by the surroundings, which may or may not prove valuable when tested by natural selection. But in the sphere of mind and society, after language and institutions have been developed, the positive suggestion has a much larger place, and the field of mere trial and error is correspondingly diminished.

Secondly, the place of true contrivance is much greater. Bergson [1] has remarked that the term " response " as often employed in evolutionist theory may mean anything from a physical reaction to a well-conceived contrivance adapted to a need. Here, in the case of Mind, we come to true contrivance ; the forecast of a situation and the combination of means to meet it. But yet here, as in the last case, and as in the case of subjective selection, the court of ultimate appeal is natural selection, or the verdict of the environment.[2] So that although the distinctive field of what we know as trial and error

[1] *Évolution*, p. 63.
[2] " If this counsel or this work be of men," etc. This is quite obviously and unquestionably an appeal to natural selection.

is at this level greatly diminished, yet ultimately and on the large scale it is trial and error that gives, or rather embodies, the conclusive and final decision. Will the universe stand your experiment, or will it not? And this after all is natural selection or determination by the environment.

In the above senses, then, social selection might be called relatively artificial or more than natural, in so far as it includes suggestion and promotes teleological contrivance. But on the whole it is well to regard it as natural, in the sense in which the whole activities of Society, as representing the necessities of man's nature and surroundings, are natural and necessary, and a better standard, than any reflective theory, of what should and should not be encouraged. In this contrasted sense, and apart from the ethical or biological opinions of individuals, Society carries on the work of soul-formation by a severe and inevitable process,[1] which it is both wholesome and true to regard as natural selection in its social form.[2]

iii. At this point of the process of soul-formation, where the environment in addition to pure external nature, and the twice-born second nature, takes on

The Individuality of Mind tends to burst the envelopes of particular centres.

---

[1] See, for example, Hegel, *Phil. des Rechts* on the Bürgerliche Gesellschaft, the hard world of industry and competition, which represents the demand that if a man is to be anything he must make himself into something. The common censure that the "fittest" who survive are not on the whole the best, though it has a considerable truth in the bad working of social institutions, I believe in the main, and in its full bitterness, to represent a deep-seated rebellion against the necessary severity of the soul-forming process ; and also to some extent a confusion as to the types of success correlative to different natures. See *Philosophy of State*, ed. 2, or Hegel, *op. cit.*

[2] See author's paper on Selection in Human Society. *Charity Organisation Review*, Dec. 1910.

the character of spiritual personalities, we have already noted that the development of Individuality begins to show itself in a new light. Not only are particular centres of experience moulded by natural selection into a deeper harmony with their surroundings, but in so far as the surroundings form a mental or spiritual system—a social mind—the particular centres begin to be adapted as members of an individuality transcending their own. (We observed long ago that *e.g.* legal "personality" implies an individuality that extends far beyond the "person."[1]) Their qualities begin to be reinforced by others, their deficiencies supplied, in a word, their immanent contradictions removed by readjustment and supplementation, so that the body of particularised centres begins to take on a distinct resemblance to what we know must be the character of the absolute. From the beginning of evolution, the demands made by the world upon a society are reflected in the demands made by the society upon its members, and more than that, the qualities of the several members are not isolated and self-contained, but overflow along the channels of interconnection and characterise the society as a whole.[2] Thus the soul or self in the process of being made or moulded more and more passes beyond its factual being ; and we see that not only it has to be made something if it is to be anything, but that whatever it has realised in positive qualities can never be enough, and there is always a greater unity which demands its further subordination and self-abnegation.

9. From the beginning, natural selection as operative upon the individual soul through its social

---

[1] *Principle*, p. 284.    [2] Cf. *ibid.* Lect. I.

environment has given rise to creatures and institu- How Soul-<br>making in
tions which have embodied the matter of souls or society
selves in creations transcending their particular passes into ultra-
existence. Language, morality, fine art, or the individual and ultra-
significance of the social monument or festival, social experience.
were alluded to above. In these the social mind Its severity.
anticipates an incarnation which at once is the
quintessence of its group-relations, and altogether
transcends the form of a given plurality of persons.
The smallest act of social duty, as Aristotle has
taught us, opens out on a wider horizon,[1] so that
ultimately the end of the State, that which is
implied in its whole structure, which is the true end
and aim of its individual members, and the standard
by which we can estimate the value of its social life,
habits, and institutions, is embodied in [2] its fitness
to subserve the ends of philosophy and religion, or
as we should say to-day in more modern language,
of religion, of art and poetry, and the higher life of
the intelligence.

This is only the relative completion of the process
which we saw beginning in the moulding of Life,
and the principle throughout has been the same.
The soul or self is formed by the requirements of
its surroundings ; that is, of the universe so far as in
contact with it. The machinery of the process
varies in detail between the phases of Life and Mind,
but its general conditions persist. It is not at all
implied that we are fully capable of estimating the
significance of situations and of the degree in which
souls are equal to them, or the value, in each case,

[1] See *Principle*, Appendix II. to Lect. X.
[2] In a duly adjusted whole *every* element has value. Thus, a
good day's work in the fields has value ; but then it has religion, etc.,
in it, as they also have it in them.

of being equal to this or that situation. Men may fail, it seems to us, in petty situations who would have succeeded in greater ones, and so on through the whole gamut of complaint. But all this does not touch our point at this moment. We are merely considering the general character of "the vale of soul-making," and noting that its processes are a constant reiteration of demand on the one hand and adaptation or failure on the other; that this is how particular centres of experience achieve their peculiar form and content; and that the tendency, on the whole, depends on the principle of non-contradiction, is towards individualisation, and even towards an individuality in which centres, formed and further formed by such a process, tend to be, as particular centres, transcended and absorbed.

One consequence seems clear: that adaptation must have a tendency to strain and conflict with the first natural endowment and foundation of the soul or self. For, as we have seen, the fullest individuality tends altogether to absorb and subordinate the finite centre, giving it indeed an expansion which it had not before, but on the other hand stretching and perhaps tearing or snapping[1] its simpler and earlier adaptations, which were not made in view of the environment which is ultimately reached.

Thus the higher value may go on the whole, as we have urged, with the higher individuality; but yet, for finite souls, this will not, though on the whole the higher harmony, be attended with the greater freedom from conflict or from destructive

[1] "He that loveth son or daughter more than me——"

readaptation of the self.    The foundation is casual, or appears so, bringing some essential gift, as yet unadapted; and in soul-formation there is therefore a great deal to be remade as well as to be made, and the process is certain to be more or less severe.

## LECTURE IV

### THE MIRACLE OF WILL, OR CHARACTER AND CIRCUMSTANCE

The
creative
power of
volition.
Its secret.

1. IN the previous Lecture we were engaged with the moulding of souls by the world through natural and social selection. It seemed to us that the marvel of life and mind lay not in their possession of any immanent and independent content, contrivance, or purpose,[1] but rather in the inherent universality which enabled them, apparently from any material starting-point, to adjust themselves to a structure and function relevant to the demands of their environment at that starting-point. Thus, we thought, the wisdom of the whole, though not primarily active in any intelligent form (except in so far as the environment might itself be largely composed of finite intelligent organisms), yet models the incarnations and effects the adjustment and the discipline[2] by which life and mind are driven to their relevant shapes. In this way it seemed as if

---

[1] Cf. *Principle*, p. 368.

[2] Sometimes amounting to what seems to us wholesale waste and destruction. This, we suggest, is only to be understood as analogous to the discipline and severity of soul-making. In sculpture there must be apparent waste as well as a good deal of cutting.

the whole wealth of finite life and experience was brought to pass through the operation of an external system—what we finally differentiate as " nature "—upon and in co-operation with an empty principle of totality called life or mind.    And organisms, souls, selves, societies are the outcome.

But this, we now have to see, was only one side of the matter.    The living being in its degree, and more obviously the conscious or self-conscious microcosm, soul or self, begins from its first appearance to exercise the inherent logic, or tendency to form a system, which constitutes its "omnipotentiality." [1]   Even in the simplest organisms, I suppose, the adaptations which the environment can exact are limited by the necessity of being "compossible" in a living creature.   The environment can destroy the organism, but it cannot make it at once cease to be a system, and remain alive.   We need not, perhaps, assume that life implies initial impulses to special and divergent zoological types.   But different as its conditions may be according to its different embodiments, it must, as a principle of totality, generate some conditions of completeness in every shape that it may assume.   Now the point for us is this, that these conditions constitute a limit upon the adaptations which *per se* might be able to satisfy features of the environment, and involve, therefore, a reciprocal selection from these possible adaptations, due to the character of the creature itself.   This fact places us, as it were, at the other side of the process of natural selection—the other side in the sense of the right side of a carpet being woven.    The world imposes its plan upon the

[1] *Principle, l.c.*

incipient centre of life and mind, but in proportion as that centre acquires a nature of its own, this nature determines what it can or will accept. Destruction may follow non-acceptance; but at least apparent destruction is essential in any self-shaping world. It is the modelling tool of the universe. Thus we have a selection *by* the organic or intelligent creature as well as a selection *of* it, and an adaptation *of* the environment as well as *to* and by it.[1] A limited externality has set up its centre and representative; but its representative, being as such an active unity, must tend to become its critic and its re-creator. Here we have the root of Will, and are close upon the secret of its power, or the power of character, to transfigure and so to conquer circumstance. This point we shall recur to later.

But what we have now reached is the initial fact that the representative centre of any range of externality can only represent it in a way of its own. And this means a selection and adaptation exercised upon the externality by the centre, in consequence of that same special character in the centre which it is acquiring by satisfying the demands of the externality.[2] Its place and function in the environment rests upon this differentiation, which necessarily involves its seeing and dealing with the environment from a special point of view.[3] When we consider this relation in the case of a fully intelligent centre, we are face to face with the problem of will. Not

---

[1] Cf. Ward's reiterated insistence on the selected and so adapted environment in which every creature lives.

[2] For an answer to the criticism that Natural Selection is negative, and not a positive modelling agency, see *Principle*, p. 151.

[3] In speaking of mere life this is a metaphor; with mind it is a fact.

only has the "contentless" principle of mind embodied itself in an outward form and inward
capacity relevant to the special environment which
has moulded it, but it has augmented this environment—the primary natural externality—by that
whole second nature which has been brought into
existence by means of and for the sake of such
differentiated functions. The second nature in
question may be indicated in two words as society
and civilisation, taken in the widest possible sense.[1]

The miracle which has been achieved in this
creation—for it is as near a creation as anything we
shall find in the universe, since even the coming to
be of a new soul depends on it more than on
physical origination[2]—is usually covered by some
such word as "elicited," which we have already
applied in a kindred context.[3] The entire content
of the finite will has been "elicited" by the contentless principle of mind from the primary externality
(say the inorganic world[4]), which at first sight includes
nothing in any way relevant to it, much as the whole
multiplicity of the organic world has been "elicited"
by the kindred principle of life from the same
inorganic background. "Elicited" is a useful
word, but covers, as we said, an almost miraculous
creation, which it does not explain. How can will
"elicit" its world, which indeed includes nearly all
of itself, from what primarily appears as a mere
external nature? How, moreover, can it display

---

[1] I mean that from a general point of view we must reckon *all*
human ways of living as society and civilisation; something built up
by the finite will upon the foundation of primary nature. Whether
the animals other than man have anything corresponding to this, we
need not discuss here.                        [2] See above, p. 86.
[3] *Principle*, p. 368.                       [4] Cf. p. 78, above.

H

the extraordinary power, parallel to some of the phenomena of natural selection,[1] of "eliciting" a fairly adequate response to pretty nearly any conceivable demand?

We have here two kindred questions—*a*, what is the source of the concrete content of will, and *β*, what is the nature and what are the limits of the power of will or character over environment and circumstance?

It may be thought that we are passing beyond the subject which we are professing to discuss, "The Moulding of Souls." But it is not so. We shall see that in re-creating its world the finite mind is only carrying forward the process of its own genesis, of having its nature communicated to it. In re-creating its world it is continuing the work which began by its own creation; for its own nature, as well as that of its world, lies in all that its world, as focussed in it, is capable of becoming.

Serious-
ness of the
difficulty
illustrated
by

2. Before attempting to answer the questions which have just been stated, we will spend a few moments in considering how real and arduous is the difficulty they involve—the difficulty of what we may venture to call the creative power of will. We may see a proof of the difficulty in the insufficiency of certain attempts on the part of ethical psychology and metaphysics to bridge the gap—the gap, I mean, between the assumed position of an intelligent being confronted with an external nature plus a number of other intelligent beings, and that highly concrete and organised web of objects and relations

---

[1] Matter, *e.g.*, seems to be able to produce any quality which natural selection demands, *e.g.* any colour, or elasticity, or rigidity, or any permeability to light, or any shape, *e.g.* of a lens.

which in real fact and experience constitutes the content and support of the civilised will.

i. When we go for our analysis of the will and its moral world to any form of naturalism, say Hobbism or Hedonism, or again to any form of abstract Intuitionism, such as that familiar in Clarke's pseudo-mathematical principles of ethics, it does not so much strike us that we are being told the wrong things, as that we are being told what amounts to nothing at all.    One or two tautologies of formal reasoning, one or two abstractions of superficial psychology,[1] worked out with an unreal show of deductive argument, and that is all.    There is no genuine recognition of the marvellous creation which we have been trying to appreciate, the intricate fulness of the object in which a human will can truly find its counterpart; all of which has somehow come out of—been "elicited" from—mere natural fact, and yet cannot possibly be held to have arisen by the mere addition of new natural facts to primary nature.

Vacancy of intellectualist and abstract accounts of the will.

Now if there is to be an Intellectualism in a bad sense, it is here, I think, that we should look for it. For the long and short of these doctrines is, that they try to deduce the content of the will from abstract assumptions—whether psychological or metaphysical makes no difference—generated by a reflective intelligence in face of an external world of nature, and of a humanity treated as external.    We may say either that they bridge the gap between

---

[1] I would not recur to these ideas, which appear to me to have lost all interest as contributions to philosophy, if it were not that a single error of fundamental principle, in which one and all of them, as I think, are rooted, seems to me not to be commonly perceived, or stated in its general nature.    I should call it Intellectualism.

will and nature by empty axioms, or rather that, not realising its existence, they do not actually deal with it at all. The actual moral and spiritual world in which the will itself has embodied its miracle—deposited the hard-earned treasure of its content, and given proof and explanation of its power to regenerate and conquer circumstance—is simply left out of sight. Thus on the one hand the true essence of will is here, by a formal Intellectualism, left unrecognised; and on the other hand, because it is left unrecognised, an opening is made for the occupation of the ground by a foolishly mysterious Voluntarism.

Problem of giving genuine effect to doctrine of Free Causality in Thought and Will.

ii. It is possible that by confessing an early perplexity of my own I may help some others to appreciate the difficulty which now appears to me so fundamental and so suggestive. At all events, I will make the attempt. After I had become, according to the best of my belief both at the time and to-day, fairly versed in the criticism which establishes the distinction between a thinking mind and a natural object, and the impossibility of applying to the former the categories relevant to the latter, I still found myself in a difficulty when it was a question of making use of any such view in accounting for any re-creation of the given either by way of thought or by way of volition. Thought—so much seemed clear—was free in the sense of being at least the apprehending centre of worlds of objects and relations, and not itself an object or relation among others. But in all this formal freedom of thought, where was to be found any real power of transforming a point of view, of looking at any group of facts more significantly or more worthily than their first appearance suggested? How could the mind, so crudely did the problem state itself, make a new relation or a new object, or generate any aspect or quality in things, beyond the organisation which it apprehended as given in the world of the given? Granting that in some sense it could "impose" relations, that is, that fresh relations became necessary to be recognised as it handled and organised fresh objects, yet there seemed no ground for treating such imposition as anything like an origination—a new light, a higher meaning. How could the thinking mind alter or re-create the aspect of a given scene or situation or conjunction of circumstance, except by connecting and developing what further content perception might chance to furnish or formal deduction to establish? Was anything effective meant by its being above its world, exempt from the application of the causal categories, a "free cause," a spiritual principle?

Ah, but—it may be replied—you should have considered *will*. *Thought* could do no more than build up worlds out of fact, but will could originate, modify, produce facts and characters; that is where you should have looked for the new spiritual world that was to supplement primary nature, and be the content affirmed in our volition. But the circle in this statement shows how little it can help us. Will was to create the content of will. Well and good, but what could it create beyond what it could conceive? and what new thing was it to conceive, seeing that thought could add nothing out of any content of its own to the object-world of primary nature. Where were the ideas, the clues, the directions of experience to come from that were to guide towards satisfaction the creative will? Was it to create first, and think its creations afterwards? Something occurs that is analogous to this in the contrast of practice and reflection, but it is impossible to push the contrast to the end. Really blind will, experimenting wholly without a clue, could not, except for the wildest voluntarism, be the power that was to build up the world of satisfaction for finite minds. What was the secret I had missed? All these questions reinforced the impression of vacancy made by the formal and naturalist theories just referred to. It seemed clear that something further must be noted in the nature of thought, and of will so far as dependent upon thought, if we were ever to understand either the inventive and expansive side of knowledge, or, what is closely akin to it, the creative aspect of will, and its practical power over circumstance.

Solution in general terms. There is always a larger point of view than the given; and will always, in principle, has access to this. Secret lies in what works *in* the mind, and *on* the situation.

3. And the solution of the difficulty seemed to me to spring from the careful and sympathetic study, anticipated by the attitude of the greatest thinkers, and developed by post-Kantian philosophy, of thought as actually at work in building up knowledge, and of the kindred side of will; will, that is, as actually employed in building up morality —amplifying and further determining the system in which it finds its satisfaction.

The difficulty as really felt—if I may repeat and summarise—was to see how the freedom or centrality, or active originality of thought and will— whatever term seems best to express their difference from external objects and their claim in some way to predominate over such objects—to see how any such characteristic could practically help us, in view of facts and situations *prima facie* given, to deeper points of view and to higher and wider possibilities of action.

Here, say, is a limited group of facts, involving for intelligent apprehension a limited complex of relations; there, again, or in that same group of facts, is a situation involving certain possibilities of action, and, apparently, no more. Can thought find characteristics in the one, or can will find openings in the other, beyond those which the direct apprehension of the complex in each case, as an outsider might sum it up, renders necessary? A solution depending on the contribution by thought of *a priori* principles of knowledge, or by will of *a priori* principles of morality, coming as if made "of whole cloth" *qua* additional gifts from "the mind," we could not find credible in itself; and experience shows, as we noted above, that it has really nothing to say. What service, then, do we practically receive from the pre-eminence of mind or its omnipotentiality and tendency to form a whole, if its operation is thus limited by presentation, more than if it were a servile faculty, registering or copying external facts and things?

In attempting to answer this particular form of the question of freedom, which seems to me to be at the root of much of the difficulty found by practical men in philosophical views of the subject, I am doing nothing more than to read in connection the logical and ethical sides of familiar doctrines. To begin with, I am working with the idea which I have maintained throughout, that the universe is one, and each finite mind a factor in the effort which sustains its unity. Therefore in every finite complex or situation there are openings into, connections with, fuller complexes and wider situations,[1] inclusion in which by the mind would transform the given. And these larger visions and arrangements—more determinate, not more superficially wide—are in principle within the capacity of mind as such, because everything is so. But how — and here is the crux we have been insisting on—is *a* mind to get at them? If it does not see them, you may say, it does not. *Ex hypothesi* it possesses no formal deductive principles covering the particulars of the case, to take it further by abstract argument. And even Inductive law, if it could find one, would, according to the common formula, only tell it that if the complex is repeated—it is repeated.

How then can it move except by a fortunate change in presentation, modifying the suggestions of the apprehended complex? I do not say that it can move without a change in presentation; but the relevancy and direction of the change need not depend on chance. The point is this. The mind, of course, has a filling before it is self-conscious, or it could never become so. Its universality or nisus to the whole is so far governed and directed by its filling. Now when a mind, whose working has thus identified itself with a concrete principle, scrutinises a concrete complex or situation, the operation which takes place is quite different from formal Deduction or formal Induction, though it is prior to both, and is the real fact which they represent. Formal Deduction analyses

[1] Plato's *Meno*, 81, τῆς φύσεως ἀπάσης συγγενοῦς οὔσης, καὶ μεμαθηκυίας τῆς ψυχῆς ἅπαντα.

such a scrutiny and its results.   Formal Induction applies negative tests of coherence to its result.[1] But the real growing point is where a mind possessed of, or rather by, a principle applies it to the given (in "apperception," if we like to say so) so as to make it a clue which selects and justifies the connection of the given with something beyond, different from it but kindred with it.   Then the result is at once a true derivative and a genuine novelty or creation.[2]

And in this way either thought, or thinking volition, may transform a complex or a situation, which is unfertile to mere contemplative apprehension or to formal inference.   You do not in such a case work *a priori*, without and beyond facts, except in the sense in which all finite

---

[1] Author's *Logic*, ed. 2, vol. ii. p. 174 ff.

[2] See the latter part of section 308 of Green's *Prolegomena to Ethics*.   It is on the combination of such ideas as those indicated in this passage, with logical analyses due to Green himself and to others since Hegel, that the doctrine of the text is founded.   I quote one or two sentences from the passage referred to : "A proposition of geometry, from which by mere analysis no truth could be derived which was not already contained in it, becomes fertile of new truth when applied by the geometer to a new construction.   A rule of law, barren to mere analysis, yields new rules when interpreted by the judge in relation to new cases.   And thus a general ethical proposition, which by itself is merely a record of past moral judgments, and from which by mere analysis no rules of conduct could be derived but such as have been already accepted and embodied by it, becomes a source of new practical direction when applied by conscience, working under a felt necessity of seeking the best, to circumstances previously not existent or not considered, or to some new lesson of experience."   With this compare my view of the real nature of Induction (*Logic*, ed. 2, vol. ii. p. 174) and the interpretation of the movement of Hegel's Dialectic given by Mr. Bradley (*Principles of Logic*, pp. 381-2) and Dr. McTaggart (*Studies in Hegelian Dialectic*, sect. 9), the point being that the whole, active *in* the mind, operates upon what is *before* the mind as a criticism and a demand.   The whole growth of society and civilisation, as objective mind and will, is due to a movement of this kind.

experience is always beyond itself. You work by a light which shows you relevant facts, or the relevance of facts, and the operation of which is the same thing which we have described in *Principle* as the reshaping of our world by itself under the influence of the nisus of mind to the whole. The facts whose relevance you are led to perceive do not syllogistically come under the principle which is the clue, as particulars under their major premiss. They are fresh applications or developments of the principle, and you make it their major premiss, if at all, after you have made the applications and developments. Work of this kind is the mainspring and essence of thinking [1] and of will.

For Logic, *i.e.* when the question is of an extension of knowledge, you find the typical case in any expert judgment. Suppose a man, full of the gold-seeker's experience and yearning, meeting with a topography and geological formation which he recognises as characteristic of the presence of gold. At once the apprehended complex becomes to him a new thing, because an application of an old thing. It is, of course, not a mere repeat. It is a new application of a principle, which is seen to be embodied in certain facts *mutatis mutandis*; and the expectation, again, is not a repeat, but new and a creation.

So with a moral situation. Consider one in which a complex of interests and even duties seems in hopeless internal conflict; seems so, that is to

---

[1] The whole of the author's *Logic*, and not merely the paragraphs on Induction above referred to, is an attempt to place the thought-function in this light.

say, *prima facie*, or to the outsider's eye.  Let it be, *e.g.*, such as might be used in a text-book for an example of the futility of rational construction in problems of conduct.  In such a situation a concrete scrutiny by a mind possessed with an unselfish principle of action[1] must, we may say fearlessly, always raise the level of rationality in the situation as a whole.  Thereby *ipso facto* a fair solution is made incomparably more possible than a formal enumeration of the *prima facie* alternatives would suggest.[2]  The situation is actually changed by a clue that reveals in it new factors.

Now of course all this reasoning is open to the criticism which depends on supposing the best to have been tried and failed—a supposition so easy to make in a text-book, for who can deny that our best efforts will sometimes fail?  But I must persist that our view is not dependent on mere chance, but relies on forces which always and necessarily produce *some* effect, and if they have failed on the whole, have yet altered the situation before they failed.  It is easy to retort, "Oh, yes; *if* you are really possessed by a principle, and *if* it is a fruitful and relevant one, then you can always promote a solution.  That is no news.  But suppose you have none; or that what you have is proved unfruitful, by the facts and circumstances remaining stubborn

---

[1] What right have we to say "unselfish"?  How is that part of its logical or solution-making quality?  Because it corresponds to the organising or guiding quality of the principle we have postulated in a parallel case for knowledge.  The whole point is that it must be a clue to a larger complex.

[2] I have heard it well suggested that when causes of failure in social help are being set down, there should always be a heading for "Incompetence of the Helper."  In principle there always must *be* a solution for the reason in the text.

and unresolved under your intensest and widest scrutiny." We shall throw a stronger light on the very knot of this criticism directly, when we instance the extreme case of overcoming moral and physical impossibility, or what passes for it. But here, before dealing with examples, I wish to insist on the matter of principle. *In principle*, a fruitful thought and course is *always* open ; for the whole of the universe is accessible by some path or other from every complex within it. In principle, again, you—the finite mind—have *always* a clue to a relatively fruitful thought or act, because every demand of mind, pressed thoroughly home, must ultimately bring you to all that mind can be.[1] Thus to fail of fruitful thought or choice is in the main to fail, as we all constantly fail, in sincerity and thoroughness. Now we have already [2] dealt with empty Free Will, and need not here discuss whether there is sense in saying that *ohne weiteres* "we *could* have been" more sincere and unselfish — or, in a scientific problem, more relevantly inspired, than we were. But no one need, or can, dispute that if we had thoroughly penetrated the necessity that vistas must be open from every circumstance and situation to a more satisfactory complex, and that what is necessary is the giving ourselves wholly to our best inspiration in its bearing on the concrete facts, we could all, under the influence of such a conviction, have been in some degree other than we were without it. If our doctrine is made out, this con-

---

[1] "It seems as if any emotion [and we might say, any line of action], if sufficiently thorough-going, would take one to heaven" (R. L. Nettleship, *Remains*, i. 96). Of course it will, as we said, take you faster if it is unselfish. Otherwise it must transmute itself, and that takes time and pain.      [2] *Principle*, p. 342.

viction is justified up to the hilt, and the *power* of thought and will, which is what people constantly mean when they speak of their *freedom*, is vindicated in a high degree. On the whole, and in ultimate doctrine, it is true that given finite facts cannot maintain their fixed narrowness against thought, and given finite circumstance cannot stand against will and character. And this is not opposed to the view we have taken throughout of mind's debt to externality; but, on the contrary, could not be maintained on any other basis. It is the dialectic of externality itself.

4. In order to attach the doctrine of the previous section more explicitly to recent theory, and, moreover, to insist on its bearing as a more effective account of the creative power of will than any view which disconnects it from thought proper,[1] we will now return to the two questions of page 98, and arrange the examples we are to offer so as to indicate the answers to them. *Examples to confirm above doctrine, arranged so as to answer questions a and β.*

*a.* What is the source of the concrete content of will ? and

*β.* What is the nature and what are the limits of the power of will over environment, or, in other words, of character over circumstance ?

*a.* I take the concrete content of will to be all that is included in the terms society and civilisation, construed in the widest sense as equivalent to a definition of humanity.[2] The source of this content is thus the environment of man, consisting of *The source of the content of will. Examples.*

---

[1] *I.e.* as I understand, the consideration of experiences with reference to their meanings, or, in other words, as members of a connected world.

[2] I take humanity not as probably all there is of finite mind, but as what we have to deal with, and as its typical case.

organic and inorganic nature, so far as we can conceive it apart from the reaction of finite mind upon it. The creation or "eliciting" of the content from this source is the work of thinking volition,[1] operating in the way which has just been analysed, upon the various complexes and situations presented before the mind, and also within it in virtue of its identification with an animal organism. In principle, every physical feature of the external world, every instinct and desire of the animal nature, is a fact, or is in a complex, of which it is true to say that an opening leads from it to some further complex in which it is transformed. The thinking will, working always through the tendency of thought to the whole, embodied in this or that impulse or desire, upon the complexes relatively given to it, finds always a path or opening which leads to this or that larger continuous complex, and, pursuing it, makes and adopts the changes which the newly presented facts and combination suggest and present.

An example of universal significance going to the very heart of all spiritual development is the case of language. Without entering into contested matter, we may safely state it thus, in general terms of our theory: The "consciousness of kind"—an animal instinct—inspired by the nascent demands of thought for communication based on a common world, and so induced to make the most of the

---

[1] It is unnecessary from this point forward to repeat the separate reference to thought. The essential character of its connection with will is plain from what has been said. But for clearness' sake we will distinguish below the concrete development of the man as a moral will from morality conceived as a system of personal virtues—an imperfect view, tending to a dangerous individualism.

existent facts of animal utterance and incipient communication through sound, must have set on both scrutiny and experiment to utilise and to adapt all possible articulations both of sound and of meaning. By attention and experiment the thinking will —itself, of course, undergoing development *pari passu*—must have thus found the way from the complex of natural sounds to the significant whole of language, the very sounds and their organs undergoing transformation *en route*. Thus was created, it might be said, a vast multitude of facts which were natural and yet not natural—not beyond or discontinuous with the organic processes of nature, but yet a complete readjustment and transformation as compared with any facts which could be given by nature apart from thinking mind. Just so a house has in it nothing but natural facts, and yet could not be given by nature apart from thought. What makes this peculiar relation possible—the relation which we called indifferently creation or " eliciting " —is what we insisted on above. There is a road from every natural group of facts to every spiritual reality in the universe ; and the essential nature of mind forces it always in some degree to traverse this road, and that in the direction from less to more.[1]

A further and very relevant example, which I have analysed in detail elsewhere, is the spiritual significance taken on by what are *prima facie* mere temporal and spatial relations in the moral development of the family and of society.[2] The mere pro-

---

[1] Except in sin and error, of which we will speak by themselves. The progress in them is indirect.

[2] *Philosophical Theory of the State*, ch. xi. And cf. R. L. Nettleship, *Remains*, i. 329, cited *Principle*, p. 56, on the further

longation of the period of parental care, the very indifference of space, which makes neighbourhood certain to become a problem of aliens as well as of kinsmen, are characters of relatively given complexes of fact or circumstance, which, when attended to and reacted on by the thinking will, "elicit" feelings, attributes, habits, institutions, which are morally and spiritually new things—and, in a sense, are new even physically. "Institutions"—here we have perhaps the most important keyword in this problem of volitional creation. Mere facts, *e.g.* the eating of food together—*i.e.* in spatial proximity—become "institutions" when the thinking will, having noted their connections and further implications, has reacted upon them so as to stamp them as symbols, elements belonging to and indicating further and larger complexes than those to which, as natural facts, they belong. It traces and notes and practically relies on this significance, because it is animated by some desire or impulse—say the "consciousness of kind"—which is one for the moment with the demand for unity and completeness possessed by will *qua* intelligence or thought. It operates therefore in the way analysed above, and this is the creative path by which the content of will—the second or spiritual world and nature—comes into finite form, as a factor in the tension by which the Absolute passes into and out of its externality.

The point is familiar, though of vast importance, and need not be laboured further. It is, in substance, the well-known doctrine of objective mind and will. We have only to repeat, what many

determination of a second of time, the highest case mentioned being its place in a moral action.

great men have explained at length,[1] that in this world of content, the work of thinking will, we have in an external and factual form the body and substance of thinking will itself.   Here is its concrete and actual content, what it finds to affirm in its volition from moment to moment, and what forms the steps and systematic connections by which its self-expression from day to day is linked with —enters into—the total world of its satisfaction in a law which is at once its own nature, and a high expression of the Absolute.   What a contrast with the abstract formalism of Hedonistic or Intuitionist axioms!  We have seen the process of creation of this world, and have, I hope, fairly analysed the plain meaning of our magical formula, that the spiritual world is "elicited" from the primarily natural by the activity of the thinking will.   We should note, further, that in eliciting this the will is by the same operation eliciting a definite and adapted shape of itself.   Thus the creative process of volition is the process of moulding by natural selection as interpreted from the point of view of the soul which is being moulded.   We are finding our self in the world as the world comes to life in our self.

This creation of a world is the fundamental proof and example of the power of will.   Every jot and tittle of this world is a volitional transformation of a relatively natural fact.

β. What is called the power of will or character over circumstances rests essentially on the relation

*Nature and limits of the power of character over circumstance. The word*

[1] Notably Mr. F. H. Bradley in *Ethical Studies*, to a great extent following Vatke's *Menschliche Freiheit*, and parallel with Green's *Prolegomena*.   The whole position comes, of course, through Hegel from Plato.

"circum-
stance"
indicates
a double
point of
view.

explained above.   There are [1] always larger complexes connected with any complex of circumstances
presented to finite mind, and thinking will is normally on the upward road to the larger and more
complete of such complexes.   The whole formation
of the world of will by transfiguration of natural
fact is the proof and province of the power of will.
And character is merely habitual will.

The only reason for devoting a special treatment
to the power of character over circumstance is that
our general doctrine might be passed over as a
metaphysical speculation on the large scale, hardly
worth denying ; while its straightforward application
to emergencies within present finite life might still
meet with obstinate opposition, as if asserting something magical and superstitious.   It is therefore
worth while to point out the nature and limits of
its actual realisation.

"Circumstance," for this purpose, is not the
imaginary world of purely natural fact which we
took as the ideal *terminus a quo* in tracing the
history of spiritual development.   It is circumstance
as we know it and constantly speak of it ; that is, as
I explained before,[2] a fragment of the world centred
in the self or mind which it "stands round."   It is
therefore, if taken in the full life and context implied
by its name, no longer a mere fact, but a self, or
living world concentrated in a consciousness ; while,
taken as a mere fact, or mere "circumstance," apart
from the centre which it implies, it admits its own
actual relativity and exposes its own false absolute-

---

[1] In what sense, in finding the larger outlooks, the will is
"creative" depends on the doctrine of *Principle*, Lect. IX.
[2] *Principle*, Lect. IX. p. 325.

ness.  Of such a nature are what we call a man's "circumstances" when externally observed and accepted as conditions common to him and others.

Thus, if we follow the track of our discussion, it is plain that, just as we observed every experience to be beyond itself, so every circumstance, taken in the full nature which the word implies, is much more than a "circumstance" in the current sense.  For in the former it is a member in a living world ; in the latter it is a fragment, endowed with false absoluteness by the assumptions of external observation.  Of course, it is possible for a man's own observation of his circumstances or situation to be external in its character, and for that of an outsider to be more concrete and vital.

The very name of "circumstance," then, we see, goes far to explain, in terms of our theory, the power of character over it.  A set of circumstances is, as currently taken, a fragment or collection of fragments of facts, hardened by external observation, while its own immediate reality, to go no further, is the world of a self, relatively ample and complete, organised, and animated by a mind which is, *ex hypothesi*, charged with connections, and has very much in it beyond what it has before it.  This is enough to explain how the organised self, with the life of thought in it, should be able to operate on any limited set of conditions within its world from a more powerful and effective point of view than that for which they are mere circumstances.[1]  There are always, we remember, open

---

[1] Here is Plato's account of what the knowledge of the ἀγαθόν can effect as a clue to life (*Rep.* 434 B).  I paraphrase freely,

ings to the larger horizons, and the thinking will is in principle always in search of them. And character is just the habitual will, maintaining the vigilance involved in thought, and a relative elevation of look-out point.[1]

Instances of transformation of circumstances by will. Rochdale Pioneers and others.

(1) Instances are innumerable. Take, for example, the history of the Co-operative movement in Great Britain. A few working men, desiring to get their groceries without a middleman, and therefore to work in the consumers' interest and not to make a trading profit, joined in setting up a shop, and contrived a simple system of dividing the profit among the consumers. From this simple act and plan of co-operation[2] sprang the vast Co-operative movement in England and Scotland, an ethical, educative, and economic force of the highest importance in the development of British democracy.

---

giving what I believe to be Plato's intention. "A man who knows the nature of good, or even recognises anything as good, must be able to distinguish in thought the principle of the good, discerning it from everything else, and, as if in battle, carrying it successfully through every theoretical and practical test, facing supreme problems, not mere whims and fancies, and coming through to the end without an inconsistency in his principle." One knows, on the other hand, too well, how, by an abstract account of his position, a man can prove to another, who cannot possibly possess the means of refuting him, that it ties him absolutely down to a given course—that which he in his heart prefers.

[1] Cf. Inaugural Address at St. Andrews, *Blackwood*, 1903, on the practical value of a lofty standard. See also Lane Cooper, *Function of the Leader in Scholarship* (Ithaca, 1911). I once asked an able practical man, well acquainted with the Society of Friends, how he accounted for their habitual success in business. He answered primarily that the habit of exercising conscientious judgment from a high standpoint on all questions of conduct tended to give them "a right judgment in all things."

[2] This, as I understand, is the history of the Co-operative movement in the sense now accepted, from the Rochdale Pioneers onwards. Of course in a full history of the kindred movements and influences many more points would have to be mentioned.

So with Trades Unionism, primarily, I take it, a scheme or combination to maintain or raise the rate of wages, but at the present day an immense power representing in a great measure the social and political ideals of working men.[1] In these and countless other instances the eager and vigilant thinking will, pressing hard upon the fundamental fact that all life is connected, and following up clues to fact and action in the manner analysed above, has "elicited" step by step, apparently out of the barest circumstances, but really out of the whole of social life implied in them, and in the minds operating upon them, constructions dealing with vast problems, far beyond the two or three simple facts in confronting which they took their origin.[2]

(2) A very instructive extreme case is in the power of character against so-called physical impossibility. Theory is here at a great disadvantage from its habit of dealing with hypothetical cases rather than with actual facts. There must *be* situations, groups of circumstances, in which will cannot possibly execute its preconceived purpose. This inevitable admission is accepted, and becomes an unanalysed factor in theory, a hard barrier, supposed to exist at some definite point, against the power of will. We are thus misled into failing to enquire how far and to what such impossibility is relative; and how far, therefore, physical impos-

*Relation of character to so-called physical impossibility. Wide relativity of physical impossibility. Distinction between strength and power of will.*

---

[1] I speak of facts. I am not entering into controversy about the merits of labour ideals and methods.

[2] It will very likely be observed upon this account that, *e.g.*, the first co-operators had *consciously* very large problems before them in germ. But, so far as it was so, this was only the beginning of the very process we are describing.

sibility is an unmodifiable barrier, how far a case of the rarity of the adequate will.[1]

And so two irrational attitudes are promoted; one magical and superstitious, demanding no *rationale* of the power of will, and so holding it to be capable of vast physical and moral achievements by its mere fiat;[2] the other fatalistic, holding it as a permanent and not an abnormal condition that

> " Things are in the saddle,
> And ride mankind."

Now what stares us in the face is this. Physical impossibility, to a very great and indefinite extent, is relative. It is relative to the agent's or agents' strength, motive, ability, and time. " Oh, yes," the retort may come, " but every one knows the outer limits of human strength and wits, and how soon you come to them." But none the less, we must insist, the area covered by the relativity is really immense. Our current estimates of impossibility do not relate to the outer limit of all human power, but to a most unreliable judgment of average ability and circumstance, modified to suit particular cases, and varying as regards even the same person according to supposed motive and occasion. Then this varying and unreliable estimate is apt to be confused with the ideal outer limit of human powers, and its unreliability, and the true malleability of circumstance to the thinking will, are therefore not attended to.

[1] It may be objected that you cannot will in face of a recognised impossibility. But then our question would be in what situations you would be right in recognising impossibility.

[2] Cf. Mr. Bradley's remark that, in consequence of extreme Libertarian ideas, people are not careful enough in avoiding temptations, which is really a plain duty (*Ethical Studies*, p. 44).

If I am locked up in a room by accident, and the bell is broken, and there is no urgency, I shall commonly say that it is "impossible" for me to get out till some one happens to come. But if the building is on fire, it becomes quite another matter, and dozens of possibilities of escape suggest themselves which otherwise would not have been held relevant.[1] Stories like that of Columbus' egg go to this point.[2]

Because, then, of the road from limited to less limited complexes, which will with thought is always seeking and finding, it is impossible on any definite principle to set a limit to the power of will. But it must be understood that it operates rationally and not magically, through transformation of circumstance conceived and carried out by means of clues by which new groups of fact are brought to bear.

And it must be noted that time is a condition of the first importance. The mind's power lies in its relation to totality, but in finite life this is subject to succession, and totality is never actually achieved at all, and never approached except through succession. Thus at and in a given moment will may be practically powerless against circumstance, of a kind that, given a lifetime of preparation and organisation, is easily dealt with. Here you have again

---

[1] We go always on a rough estimate of relevancy, which is essential in practice, but may be very misleading. Cf. Mr. Chesterton's clever story in which four sensible and honest watchers declare that "no one" had entered a certain house between certain hours. A postman had; but he "did not count."

[2] So in our novels of adventure we watch with complacency circumstances of physical impossibility, say, of an escape, being heaped up. For we know that the invincible hero will dispose of them by some simple contrivance or observation. The moral is in itself quite sound.

the abstract hypothetical case. Put a sensible and determined man in a canoe just above Niagara, and what can he do? But if you give him a day or a week of his life before the time suggested for the catastrophe, it is very unlikely that it will take place. Or, if a capable man has no food and no money and no employment, how can his character help him at the moment to feed his children? But you must qualify the man by his previous life, and not treat him as if he was just created, capable, and starving, and a father, at the same moment; and indeed one knows that some people would manage to feed their children in such an emergency, while others would not. The abstract case, taken as adequate, is the enemy here as throughout.

There is a final case which must be mentioned, and which may be set off against the acknowledged fact that some achievements are absolutely impossible. For, on the other hand, we may say, it is *never in principle* impossible for an adequate solution to be found by will for any situation whatever. But the solution may not solve the problem *qua* physical.

In following the road to larger horizons, the will transforms, not only its problem, but itself. The physical impossibility may be shelved by a new purpose. And here undoubtedly is a secondary sense of the power of will, which supplements the first, and while useless by itself, seems to many the principal factor in it. I mean courage, resolution, decision.

The nexus is this. The larger horizon will not in finite life always include the lesser without interference. In other words, the higher solution, which transforms the will as well as the circumstances, may demand a sacrifice. It may show that the desired good can be achieved, and more perfectly than the situation seemed to admit. But the achievement, it may become clear, must involve parting with something which is dear to us. Courage and decision will then have to be prayed in aid of the thinking will. "*Strength*" of will—courage and resolution—becomes a condition of the *power* of will. But mere courage or strength of will cannot work the miracle by itself. We must have the transfigured outlook, before we can grasp the sacrifice that will bring the longed-for solution.

5. The above view depends on taking the power of will to be essentially connected with the character of thought. The power of will, if we are right, lies in "being equal to the situation," or on "seeing and dealing with things as a whole," or on "seeing life as a whole." And this is the fundamental nature of thought and mind, viz. to grasp things as a whole. I fully recognise that in will proper there is a felt want of some special kind, working in the mind, which is the peculiar guide and clue of thought on the particular road to totality which may be in question. The intensity of this want, along with the formal habit of constancy and resolution in adhering to the path one has started on, just because one has started on it, may be called *strength* of will, or formal self-determination, in contrast with *the power* of will, or its ability to command success, as explained above.

*Will and cognition, how respectively dependent on thinking.*

These remarks apply alike to cognition and to volition proper. The difference between thought as will and thought as a cognition is really a matter of degree, and lies not on the side of production or initiative—for in both cases something is produced or initiated, and by essentially the same psychological movement—but on the side of the result produced. In cognition proper this is a system of ideas, fulfilling a general conation, a roving commission so to speak, towards the introduction of ideal order; though huge exertions of will proper, producing external changes through external appliances, may be subsidiary and essential to this result. In will proper it is an external change as such, fulfilling a more or less special conation to a more or less foreseen and definite end.

In spite of all that has been said to the contrary, the distinction, though inherent in finite life—because of the dual form of thought and externality—still seems to me in the main one of degree, and one that becomes arbitrary where the margins meet. When you write a book, is that—I do not mean the distribution of time or the manual exertion, but the essential work itself, the production of ideas in an order, fulfilling generally a previous idea and intention of producing such an order of ideas—is that cognition or volition? And if we change the example to laying out a garden, the production of an order at once ideal and external, fulfilling specially a previous idea and intention of producing such an order—is that cognition or volition? Of course, if you stop at the superficial distinction which makes cognition a copying of things and will a making of them, you get an apparently simple and radical difference. But that distinction is plainly false.[1] The two attitudes are sub-cases of introducing order into experience, and either turns at once into the other, if it meets the resistance characteristic of the

[1] See author's *Logic*, ed. 2, vol. ii. ch. ix.

other; cognition to volition if I have to strike a light to see the time; volition to cognition if I have to ask my way to Charing Cross.

There are two points which call for remark in the relation of this view of will to the opinions of to-day. They are

*a.* The difference between thinking will and will as conceived by voluntarism, and

*β.* The degree in which our view, both in principle and in actual results, meets a demand which has been made with great emphasis, for more study of ethical fact and experience, in contradistinction to argument from postulated principles and ideals.

*a.* I spoke of certain views of ethical principle as deserving to be called Intellectualism in a disparaging sense.[1] Their essence appeared to lie in arguing out the content of will from selected general postulates, without analysis of the concrete ethical worlds. To such Intellectualism our view is decisively opposed. But if Intellectualism were to be the name for every view which refuses to divorce volition from the essential nature of thought, an attribution unwarranted, we hold, by theory or usage, then, and then only, we should be found among the ranks of the Intellectualists.

The differentiation of voluntarism from our view is the counterpart of this. If Intellectualism relies on naked principle, Voluntarism relies on blind impulse. For voluntarism, as I understand it, the nature of thought, the nisus towards the whole, to utterance, that is, in the form of the concrete universal,[2] is not present in will. Will is for it the blind underlying

Relation of contrast between thinking will and the will of volur'ta'-ism to the opinion of to-day.

---

[1] Above, p. 99.      [2] See *Principle*, Lect. II.

impulse of all change, life, and action.[1]   Its unity, if
any is implied in it, is that of an initial impulse
which has not attained self-distinction, rather than
that of an immanent whole; and the impulse is
readily conceived as one tending to divergence, in
which no more than echoes of the initial unity—the
only unity in question—survive.   A final unity is, as
I gather, not excluded, but it is not implied.   There
is no necessary return or reconciliation of elements
to inclusion in a totality—there could not be, if will
is divorced from thought.

Thus the theory naturally links itself with
pluralism and with pessimism; with pluralism, for
development is primarily divergent, effected through
trial and error in an environment without unitary
significance;[2] with pessimism, because such a will,
excluding the guidance of ideas, is *ex hypothesi*
debarred from satisfaction, which is the coincidence
between idea and existence.   In a word, if we recur
to the language of the previous section, such a will
may possess strength or intensity, but it cannot
possess power.   For power comes only by the
approach to totality through thought; and to the
will of voluntarism such access is interdicted by its
very nature.   It is by its definition a striving which
excludes satisfaction.

This being so, it seems worth while to draw
attention to certain facts, which would be paradoxical
if voluntarism were the true account of will, but as

---

[1] Note, what I have insisted on throughout, the polar antithesis
between the term action as thus employed and the sense which it
carried for Leibniz and Spinoza.

[2] Where, therefore, trial and error cannot be superseded by the
power of will, because there are no roads through thought to the
larger horizons which give will its power.

it is, seem just what we should expect. I would never attempt to rest a philosophical doctrine either on its acceptance by any section of the public or on the success of views akin to it in the treatment of affairs ; philosophy is the judge of philosophy, and . there is no appeal.   But if defects are alleged, and excellences claimed, in which fitness or unfitness to do justice to special sides of experience are cardinal points, then it seems right and necessary to observe, in connection with relevant theoretical argument, on the *de facto* exhibition of such fitness or unfitness. If the side of experience which is being made into a test is the will-to-live, energy, activity, then it is fair to observe that over a familiar theatre of arduous progress and activity in important human concerns —concerns of social improvement—the one view has been operative in all that has been done, and principles akin to it have commended themselves to the doers ; the other is remarkable for the fact that it has never been operative in any advance at all, and has commended itself in the main to minds out of touch with social energy.

Now I have ventured to point out elsewhere[1] how much more deeply rooted in human nature and how predominant in practical influence and inspiration is such a work as Green's *Prolegomena*, as compared with anything that has emanated from the voluntarist movement — the movement that is supposed to represent will, activity, practicality. It would not be far wrong, in my judgment, to say both that the great and effective movement of social reform which has permeated the civilised world during the last fifty years has been directly or

[1] *Philos. Theory of State*, ed. 2, Introduction.

indirectly in a very great measure inspired by ideas
of the general type which Green advocated ; and
also, a still more interesting and important point, that
the actual substance of this movement as a practical
method of action—though I most carefully disclaim
the idea of assigning it any conscious relation to a
philosophical theory—has itself given rise to and
adopted principles in harmony with our above
discussion of character and thinking will.   Every
one who knows anything of social work behind the
scenes, knows that such watchwords as working
with a plan, of power belonging only to the thought-
ful will, of success attending only the inclusive point
of view, of the magic and miracle which attend the
attitude of considering life as a whole, have during
the last half century, in the English-speaking world
at least, been the operative ferment of social enterprise and advance.[1]   It is, if I am right, a noteworthy
phenomenon that the great works of will in the
province of greatest practical advance have on the
whole proceeded from or in accordance with the
principles of thinking volition and not those of
voluntarism.[2]

In the sphere of art, I am aware, a conflicting
claim might be set up, though as I hold on very
insufficient grounds.   It is in the appreciation of
this realm that Schopenhauer's very one-sided excellence chiefly lies.   But here we are no longer in the
strictly volitional sphere, and Schopenhauer's merit

---

[1] Green's philosophy was drawn quite as much from social
experience of life as from post-Kantian ideas.   And that is why, in
my judgment, it is likely to prove of permanent value.

[2] The relation is anticipated by that of Hegel and Schopenhauer.
Wherever you come upon their traces Hegel is fertile and Schopenhauer is barren.

is precisely *not* in his account of volition, but in his account of the refuge and escape which art affords from it.

It remains to be mentioned that the analysis of the actual moral world of objective mind (*Sittlich-keit*) both is an element of theoretical strength peculiar to the theory of thinking will, and has also, in and through the practical standpoint referred to above, been commended by that theory to the actual and active social consciousness which it thus reinforced and brought to higher energy.

β. It appears to me also that the demand of those who ask for a wider study of actual ethical conduct and its standards has been met much more largely than they recognise by the social movement of the last half century, under the influence of the view we have been discussing. There is a curious but quite genuine spiritual heredity from Plato's study of class-morality in the *Republic* to Hegel's analysis of the actual social mind as an objective structure; and from Hegel's analysis to Green's study of citizenship,[1] under parallel influences to which, but without conscious connection, came Le Play's methods of concrete observation, and then again, with full awareness of connection, the interest awakened by Toynbee, Edward Denison, and others, opening out into the full detailed study of social conduct which forms the equipment and the instrument of the sociologist and social worker[2]

*Relation of our theory to demand for ethical fact.*

---

[1] No one can here forget Mr. Bradley's masterly analysis of the actual moral world in *Ethical Studies* prior to the publication of Green's *Prolegomena*.

[2] There is a great deal of bad investigation as well as good. But the good exists, and that is all that concerns us here.

of to-day. Just as a great addition was made to the foundations of ethical knowledge when Hegel analysed *Sittlichkeit*, so another great step has been made during the last century in the critical and almost experimental study of social and ethical forces throughout the larger part of society. We may say now, I am convinced, without presumption, that we know by critical experience, and not merely infer, such truths as those we have been discussing about the power of will. We know much of the difficult subject of the morality of classes, and we have been able to rehabilitate in our estimation the character of the people, *not* in respect of the conventional moral " virtue," but in respect of the standards which belong to our more concrete view—in respect of their virile and human qualities. It is not too much to say that there remains no unknown class from among whom a revaluation of our ethical values could be sought or found. A further proof of this is our attitude (just alluded to) towards the personal virtues of tradition.[1] We are now disposed to praise and blame not conventional qualities, like a kind of " accomplishment," but rather the whole energy or weakness, the love or unlovingness, manliness, womanliness, and their opposites, with which people face the world. The will, we feel, is the man, a single energy, and not an aggregate of attributes.

Is Power of Will part of subject " Moulding of Souls " ? Yes ; will not be ulti- mately

6. With the argument of this Lecture we complete the two-sided idea of the moulding of the soul, and now find ourselves prepared to attempt some outline of the hazards involved in selfhood, and of the destiny of the finite self.

[1] Hegel, *Rechts-Philosophie*, sect. 150.

It would be an error to suppose that in discussing the miracle of will we have transcended the consideration of the world as moulding the soul. The soul—I use the term in the most general sense to mean the centre of experience which as a microcosm has acquired or is acquiring a character of its own and a relative persistence—the soul is not to be contrasted as a detached agent either with its constituent externality on the one hand or with the life of the absolute on the other. Our idea has been throughout, as we have naïvely expressed it in language which seemed the aptest we could find, that the soul is a range of externality "come alive" by centering in mind. And when we speak of the soul as a will creatively moulding circumstance, this is another expression for the microcosm, including the centre which its circumstances "stand round," remoulding and reshaping itself. It is, on the other hand, a thread or fibre of the absolute life, or rather, as we said before,[1] a stream or tide within it of varying breadth, intensity, and separateness from the great flood within which it moves. For the idea of a persistent isolated unity which the term soul conveys, or any such metaphor as that of a thread in a tissue or a fibre in a bodily organ, must not conceal from us the constant fluctuation of its range, the amplification and diminution of its microcosm, which is involved in our whole conception of the being of self and the power of will.

Being moulded, on the one hand, and moulding circumstance on the other—coming alive as a world, but as a world reshaping itself and transcending itself through striving towards the unity which is

*opposed either to environ- ment which selects, or to life of Absolute.*

---

[1] *Principle*, pp. 372-3.

completeness—are the double aspect of the soul or self which is, as we have seen throughout, essentially a world. As such, though fluctuating in range and energy, it has a relative and finite individual nature [1] —an apparent individuality—and a certain seeming persistence in time. Yet it has no barrier of division against the absolute, with which it is continuous, to speak in spatial and temporal similes, before and after and on every side of its spatio-temporal being. [2]

From this point forward we may consider the soul as relatively or in appearance a finite individual. And we pass on to make some attempt at analysing the hazards and hardships which are inherent in any pretension to fill such a place in the universe, to point out in what way they are incidents of the logic which determines its value, and to examine what sort of ultimate destiny we can seriously or critically desire for it, assuming, as our whole argument requires, the conservation of its value in the absolute, or, more truly, the being of its value solely in the absolute.

---

[1] See Lect. II. of the present volume.

[2] See on inclusion *Principle*, p. 272 ff. This continuity does not bar private pre-existence or survival. There is no question of being "in the absolute" or not, but only of the mode.

# B. HAZARDS AND HARDSHIPS OF FINITE SELFHOOD

## LECTURE V

### THE WORLD OF CLAIMS AND COUNTER-CLAIMS [1]

1. FINITE selfhood, the attitude of a self which thinks of itself as a finite thing, and considers the universe under the aspect of finite terms and relations, may be said to belong to a world of claims and counter-claims. *The world of finite beings in relations.*

It is burdened—I had almost written "oppressed"—by the sense of a duty to a superior being, with whom it is in relation, and this duty constitutes its morality, its sense of good and bad. The self makes on its side a number of demands upon the superior being and upon the other beings which are the terms of its universe, and their fulfilment and non-fulfilment impress it with a contradictory sense of justice and injustice. One remembers the heading of the sermon which O. W. Holmes's minister wrote under pressure of such a feeling, "On the Duties of an Infinite Creator to a Finite Creature."

Thus its life is essentially and inherently one of hazard and hardship. It is bound to the hazard

---

[1] Cf. *Ethical Studies* (F. H. Bradley, 1876), p. 279. I am even more than usual indebted to Mr. Bradley in this chapter.

of attempting to live by the command of a superior, which is outside and above it—an attempt which in the nature of the case must prove a continual failure; as is shown by the oscillation between the good will and the bad, which is all that, as thus considering itself, it can realise. It is bound to the hardship of constantly making demands for respect and assistance from God, nature, and fellow-men, which are recognised, as it appears, most capriciously and imperfectly; for, as we have seen, the environment rather moulds the self by a severe discipline than nourishes it without interference, and if we look at the miracle by which the self trans-mutes circumstances to its will, we see that in this very act it is no less in the furnace, recasting itself.

For the finite self, taking itself and the universe and—though not in so many words—God himself, as parts of a complex of finite beings in relation, is inherently a contradiction. It is a finite being which is infinite without realising it, and so, like all finite experience, is always beyond itself. It has working in it the spirit of the whole, and cannot, though it does not know why, find satisfaction in its limited self, and in the relations which, while they connect it with other beings, yet exclude it from them.

It is this double being which necessitates the atmosphere of hazard and hardship which surrounds the finite self when it tries to take itself as such. It finds itself always inevitably discontented and on the strain, in varying degrees according to its sensitiveness. It never feels that it does its pure duty, nor that it gets its whole rights. It cannot make its own claims good, nor satisfy the counter-claims upon it. It is, to borrow a lawyer's phrase (and the aspect of things thus considered is legal), "at arm's length" with God, man, and nature. It is over against them in relation; and claims and demands arise, as between independent terms or subjects, which`yet are forced into connection and collision.

The position, and the illusion that is involved in it, may be illustrated by a familiar conception in Hegel's social philosophy. He treats, it will be remembered, the economic world—the economic association of citizens as distinct from the spiritual unity of the social whole—as a world of units at arm's length to each other, governed by what may be compared to natural laws. This world has the peculiar characteristics which belong to these quasi-natural worlds of isolated units—severe natural selection, formative discipline and hardship, a condition where every man is for himself, subject to claims arising out of relations. Just such, we might say, is the world of relational morality with its machinery of duties and rights, for the finite being who takes himself seriously as finite—the world of individualistic morality.

And an illusion of the same type is involved in both. There *is* no such world of isolated terms in relations as these worlds appear to be. The economic world is not really a self-complete world. It is an appearance, a way of behaving and thinking, within the organic whole of society, within which alone its existence is possible. You could not have a world of the Stock Exchange which did not rest on the family, on social relations, and on the State. It would be a rope of sand.

So with the apparent world of moral relations between independent beings. It could not really exist, except as an appearance within something more single and self-complete. Our duty towards God and our neighbour (and our rights, which at this stage we tend to insist upon, against both) rest on relations that could not spring up between really independent terms. In envisaging the universe as an aggregate of such terms the finite self has construed the infinite in the language of finiteness, and the proof is that he finds himself in a contradiction whichever way he turns.

*Theism involves such a conception. Vatke's criticism on "Creator of Creators."*

2. It is characteristic of this world of claims and relations that to it Theism characteristically belongs. It is true, I think, that a Theist of to-day would deny that his views involve in full the attributes of such a world. He would deny that he considers God as merely a supreme ruler, the author of laws imposed *ab extra* on other beings; or merely as a governor of the world by rewards and punishments; or merely as a providence who compensates for apparent injustice in and by a future life; or merely as a Creator of subordinate beings, whose life is thereby predetermined (as, *e.g.*, Kant points out); or merely as an ideal and superior will, which finite beings can make their own only through an unending approximation (again involving the future life); or merely as an existence apart from the universe and from created minds, so as to become, in reality, himself a finite being. Yet these doctrines, which in their full abstractness would to-day be disowned, nevertheless must always influence Theism, because it is an outgrowth of that mode of construing infinity in the form of endless finiteness and related

plurality from which all these doctrines in their distinctive forms are derived. Thus the modern Theist might disclaim with Kant the moral government of the world through rewards and punishments, denying that the adjustment, which he demands, of happiness to desert is to be considered as a motive to action; but he would insist, I think, as a rule, on the necessity of a future life with a view to compensation for the injustices which the eye of individualist ethics everywhere detects, and probably also with an idea of giving room for the endless approximation [1] to the ideal will. Guidance of the universe *ab extra* so that ends are fulfilled, separateness and independence of God and man, need of the future life, as just observed, for compensation and ethical improvement, and, we may add, the direct and personal, and therefore miraculous dealing with the individual soul through grace (social solidarity having no place in the relational world [2]), continue on the whole to be the marks of the Theist, even though it seems to him desirable to claim a measure of immanence, which being made complete would destroy his position.

Here is a test point. The modern Theist sees that God must not be a literal creator; he must somehow not wholly make finite minds, but leave them to make themselves, or their freedom is destroyed. Now the Creator in the natural sense—if the term

---

[1] We must always remember that Kant in effect transcended this primary view of his, as he did also the idea of the literal Creator, and that of rewards and punishments in a future life.

[2] The question of the *actual* (*e.g.* social) character of the means of grace, as opposed to a magical and unintelligible account of them, is all-important for the theory of freedom and the connection of God and man. See Green, *Prolegomena*, sectt. 110-11 and Vatke, p. 459.

has a natural sense—can obviously not do this,[1] and in the world of separate related beings, and therefore in Theism, this kind of Creator is what we should expect to find.

Therefore on this point we are confronted by an evasive modification, which takes us too far and yet not far enough. We are met by such phrases as that "God actuates" or "produces the free as free,"[2] or "God is only a true creator if he creates creators."

Now on the ground *on which relational Individualism stands*—and this is the pure and normal ground of Theism—it is futile to pretend that these can be anything but phrases disguising a contradiction.[3] In will the particulars are essential, and if a separate personal God wills the being of the human will, that must mean that the detail of the human will is absorbed in the divine will. It is a contradiction to say that God, being a person separate from man, wills that man should have a will; but that man can use the will as he pleases. To will a will is to will its detail.

The contradiction is the same throughout. Finite self interprets its consciousness of the universe as a

---

[1] See Kant's discussion, *Krit. d. Praktischen Vernunft*, p. 234 (R.).

[2] Vatke, *Menschliche Freiheit*, p. 401, cited below.

[3] Vatke's profound and judicial discussion leaves no escape, I feel sure, from this conclusion, so long as we remain on the ground of mere related being and do not advance to the identity of the human-divine will. I cite a passage from his argument to show its carefulness and judicious temper (*Menschliche Freiheit*, p. 401):—

"Da nun aber die menschliche Thätigkeit erst mit dem wirklichen Wollen beginnen soll, so muss die durch Gott gesetzte Möglichkeit der Freiheit auch bis zu diesem Punkte geführt werden, und man muss sagen: dass der menschliche Wille Freiheit ist, hat er ohne sein Zuthun von Gott, wie er sich aber als Freiheit selbst bestimmt, hängt allein von ihm selbst ab.

"Hier zeigt sich nun aber derselbe Widerspruch, den wir oben

consciousness of independent beings in a world of claims and counter-claims, and views their closer union as something to be attained by endless approximation, the root-difficulty of their separation not being in principle removed. But such a conception is self-contradictory, and makes freedom, morality, the channels of divine grace, the realisation of perfection in finite beings, contradictory and unintelligible. The uneasiness incident to the position betrays itself in all that concerns the problem of progress. Apprehending no attitude but its own, the self in ethical individualism clamours for the

---

schon bei der Formel bemerkten, dass Gott das Freie als Freies hervorbringe [in other passages also 'wirke']. Alle Theorieen, welche die concrete Freiheit nicht als Product zweier in einander wirkender Factoren auffassen, führen zu einer abstracten Einerleiheit des göttlichen und menschlichen Willens, und können dieselbe nur durch verschiedene Arten der Selbsttäuschung von sich abhalten. Sagt man nämlich : dass der Mensch ein wollendes Ich ist, hat er von Gott oder durch den Willen Gottes, und zwar *ohne eigenes Zuthun*, so heisst dies ja so viel als : das menschliche Ich ist als Selbstbestimmung nicht durch sich thätig, sondern Gott allein ist darin thätig, es ist also blos Selbstbestimmung Gottes. Führt man denn fort ; aber *wie* das Ich sich bestimmt, *was* der Mensch als freies Wesen ist, hängt allein von ihm ab, so fällt dieser zweite Satz schon durch den haltunglosen Widerspruch des ersten ; ist die Selbstbestimmung des Menschen in der That *nur* Selbstbestimmung Gottes, so auch die Qualität derselben. Dazu kommt nun aber noch, dass die Selbstbestimmung überhaupt gar nicht ohne die Bestimmtheit, den Inhalt, das Wie und Was gedacht werden kann, da in dieser Besonderung des abstracten Ich die Bedingung liegt, unter welchen dasselbe Wille ist. Obige Formel sagt daher in der That das Gegentheil von dem aus, was man eigentlich meint. Da das Dasein der Freiheit von ihrer Thätigkeit nicht verschieden ist, so gewährt es auch keine Hülfe gegen die abstracte Identität beider Seiten, wenn man den Willensact Gottes, durch welchen er die freie Persönlichkeit der Creatur setzt, als eine göttliche Selbstbeschränkung auffasst. Denn da das Dasein der Freiheit das Wollen selbst ist, so fällt gar keine Grenze zwischen das göttliche und menschliche Wollen ; der göttliche Wille kann daher auch seine Bethätigung nicht zurücknehmen ohne damit zugleich das Dasein der menschlichen Freiheit zu vernichten."

unending progress, as we observe both in the fundamental importance attached to the future life, and in the tendency to make the standpoint of amelioration, advance, actual modification of the whole reality by the work of finite minds, applicable to the universe.

Morality (as duty for duty's sake) the central expression of the contradiction of such a world.

3. The contradiction of this world of claims and counter-claims centres in its morality—the conflict of good and bad. The finite self, construing its universe in finite terms, feels bound to be what as a finite term it cannot be—that is to say, one with the divine or ideal will. It feels this because, though finite, it is not merely finite, and throws its inherent impulse to identity of love and will with the universe into the shape of an impossible union of two independent terms. The position has often been analysed in philosophy, and here we need only draw attention to it, and to the light it throws on the finite individual when he construes himself in terms of his finiteness.

The essence of his being—the central claim which the universe makes upon him, appears as involving a contradiction. He has a finite will, which is *ex hypothesi* not the ideal will—this must be the will of another and independent being, the supreme Ruler—but the ideal will is imperative upon him because his nature is really, though he does not know it, more than finite, and is that of the whole. Because of this imperative set against his finiteness his own actual will is in opposition and is evil. The ideal will, again, is determined by opposition to the actual will, and its goodness, as also the badness of the actual will, is in this opposition, and they are essential to each other.

Thus—the point has been made quite familiar by
Mr. Bradley and others—the sides of the moral
agent's being, so far as this attitude goes, are in
contradiction to each other, but their contradiction
is necessary to the nature of both.   To be good
is to overcome the evil; to be evil is to be in
contradiction with the good.   If the evil were overcome in a man there could for him be no good;
for the definition of good, that it lies in overcoming the evil will, would no longer be applicable
to his will.   The paradox shows itself in the well-
known difficulty [1] of finding a content for the ideal
will.   The miracle of will cannot here take place.
It lay in developing an identical world as the object
of ideal will—the true human will—out of the substance and content organised by the rational will
fore-feeling itself as one with the organisation of
life in society and institutions.   But here—if the
point of view could be kept pure, which is impossible—we have no such faith and outlook upon
concrete unity with the whole.   We are bound,
by our sense of being more than we seem, to
identify our will with a superior law, but as, to this
view, the universe contains no substantial whole
which expresses in its organisation the identity of
finite wills, we cannot actually make the ascent out
of our finiteness which the relation to the supreme
ruler binds us to make.

Thus, so far as we remain in this point of view,
we are bound to an impossibility.   This makes us
restless and uneasy.   We demand, in the strength
of our solitary finite mind, or of a mere aggregate
of such minds, to reform the universe and change it

[1] See p. 98, above.

from evil to good. And all the while we carry *ex hypothesi* our evil with us. It is true, of course, as we amply saw in the former course of Lectures, that we *are* responsible for all possible amelioration ; the world *does* rest on our shoulders, and our finite mind *does* determine great issues by the next step that it takes. This is all true and valuable, but, as we saw and shall further see, it is not the whole truth. In asserting it barely, we are ignoring the real roots and complete nature of our being, and though "our" responsibility is a true and tremendous fact, it changes its shape very completely when we come to analyse the meaning of "our."

In this world of finite morality, however, what we want is to exchange our finite for a better one. But the better finite is a finite still, and our progress makes no change of principle. We remain, so far as it goes, in the world of claims and counter-claims, with the supreme ruler out of reach above us, and our fellow finite beings of mind and nature at arm's length around us. We get no nearer to the one, and no closer to the others.

All this, we must remember, is on the hypothesis that we maintain the attitude of insisting on our finiteness, and of treating the universe as an aggregation of related finites. But if so, we are treating ourselves as what we are not, and contradiction must inevitably result.

In the actual world, indeed, this illusion prevails only in part.[1] For, from the beginning, the

---

[1] Bradley's *Ethical Studies*, p. 279. "So we see that the moral point of view, which leaves man in a stage with which he is not satisfied, cannot be final. This or that human being, this or that passing stage of culture, may remain in this region of weariness, of false self-approval, and no less false self-contempt ; but for the race,

miracle of will has been enacting itself, and the common substance and content which it has "elicited" have begun to form a genuine possession of our self, precarious indeed, but having some degree of true individuality and self-completeness, and forming an earnest of a true satisfaction other than and transcending the endless progress.[1] The miracle of will, we saw, is founded on our divination of the whole as the only true expression of ourselves, and proceeds by search and construction to bring this whole into explicit being. So in the realms of beauty and of knowledge. In all of these we are in some degree taken beyond the contradiction of connection and relation between isolated terms. In the case of beauty, for example, we have made for ourselves, and are able to possess, a reality which is an expression of what is deepest in each of us, and yet—this is the essential point—is not finite in the sense in which we are severally finite. It is our belonging—nothing could be more so—but it has the character of what is much more than we are. It is, in short, an earnest and manifestation of the self-complete and thoroughly individual nature of the absolute. In it we see how the limits which make us finite and isolated are, and therefore can be, absorbed.[2] So too in the social whole and in civilisation, which we treated as the special embodiment of the will, a satisfaction in which separate finite wills unite in the possession of themselves and each other.

---

as a whole, this is impossible. It has not done it, and while man is man, it certainly never will do it."

[1] This point is thoroughly explained in the well-known chapter "My Station and its Duties," in Bradley's *Ethical Studies*.

[2] See *Principle*, p. 375, on participation in poetry compared with participation in the absolute.

And so too with knowledge, itself no doubt a system of terms and relations, but implying and revealing a unitary reality which underlies this system and in various degrees attains appropriate revelation through it.[1]

It is the existence of these realised anticipations of the absolute that makes life possible, in spite of mind's ignorance of its own nature. In a world of sheer morality—individualist ethics—the abstraction of the necessary contradiction and concomitance of good and bad, it would be impossible to live. As we said at starting, there could not really *be* such a world. The solution is, that the mind is only in part aware of its own nature, and it has already in some degree possessed itself of the substance of identity with God, man, and nature before it awakens to the reflective conception of an individuality and apartness in its life, eked out by relations, connections, claims. In realised social morality, for example, we have the beginning of that refutation of the empty contradiction and the unending progress which will find its consummation in religious faith.[2] But with this relatively self-complete and organic world, the substantial and real correlative of thinking will, we have already transcended the world of claims and counter-claims, and have entered the sphere where relations are superseded by a true identity, and where finite beings,

[1] Wherever, *e.g.*, in knowledge we meet with a truly categorical element, as in the categorical basis of the hypothetical judgment, or, what is much the same thing, in the categorical judgment of philosophy respecting the universe. As resting on and developing them *all* knowledge becomes a revelation of unitary reality.

[2] For the strength of collective feeling *ab initio* cf. Cornford, *From Religion to Philosophy*, p. 77 ff.

though still in the main finite, are no longer at arm's
length, but are " pulse-beats of the whole system." [1]

4. In the first lecture of the earlier series I
censured, as it might seem too audaciously, that
commonplace form of the cry for justice which fills
our everyday fiction and our popular literature of
pessimism. This is a problem which is rooted in
the contrast of the world we are now considering,
the world of claims and counter-claims, with the
deeper reality of spiritual membership of one another.
It deserves notice both as a characteristic revelation
of the attitude which constitutes that world, and
also because this individualistic [2] justice, like the
individualistic morality which we have been exam-
ining, plays a very great part in a widely current
pessimism and discontent.

Let us remember once more Hegel's economic
world, and the severity of its discipline, the root, as
he thinks, of so much futile pessimism which rebels
at the formative influence thus rudely applied. To
live mainly in a world of claims and counter-claims
is indeed a training for pessimism. It would not be
so, we must observe, if such a world was solidly and
effectively what it claimed to be. If we were finite
terms at arm's length towards each other, and could
live by a scheme of relations dictating claims and
counter-claims, nothing could be simpler or more
mechanical. And for a time such an appearance
may hold good, in some stages of economic fixity, in
some phases of moral and social stagnation. But, as
we have noted, these worlds of fixed relations are

*Individualism of idea of justice as apportionment of external goods according to a standard.*

---

[1] Hegel, cited in *Ethical Studies*, p. 156.
[2] The term individualistic is a term coined to express and insist
on the appearance of finite individuality. For us, therefore, its suggestions are opposed to the truth of individuality.

derivative and superficial and do not exist in their own right. Great world-movements, even everyday social change and progress, make our fixed scheme of relations crack and shiver round us like ice on a river in spring, and the world of claims and counter-claims manifests by its flux and variation its inability to express and include the real elements of human nature. The point and the solution is that no one should or really can live merely in such a world, though it is an aspect which life under certain limitations assumes for the following reason.

Comparing different persons as separate units, and their fortunes in the same way, we are struck by inequalities. And in face of these inequalities, standing on the ground of separable and comparable terms, characteristic of this whole world of claims and relations, we are led to frame some sort of *prima facie* scheme of claims or pretensions, dealing with some kind of apportionment of external advantages to individual units—apparent finite individuals—each to each.

It is very hard to make out what standard we instinctively resort to in the erection of these claims; the fact would probably turn out to be, if we took a comprehensive survey of current pessimism as it regards the injustice of the world, that we make use of a great variety, whose results would by no means be compatible. Thus, as we shall see, you cannot by the same rule claim advantages for weakness and for strength, and if in formulating claims you adhere to the word "merit," that is simply to leave it open upon what ground of claim you are proceeding.[1]

___

[1] I quote at length an interesting discussion by Mr. Stephen Reynolds, because it illustrates strongly the natural claim for justice,

But this does not alter the general fact that when
we regard each other as finite units in a world of
externality we tend to frame schemes of apportionment according to which, by some rule or other,
each separate unitary being has some claim to a
separate unitary allotment of happiness or oppor-
tunity or reward—of something which should be
added to him, it seems to us, by God or man or

and the impossibility of satisfying it *on the ground of claims and counter-
claims* (*Seems So!* by Stephen Reynolds, pp. 111-112): "You put it like
this, sir ; suppose you, being a gen'leman, had ten thousand pounds ;
an' me, being only a working man, had scraped together a hunderd ;
an' s'pose the interest on money was four per cent.    You'd hae four
hunderd a year, wouldn' 'ee, an' I should hae four?    Which is all fair
as far as interest on money goes.    That'd be our incomes if *we* was
nort an' money was everything.    But now, s'pose we lumps you an'
me in 'long wi' the capital us got, an' reckons out the proper incomes
us ought to have then, not as money-boxes, but as men.    'Twouldn't
be near so much difference.    You might hae a quarter or half as
much again as me, but 'tis a sure thing you wouldn't hae ten times
as much.    I bain't saying there's all that difference really, but that's
the two ways of reckoning justice—theirs an' ours.    They'm always
pushing for to reckon up things the first way, an' we says the second
way is right.    An' so 'tis.    A man counts more than ort.    *They*
says, ' What's a man worth?' meaning what's he got.    *We* says,
' What's a man worth?' meaning hisself an' his money together.
They says, ' What's just between this rich man an' that poor man?'
on the supposition that they'm to stay as they be, one rich an'
t'other poor.    But us says, ' What's just between this man an' that
man?    An' how is it that one o'em *is* rich an' t'other poor?'    They
asks, what was a man born to?    poverty or property?    an' works out
justice between 'em accordingly.    But *us* says that us was all born
naked, wi' nort at all till 'twas gived us.    That's the difference, an'
there can't be no agreement till they sees it."    I am sure you can
get no standard in this way.    The language reminds us of Aristotle,
*Eth. Nic.* 1133 a 22 ; but then he, I take it, has read economic
demand for the product (or cost of production) into the shoemaker or
builder.    But the man, apart from a selected standard, gives you no
rule.    I am sure the only way is to go to the facts of membership
and function, and attempt to arrange a system which assigns what is
necessary in their light.    The fundamental difficulty is that we want
the system to be as nearly as possible automatic, and that is very
hard to contrive.    We put up with many abuses rather than risk
complete new departures.

nature or fortune. And when our scheme proves wholly and absolutely alien to facts, we foster a pessimistic sense of injustice. We ask, " Why is it not as we so reasonably expected ? "

Now before discussing any such scheme of apportionment as a principle of justice, we are to note in the first instance that it is an individualistic scheme, in the sense of starting from the apparent finite individual *wie er geht und steht*, and building up, on and for him, a claim to equal or proportional treatment according to some rule or principle realised in him as a unit. Such an individualistic scheme, compared with the actual texture of the world of events, is of course a perpetual source of disappoint-ment, and for minds which are apt to take such schemes as ultimate, passes into a deep and abiding sense of injustice and injury. " What had this man done or his parents that he was born blind ? " Scrutinise the unit as a unit—it is needless to furnish instances, the whole of life is an instance. In multitudes of cases — those common ones, *e.g.*, of innocent sufferers—it is obvious, and in all ultimately true, that you will not find within him what will explain and justify his fortune by any of your rules of apportionment. It is impossible in a differentiated universe that it should be so, for ultimately *he*—the unit you are to take as basis of the arrangement—is himself a case of the apportionment. His qualities are his "gifts," and if you apportion fortunes to them, you are apportioning to a prior apportionment. Thus your expectation is, as a rule, materially disappointed, and in any case it never has a really reliable basis. The world of claims is a hard world, just as Hegel said, because it takes you apart from all your deeper spiritual supports, family, love, God, and demands apparently of the finite individual as a unit to fight for his own hand; and, secondly, because your deeper spiritual supports are not really gone, but inconveniently reassert themselves through the full reality of life, shattering the world of claims and counter-claims erected with such pains and labour, like the warm floods of spring shattering an ice-bound river.

I may venture perhaps to explain the light in which this contrast of worlds appears to me by referring once more to a phase in my own experience. When critical ideas directed against current orthodox Christianity first made an impression on my mind, it was more than anything else the doctrine of vicarious atonement, literally construed, that seemed shocking and unjust. And it was with some interest, and not without surprise, that, taking stock of one's convictions after a long development, one found that what was obviously the intention of the doctrine in question, so far from remaining the great stumbling-block in Christianity, had become pretty nearly its sole attractive feature. One had passed, I suppose, from an individualistic rationalism to an appreciation of the world of spiritual membership.

That a law shall accept an innocent man's death or suffering in lieu of that due by this law from another man who was guilty under it, is a thing conceivable according to some ideas of law, *e.g.* if its object is pure deterrence, or if it is construed, as in the world of claims, on the strict analogy of the exaction of a debt. But yet, in this same world, it is opposed by the sharp contradiction that the person who suffers, taken as a sharply separate individual, was never guilty at all, and had nothing at all to do with that, whatever it was, that caused the law to apply.   On the other hand, *upon the same quasi-legal basis* of separate individuality, you may urge that a person—a subject in the world of claims—can consent to what he pleases (*volenti non fit injuria*).   And thus individualistic rationalism may take, as it does take, either view at its choice : that vicarious punishment is made justifiable by consent, and becomes in this case a true satisfaction of the law (as might be more or less the case with a pure debt or for pure deterrence) ; or that it is irrational and contrary to the purpose of law, which is, at least, to connect a consequence with an act, and so a horrible injustice. In taking *either* of these views, I imagine, whether with rationalistic orthodoxy or with critical rationalism, one is in *the same* world of persons in relation, "at arm's length" to each other.

But on the assumption of any spiritual identity or solidarity, whether social or of a deeper kind such as we have in religion, all suffering of any member, we see at once, must in principle be borne by all ; and, owing to the nature of the power to endure, will continually be borne in chief measure by " the best "—the completest, most capable, least obviously guilty members of the whole.   This is an obvious and primary truth, and, on the whole, no decent man could wish it to be otherwise, for it is the principal characteristic which ennobles life and gives greatness to suffering.

In spiritual membership you have the root of the hazards of selfhood, which display themselves by shattering the relations of the world of claims, itself a hazard, as we have suggested, like an ice-floe on a warm ocean. "*Mea virtute me involvo*" is no phrase for the member of a spiritual whole. He is one with the child, the beggar, the criminal, the revolutionist. They may throw horrible burdens on him, and he has to shoulder them ; nay rather, in his nature and spirit, he has implicitly shouldered them *ab initio*.

This, I take it, is the fundamental truth which the doctrine of vicarious atonement was intended to express. It is quite familiar to us as a great doctrine of Plato and St. Paul, and of later masters of philosophy. It is the doctrine "die to live," the only idea that makes life worth living. The difference lies in having passed from regarding the finite individual as the unit, in a network of claims and counter-claims, to grasping the identity of a life of membership "one of another."

5. Following up this distinction we may finally explain the nature of that pessimistic sense of injustice which, as we have seen, attends upon the world of claims and counter-claims. The point clears itself up in this way. The common basis of the notion of justice is to treat every one by the same law—insisting on the point that this law is a general rule—to make no distinctions which have a source outside the law on which you profess to go ; in short, to observe equality before your principle. But the Greek theorists saw, and it is an all-important truth, that the idea of an organic whole may take you out of the range of any practical application of such a principle, because of the spring of differentiation which it contains. If your principle of justice is "the best for each, consisting in the fullest service

Nature of Pessimistic Sense of Injustice in world of claims.

to all which his peculiarities allow," the apportionment of advantages which commonplace justice contemplates is thrust out of the scheme, and a development of the differentiated structure of the totality—society or spiritual kingdom—takes its place. Individualistic justice—the apportionment of advantages to units by a general rule or scale—would be absorbed in "the best," and there would be nothing separate to count as "justice" over against the realisation of the completest development of each that its nature permitted.[1] There could not be, beside and outside this realisation, a scheme of equal or proportionate claims of individual units depending on some scale of a selected characteristic belonging to them as isolated beings. Concrete justice as above is the organised righteousness of Plato's *Republic* or the mood of religion. Separate units, *qua* separate with their respective claims according to general rules, do not survive at this level.

But this attitude is not wholly possible for a finite society in space and time, composed of finite individuals having many characters of isolation and distinctness—material characters such as a body, and its accessories in the way of property. Here the principle of the unit as such must receive some sort of recognition and protection. You must provide not only, so far as you can, that the unit shall have open to him the best that his nature in relation to the whole allows him, but that the simple

---

[1] It is the old story of Cyrus and the boy whose coat fitted another boy better. Cyrus, the story says, judged wrong in giving the coat to the boy it fitted best. He should have thought whom it belonged to. But from the standpoint of membership and function the best for each when admitted must supersede justice as equal treatment, whether by the general rule of ownership or any other general rule.

material conditions on which as finite he depends shall be in some way and degree accessible to him, and that he shall be furnished with some apportionment of a limited and separate degree of self-maintenance. You cannot allow an omnipotent principle like that of spiritual membership to be used and abused at the discretion of finite societies. The rule, in itself perfectly sound, " It is expedient that one man should die [or starve or lose his goods or his health] for the people," is apt to be applied inexpediently in the practical government of terrestrial communities. And so it comes about that our distinctive sense of justice is divorced from our sense of the best, and is hardened into what might be called a protective or conservative rule, or rule for ensuring the minimum, by which units are to be conserved in some simple degree and proportion to their mere existence and presence as numerable factors of the community. This is the justice which the courts maintain, rooted in the fact that every finite unit as such has (rightly or wrongly from an ultimate point of view) claims and accessories belonging to his separate existence, in which, if there is to be a visible social order, he must be guaranteed security. There must be in finite life a justice which maintains some apportionment of externals to individuals. This is what gives us our current idea of justice ; this individualistic apportionment is what, as a rule, we mean by it.

Now this conception of justice throws us back on the world of claims and counter-claims, the world of individualistic justice, with, as we saw, most insufficient data for establishing schemes of proportion. But yet, following the analogy of a finite community, we adhere to the conviction that there is something definite and anticipable, some apportionment of fortunes, some routine in the ordering of externals and incidents and the trend of events, which is what we call "just," *i.e.* suitable to our unitary finite existence, in virtue of whatsoever feature of it we may happen to choose. This, as we hold, we have a right to expect and demand from God, Man, and Nature as our counter-claim to the claims which we acknowledge that, as terms in certain relations, they have upon us.

Here, then, is the crux. The great world of spiritual membership, to which really and in the end we belong, takes no account at all of any such finite claims, for reasons to be stated directly. Therefore our "individual" fortunes betray no approximation to any single standard of individualistic justice, to any claim for apportionment of external advantages either by equality *qua* human beings, or by any other standard. The real principle of things is quite other, and dashes our world of individualistic justice to shivers wherever for a moment it has seemed to assume consistency. Therefore the world of claims and counter-claims is oppressed not only with a claim for goodness which can never be realised, but with a claim for considerate treatment from without which bears no relation to spiritual reality. And, therefore, to acquiesce in the ideas of that world is to be always in moral despondency and also in pessimism, and filled with a sense of injustice.

For, as we have urged,[1] the spiritual world, as a

---

[1] Aristotle's distributive justice, though itself a form of individualistic apportionment, is yet by its recognition of an organic differentiation in society akin on the whole to a principle of spiritual membership,

world of true membership, affords no encouragement to ideas of justice turning on apportionment of advantages to units by any rule whatever. To begin with, the very basis of apportionment is cut away. The unit makes no insistence on its finite or isolable character. It looks, as in religion, from itself and not to itself, and asks nothing better than to be lost in the whole which is at the same time its own best. Such an attitude gives no fulcrum for the principles of the world of claims and counter-claims. There *are* no claims and counter-claims.[1]

6. And, secondly, if you could, or so far as you think you can, find a basis and rule of apportionment to units taken as separate, the results considered from an adequate point of view would certainly be repulsive to us in their details, would contradict the conception of unity in happiness and suffering, and would take us back to the ground on which it appeared irrational and inequitable that one—to recur to the terminology of that level—should bear the suffering or the punishment of another.

Why not have a standard of justice according to spiritual membership? Self-contradiction of such a standard.

This second point was referred to in the Introduction to the former volume, but a few remarks may be added here by way of elucidation.

If we are arranging any system or enterprise of a really intimate character for persons closely united in mind and thoroughly penetrated with the spirit of the whole—persons not "at arm's length" to one another—all the presuppositions of individualistic

---

as against the justice which merely recognises the necessity of securing units, *qua* units, in their apportionment.

[1] We discussed what is pretty nearly the equivalent of this principle in *Principle*, pp. 5, 16.

justice at once fall to the ground. We do not give the "best" man the most comfort, the easiest task, or even, so far as the conduct of the enterprise is concerned, the highest reward. We give him the greatest responsibility, the severest toil and hazard, the most continuous and exacting toil and self-sacrifice.[1] It is true, and inevitable for the reasons we have pointed out as affecting all finite life, that in a certain way and degree honour and material reward do follow upon merit in this world. They follow, we may say, mostly wrong; but the world, in its rough working, by its own rough-and-ready standards, thinks it necessary to attempt to appraise the finite individual unit; this *is*, in fact, the individualistic justice, which, when we find it shattered and despised by the universe, calls out the pessimism we are discussing. But the more intimate and spiritual is the enterprise, the more does the true honour and reward restrict itself to what lives

> "In those pure eyes
> And perfect witness of all-judging Jove,"

that is, to the spiritual fact, the realised unity in which the higher is higher by his completer self-surrender. We may think of the "honours and rewards" that have come to the great poets of the world. Plainly, there is no word to be spoken of any proportional relation between these and their services to the world—there could be no proportion between such things. As finite material beings it would have been well, we think, if due preservation and attention *qua* human units had come to them; and so, no

---

[1] Cf. John Brown, *Rhodes' Hist. of U.S.A.*, ii. 387, "God has honoured but comparatively a small part of mankind with such mighty and soul-satisfying rewards" of an enterprise in which death was practically certain.

doubt, founding ourselves on the general duty of humanity to its members, we are right in thinking. But we cannot put it on the ground of a just proportion between their deserts and their treatment. There is no such proportion, and the justice which we are inclined to invoke is the necessary regard of a decent society for its units, and not any apportionment of advantages by a standard of merits. No advantages that we can apportion count in the scale.[1] We feel that to make a great poet, say, the richest man in his community, would be irrelevant and self-contradictory. It is not what he wants, and would probably choke his work and do enormous social mischief.

If we tried to embody our highest instincts, founded on the sense of spiritual membership, in the form of individualistic justice, *i.e.* legislating for the inherent need and claim of isolated units, we should more plausibly get some such result as when we send women and children first to the boats in shipwreck. "Happiness to the weak, cowardly, over-sensitive; hard service and endurance to the capable and the strong." But the fact is that this, like any other plausible principle of individualistic apportionment, would break down after a step or two. The weaker souls would prove unable to contain and possess the happiness you would offer them, and you would find, as you do find, every individualistic principle superseded at any chance point by the working of the spiritual reality, which admits of no such principles by the side of its law, "realise

---

[1] It sounds ridiculous to say that a man is allowed to starve because no material recompense is adequate to his merits. But I have no doubt it is a wide-reaching principle, and not in every degree wrong. Such people do not want our rewards.

the best." For each the only real claim is for the best it can be, at once the highest self-surrender, and, no doubt, the completest self-affirmation. If we say, as indeed we well might desire to say, that in this fullest self-surrender there lies, as the truest self-realisation, so too the greatest happiness, we should be coming in sight of a principle which undoubtedly has great effect upon our judgments even in common life, and which would harmonise well with our views of the nature of reality and satisfaction.[1] But it would not in any way appease the pessimistic sense of injustice rooted in the world of claims and counter-claims. For it would set all claims at defiance.

*To make the finite mind, through its claims, the judge of its own need for hardship, is to make the universe a farce.*

7. I do not mean to say that the actual apportionment of fortune to finite units could ever seem to us wholly intelligible. I only say that one plain and universal principle of false judgment, the principle of individualistic justice, is got rid of by the above considerations, and so far we are gainers, and the pessimistic sense of injury, analogous to moral despondency, is done away. The view we have taken paves the way for a treatment which at least harmonises better than current pessimism with the demands of actual fact, and destroys the necessity and inclination for the wearisome "why?" of the popular pessimist, and the equally wearisome sentimentalism, of compensation to be found in a life beyond the grave. The principal difficulties which remain are not so much about the proportion of fortune to merit—not really an idea which has a strong hold on healthy minds—but about certain existences whose contribution to any possible whole

---

[1] *Philosophical Theory of the State*, ed. 2 p. xxx.

we find it hard to understand,[1] and about certain extremes of suffering and hindrance which seem to raise the same question.  To these matters we shall have to return when we deal expressly with pain and evil.  I will here do no more than repeat the principle touched on in the Introduction to the former course, that there must be in the universe something *bona fide* above and beyond the finite being, from which he has to learn, and to which he has to go to be moulded and disciplined.  Once refer the degree of suffering and difficulty necessary and permissible in the realisation of the best, to the judgment of the finite beings whom it is to affect, and you have turned the whole idea of a universe into a farce.  Who would submit, if he could help it, to the discipline inherent in his membership which makes him a real man and a soul?[2]

I have been reading, like many others, I suppose, Miss Johnson's *The Long Roll,* the terrible story of certain campaigns in the American Civil War.  I might be challenged, "Would I maintain that such things could exist in a just universe?"  I am not going to answer the challenge, but to point out what I hold an absurd implication in it.  Am I, an elderly gentleman almost tied to his arm-chair, to be asked to dictate the limits of heroism and suffering necessary to develop and elicit the true reality of finite spirits?  Why, even if the question were, should we ourselves *like* to have taken part in those campaigns, or to take part in such struggles con-

[1] Imbeciles are a typical case.  Of course, in all these extreme cases we must not judge them *both* as capable of spiritual life *and* as not.  If they are not, we can hardly treat them as deprived of it.

[2] Cf. Francis Thompson's wonderful poem, "The Hound of Heaven."

ceived as still future, I imagine that very different voices would be heard from different sections of mankind. And, to go deeper, take more cruel and less brilliant suffering, of which, if offered, every one would pray that the cup might pass away from him (is not this reference, indeed, sufficient for my argument?), is it not clear that finite judgment would practically always be wrong, and one would refuse what alone could recast one as a less worthless being, or what made the value of an age or a nation? And in principle is it not clear that to set within the judgment of the finite spirit those depths of the universe on which its being more than finite are to depend, is a contradiction in terms, and makes futile the whole notion of a finite partaking of and reaching into infinity? The whole point of the connection is that the finite spirit is more than it knows. If we let it, taking itself as finite, lay down its own ultimate limits, why then, of course, all that it dreads is gone, and with it all that made life worth living. I venture these remarks because I seem to observe an extraordinary eclecticism in the toleration of pain and trouble, as if Marathon and Salamis were somehow obviously fine and desirable events, while modern battles of a less picturesque type, and attended no doubt by miseries on a more enormous scale in the way of neglected wounded and the like—not to speak of the thousand-fold horrors of our civilisation in its grimmer and dirtier parts— were obviously and self-evidently to be ruled out as intolerable.[1] I am not at present arguing that this

---

[1] I confess that eclecticism of this kind always reminds me of Hotspur's interlocutor:

> "And but for these vile guns
> He would himself have been a soldier."

view is wrong,[1] but only that it is very startling, and that it would need a great deal of explanation and defence to make it in any way plausible. The following lectures will attempt a more thorough treatment of the subject.

[1] Vatke thinks you may distinguish between evil which ought (so to speak) and evil which ought not to exist. It seems to me scarcely possible to maintain the view. See, however, Rashdall, *Theory of Good and Evil*, ii. 236.

## B. HAZARDS AND HARDSHIPS OF FINITE SELFHOOD—*Continued*

## LECTURE VI

### PLEASURE AND PAIN

Failure of the World of Claims. What our account of our troubles aspires to effect—maximise rather than minimise. 1. WE saw in the last lecture that the hazards and hardships of which man is so deeply sensible seem not to be accidents of his lot, but rather to be rooted in the double nature which he possesses as a finite-infinite being. The World of Claims, we held, was an attempt to satisfy the demand of this double nature by a sort of debtor and creditor account, expressing our relation to the universe as claims and counter-claims between self-existent beings at arm's length towards one another. And we saw that such a scheme could not but leave us dissatisfied, because an external relation to a quasi-finite God and to other finite beings remains wholly inadequate to the spiritual membership which underlies our apparent isolation. Thus it seemed that our moral imperative is a hazard—an arbitrary obligation imposed by a power unconnected with our will—and our rule of individualistic justice must leave us under a sense of hardship when we find it fail to control our true nature and destiny. No conceivable rule can satisfy us so long as it treats us as units to be considered on our several merits.

There is indeed a more substantial world of

morality, in which spiritual membership has attained a certain degree of realisation. The consideration of this belongs to the philosophy of society, or, in our enquiry, to the hopes rather than the hardships of selfhood. And there it will fall to be considered under the general heading of religion. But our immediate purpose is to trace to their common root the troubles of the finite self, and to display, not their unreality, not their certainty of compensation, but in the first instance simply their source and nature. If this can be done, as we have attempted, and are attempting, the result should be interesting, and perhaps something more. To think that there is any sort of rhyme or reason in our sufferings, that they are not a dead fact of destiny, nor a cruelty of an omnipotent tyrant, would be helpful, I believe, at least to certain minds. And if it further appears that our troubles and our value have one and the same root—and this again we have attempted and are attempting to make good—it will not indeed directly make the former less. Our business here is truth, and not a *théodicée*. It would rather, we might say truly, make more of them, make them deeper, greater,[1] more significant. But yet in doing

[1] Cf. T. E. Brown's poem, "Pain"—

> The man that hath great griefs I pity not;
> 'Tis something to be great
> In any wise, and hint the larger state
> Though but in shadow of a shade, God wot!
>    *    *    *    *    *
> But tenfold one is he, who feels all pains
> Not partial, knowing them
> As ripples parted from the gold-beaked stem,
> Wherewith God's galley onward ever strains.
>
> To him the sorrows are the tension-thrills
> Of that serene endeavour,
> Which yields to God for ever and for ever
> The joy that is more ancient than the hills.

M

so it might make them less unwelcome, though that is not here our primary aim. We remember how Dante's souls in purgatory passionately desired the pains which assured them of their place in the eternal love.[1]

Pleasure and pain ; their common root in the double nature of finite beings.

2. Another set of experiences, then, which may well be counted together under the head of hazards and hardships, are what we call pleasure and pain. Pleasure is certainly a hazard. It may come from anything, good or bad, and we cannot tell what in a given context it indicates. Pain is both a hazard and a hardship. Not only may it come from anything and indicate anything, but it seems to be in itself a cruelty exercised by the universe upon us. Pleasure, taken by itself and out of context, would for us need no explanation. Pain *prima facie* leaves us discontented and enquiring.

Pleasure and pain, it is suggested, are rooted in the same characteristic of our nature. And, moreover, this is the same characteristic which is the source of all the hazards and hardships of selfhood—our finite-infinite being. The essential point which I hope to illustrate is that the finite being is always passing out of itself, which also means into itself. And this passage, while on the one hand the condition of expansion and attainment, is on the other hand inevitably attended by some degree of contradiction, friction, sacrifice.[2] It is in the tension and its incidents, which this self-transcendence implies, that the very life of the universe consists. And, as we partly saw in the former series, and shall further

[1] They took care not, in the interest of seeing and addressing Dante, to extend any part of their persons beyond the flames.

[2] Cf. *Principle*, Lect. VI.

see, the nature of finiteness forbids a frictionless union.  If experience seems to show something of the kind, it must be a partial exaltation, and not the full union which alone is relative to full satisfaction.[1]

3. It is commonly assumed that pleasure and pain are plus and minus quantities on the same scale—that it is possible to find a quantity of either which will cancel any given quantity of the other. And in common experience something like this appears true.  We do seem to treat the two as opposites which can only come together in a whole by subtraction of the one kind from the other.  But the more serious, the more deeply implicated in life our action and feeling become, the less possible is it to acquiesce in this simple opposition.  Even in some of their commonest forms the two refuse to be finally distinguished, and force themselves upon us as kindred aspects of some condition essential to our lives.  All the classical instances of pleasures inseparable from pains are here more or less in point.  For the fact is that they are not merely linked by causation and in succession, but they infect each other's character.[2]  The fact is obvious in the quasi-satisfactions of the fiercer desires, the pleasures of pursuit, the pangs and delights of production.  It needs some attention and imagination to realise the extraordinary aptness of the metaphor by which Socrates treated creative activity as a travail of the soul.  It is not merely a question of a craving and

*Common character of pleasure and pain ; not opposite quantities on the same scale.*

---

[1] Cf. *Principle*, Lect. I.

[2] I think it quite probable that in saying that certain pleasures and pains "take their colours from" one another (*Rep.* 585), Plato meant not merely that pains give a false intensity to pleasures, but that they infect them with some of the fierceness and restlessness of pains.

its relief. The self-expression or self-expansion itself tears its pathway; and the poet or artist, I take it, if asked whether first-rate production were pleasurable or painful, would not be able to analyse the experience into a balance of opposites.[1]

Pleasure and pain imply self-transcendence; in pleasure harmonious, in pain, obstructed by contradiction.

4. It would be beyond my purpose and my competence to attempt a complete investigation into the nature of pleasure and pain. But I will try in a few words to connect our doctrine with the best ideas on the subject.

Pleasure, I think it is generally agreed, accompanies activity in which the self is maximised; that is to say, either attends upon expansion of the self as such, or, being an incident of activity, is dependent on the harmoniousness of conditions which relatively increases it by negating all that baffles or obstructs it. This statement includes, I hope, what is clearly true about the connection of pleasure with conation. We cannot disregard the classical instances of the pleasures unattended by the pain of previous craving; and if we make conation the condition of pleasure, it must be a conation which can be continuously merged in fruition.[2] All the special theories of pleasure, which it will be sufficient to imply in describing theories of pain, come back, I think, to these general characters. By "activity" I only mean a change accepted by the self as issuing

---

[1]. I suppose we common people know something of the kind when we have, *e.g.*, to make a speech. We are miserable, no doubt, but this is partly because we are above our usual level, and are living at a pitch of effort and excitement to which we are not normally equal. And in this exaltation there is also enjoyment, and enjoyment inseparable from the misery. The instance, though commonplace, goes to the heart of the whole argument of this lecture.

[2] *Principle*, Lect. IV., sect. 3, and *Ar. Proc.*, 1912, on Mechanism and Purpose. Cf. Bradley, *Mind*, xxxiii. p. 43 note.

from itself.    Persistence or self-maintenance against possible cessation or diminution must count as such a change.[1]

The nature of pain has been stated in very many ways.    But they all, so far as I can see, come back to the diminution of activity or self-maintenance by baffling or obstruction.    It will not do to say that the mere diminution of the world of consciousness involves pain.    Falling asleep, and other forms of narrowing consciousness, are obviously painless.    If what is lost vanishes wholly, so that nothing remains of it,[2] the loss does not cause pain.    It is when the roots of what is gone remain, and struggle to reinstate it, that contradiction, which is painful, is produced.

The familiar observation that pain accompanies what is organically injurious, and pleasure what is advantageous, is rather a theory of how they come about in evolution than an account of their actual conditions.    And, moreover, the injury or advantage which is attended to is normally local and partial (a sweet poison is the classical instance), so that the mere feeling produced by an agency is no guide to its total effect on the organism.[3]    Nevertheless, this general principle is akin to a whole group of theories, beginning with that of its great advocate, Herbert Spencer, that pleasure attends medium exertion, and pain repressed or extreme activity.[4]    It is not much more than a specification of this

---

[1] See Bradley, *Mind*, xliv. 439.

[2] I am here following Bradley.

[3] Spinoza's account of partial pleasures and pains seems to me still the soundest.

[4] The whole group of theories is closely akin to Aristotle's connection of pleasure with an ἀνεμπόδιστος ἐνέργεια, and does not make very much advance upon it.

doctrine when we have pain ascribed to fatigue of an organ, to excess of wear over repair, or to excessive intensity of the object. An analogous account gives a fuller rationale of the experience when it says that pain lies in the stimulation of an organ combined with repression or obstruction of its activity.[1] A simple example, very relevant to theories of this class, is the discomfort to the eye, amounting sometimes to actual pain, of a light flickering at certain small intervals.[2] It is a case, the conditions of which can to some extent be analysed by attention, and which yet is on the border of actual sensation. Pleasures and pains of sensation cannot as a rule be analysed in terms of any theory, and our direct account of pleasure and of pain is restricted to cases in which psychical antecedents are traceable.

The conditions of pain, then, as explicitly or implicitly recognised by all these theories, are twofold. We want an activity—mind or body reacting to an object, not necessarily by conation unless in a very wide and unusual sense—and also a baffling or obstruction of it. It is not going far afield to summarise these conditions as a felt contradiction.

[1] It has to be admitted that there are certain kinds and amounts of obstruction which serve pleasantly to augment activity. In fact, how distinguish obstruction, technically, from the work in doing which the organ is exercised, and which is, *ex hypothesi*, the condition of pleasure ? It is difficult to get away from inserting in the standard of pleasurable activity the condition "pleasurable." Still, we know what baffling and obstruction are. They come from outside the relevant object. Cf. Sidgwick, *Methods of Ethics*, ed. 6, book ii. ch. vi. sect. 2.

[2] There is some analogy between this condition and that which is felt as discord in music. The latter has been compared to the feeling of trying to do sums in one's head, and finding the numbers too high. The ear demands a smooth tone, and is baffled by the irreducible beats.

The general nature of contradiction, we have seen, is an attempted union rendered impossible by inadequate adjustment of the terms. Hence pain now appears to us as correlative to contradiction, while pleasure is correlative to successful union.

Thus these two experiences seem to reproduce in the realm of feeling the general structure of satisfaction and reality. The nature of the finite-infinite being involves constant self-transcendence, union with a not-self and reshaping of the self. The distinction between pleasure and pain is the distinction between this union when unobstructed, and when obstructed, or realised with friction and sacrifice.

Both experiences, therefore, in a sense encourage movement. Pleasure encourages the unobstructed activity to persist ; pain forces the mental or bodily organism to changes of attitude in seeking for relief.

5. Now we can carry further the suggestion of sect. 3, that pleasure and pain are not plus and minus quantities, reciprocally exclusive, and only to be brought into one whole by subtraction. Rather, in accordance with Plato's indication to which I have often referred, we are to consider them as pointing to an inclusive experience, which should participate in the character of both while transcending either. For the preceding considerations suggest that both have the same root in finiteness, and partake of the same character in different modifications. It may be urged that according to my own contention I ought to take pleasure as the perfection of the experience which, when imperfect, is pain, just as satisfaction corresponds to the perfection of the experience which, when imperfect, is

*Satisfactory self-transcendence of a finite being must include something which has been pain.*

contradiction. But *such* a pleasure would have to carry in itself the significance of all pains, as a perfect satisfaction carries in it the reconciliation of all contradictions. Common or easy pleasures merely omit or pass by obstructions, as common and easy satisfactions—practical or theoretical—merely omit or pass by contradictions. The union of an imperfect self with perfection cannot be mere inclusion. The finite being, having a false completeness in itself, and being based on a casual range of externality, *i.e.* being "natural," has not merely to be added to in its lifelong struggle towards the Absolute. It has also to be taken from, to be recast and opened up to services and vistas *prima facie* beyond it. And this, like the readjustment of terms which removes contradiction, means a profound rearrangement and transformation. The sum and climax of such an experience, though we are aware of it in its factors rather than in its unity,[1] must be in principle something great[2] rather than something easily pleasant. Of course, it is well seen that the greatest things may possess the profoundest charm.

Pain has no special relation to evil, nor pleasure to good, or only in a secondary sense.
6. Thus we are brought to a theoretical result of some importance. It is impossible to hold pain to be the effect or concomitant of evil as opposed to good; of evil either in the form of moral badness or of sin as known to religion. In the very widest sense we may say, indeed, that pain is itself a form

---

[1] *Principle*, p. 273 ff.
[2] Cf. Dante's *Purgatorio*, and the kindred theory of Purgatory in the "Dream of Gerontius." Most people will admit there is a great deal which must be burned out of us. But it seems redundant to add on this process after our earthly life, when it is so sorely needed in helping to make that life less unintelligible.

of evil, being an experience, so far as it goes, incompatible with complete satisfaction. And this is the same thing as recognising that it has its roots in the same condition which is the root of moral badness and of sin. But goodness has also its root in the same condition, and involves the same contradiction, which is fundamental in finite being. Thus pain, being simply the feeling of a *de facto* contradiction, belongs to goodness as well as to immorality and sin. We have, moreover, to bear in mind that in a world of spiritual membership the pain or wrongdoing or extinction of any member in principle belongs to the world throughout, so that it is wholly impossible that pain shall be confined to those who in the normal sense, considered as units, are authors of evil.[1] Pleasure, on the other hand, as it escapes the contradiction which is pain by being, like pain, partial and abstract, may, like pain, be met with in any one of the three, or strictly four, types of experience in question—moral or religious good, moral or religious evil. So complicated is the context of life. If we are asked how a distinction can be drawn between pleasure and pain on the one hand, and good and evil on the other hand, if both are antitheses rooted in the fundamental nature of a finite being, the answer is indicated in what has already been observed. Pain and pleasure attend upon contradiction and non-contradiction wherever they are found within the varying complications of finite life. Good and evil are characters of selves which mark a definite advance

---

[1] In a sense, plainly, as all are liable to the pain of some, so all are authors of the evil done by some. But this is not a sense accepted by the mind which expects the good to be protected from pain. Of course in all finite life there is at least the loss by death of others.

in a certain direction. The good self has so far
attained a harmony of being that by it the general
contradiction of finite life, without being set aside,
is determined to definite factors and a definite line
of conflict, in which a partly realised harmony
stands over against the embodied principle of discord. Thus, it might be urged, we have admitted
that pleasure has a certain ideal and ultimate kinship with the good, as with a principle of harmony,
and of antagonism towards the bad; and this is
true. But in finite being the affirmation of a principle of harmony is in itself, as it were, the very
watchword and banner of a radical discord.

The good self is not merely at strife with the evil
self. It is hampered by all that constitutes finiteness in itself and others, by natural conditions, by
ignorance, by accident and circumstance, by the
sufferings and sins of others. In all of these, and all
of which they are typical, it meets pain as inherently
attendant upon its goodness. So that practically
and in particular, with regard to the connection of
pleasure and goodness, it is impossible to say more
than that goodness undoubtedly stands on the side
of a principle which it has in common with pleasure,
and is sure of a certain basis of harmony. But as
it falls within the great ultimate contradiction of the
finite-infinite nature, it is impossible to say how far
in detail and in comparison with badness it may
escape the experience of contradiction.

One further point arises out of this discussion.
We saw that it was impossible to analyse the conditions of pain-sensation so as to bring it under any
general theory. But with regard to pain-sensation
in the animal creation, including man as a sentient

organism, it is obvious that in a certain sense there is present a kindred contradiction to that on which we have just been insisting. Organisms are members of a universe which transcends them, though we must suppose that, in so far as merely sentient, they have no realisation of what membership means. Still, what we call evolution involves this at least— that organic nature develops its wealth of forms under pressure of a changing environment, which in general conditions it as a whole, and which in particular is furnished by the organic world to every individual organism. Thus in the recurrent non-adaptation of organism to environment we have both the direct cause of pain in obstructed functions of organs, and the evolutionary ground for the acquisition of the pain-sensation, as a warning and deterrent from habits injurious to the organism.

Hence it appears that the general pain and struggle of the organisms below man, and of man as a sentient being, are not of the nature of a special curse, or consequence of sin, or of a fall from perfection, which we should look to see one day removed. They seem to be rather a characteristic, belonging, like the hardships of selfhood, to the position of finite members in an infinite universe, which is perpetually remoulding them by struggle and death to a wealth of expressions of itself, including, at least in our case, the becoming the vehicle of intelligence.

So far as we can see, in short, if there is to be a self-directing system of life, adapting itself to a universe which is its environment, there must be pain and death. We can see in the case of the animal creation that by domestication the former can be, to a large extent, avoided. But so far the system is no longer self-directing, nor in free evolution. Thus the same nature seems to reveal itself in the unconscious or barely sentient organic world as in the world of self-consciousness. And if we cannot see how the former participates in the membership which so affects it, perhaps this very difficulty should suggest to us that our view of the attitude involved in such participation is not sufficiently elastic. Many would find such a difficulty, as we think mistakenly, in the destiny of the rank and file of mankind. We perhaps are unfaithful to our own insight when we find it in that of sentient or even of inorganic nature. In that case our hardest problem is nearing solution. However that may be, the typical occasions of pain and of the pain-sensation seem of the same kind throughout; and we are not professing to do more than trace them home to the general nature of the universe.

Our main problem, however, is in the suffering of finite self-conscious beings. And here, I think, we have come to some result. Both it and pleasure are inherent in such beings. They do not belong to good and evil, each to each. Both of them are hazards, and one also a hardship, rooted in the finiteness of the self. Neither is a safe guide to perfection ; and although good has a certain kinship with the condition of pleasure, yet the inadequacy of finite good to reality is such that a very general human instinct as well as the voice of the teacher points us to the strait gate rather than to the primrose path.

And though in truth a perfect experience would formally be of the nature of pleasure, it would carry such a weight, in enjoying such a fulness of contradiction overcome, that it would transcend the nature of both as they appear to us. Our highest experiences—those which have in them most of being and of reality—indicate to us the line of the transformation. I cite an often-cited passage which can hardly be bettered :—

"We can only have the highest happiness, such as goes along with being a great man, by having wide thoughts and much feeling for the rest of the world as well as for ourselves ; and this sort of happiness often brings so much pain with it that we can only tell it from pain by its being what we would choose before everything else, because our souls see it is good." [1]

7. Pain is a fact which *prima facie* gives rise to a theoretical difficulty. It is incompatible, as it stands, with the satisfaction of our nature as a whole. It is, as we have seen, a felt contradiction.

Now it may be held that such an obstacle to satisfaction need give rise to no theoretical difficulty. If, it may be said, we could see a theoretical necessity for the total misery of every sentient creature, our nature as a whole would be revolted, but our theoretical satisfaction might be complete.[2] This, however, does not seem possible. Pain means an obstruction to activity, though there are activities which are its by-products.[3] Now whatever ultimately obstructs my activity also obstructs my understanding. I do not mean merely interferes, as toothache may, with my actual thinking, though this is not a negligible effect of pain. But I mean

*What should make pain antagonistic to theoretical satisfaction? Suppose it extreme and universal. Its ground is its limit.*

---

[1] Epilogue to *Romola.*

[2] On this discussion see Bradley, *Appearance,* 155 ff.

[3] The barring of an activity by way of pain therefore means unrest, not tranquillity.

that it prevents my thought from reaching its goal. Activity is a mode of union with the world, in which, as in theory, thought is operative.    In so far as activity is barred, some thought is prevented from completing itself, and the possibilities open to theory are so far curtailed.    Misery, not in any way trans-cended, would in the first place be self-contradictory; for pain itself, as we have seen, needs a basis of harmonious activity, at least of life, as something to obstruct.    But in the second place, admitting *per impossibile* a life made up of just enough harmony to be obstructed, it would mean an inability of thought to reach any goal of completeness.    Thought would be barred by contradiction on every path.    And therefore even theoretical satisfaction would be impossible.    If, so to speak, you were met by con-tradiction on every path except the theoretical, you would be met by it on the theoretical also.    The separation of the different paths of thought is not ultimately tenable.    To explain is to think as a whole, and if practical and emotional experience were nothing but unsolved contradiction—and that is what it would be on the impossible hypothesis before us—even the theoretical intelligence would have no clue to thinking it as a whole, and there-fore could not explain, and therefore could not be satisfied.

But no one actually suggests that there is complete misery, or that, as would then be inevitable, we have no experience enabling us to conceive the trans-cendence of pain.    What really, I take it, is apt to terrify us, and leads to the idea that pain has the upper hand, is the startling recognition that pain belongs to good, almost, if not quite, as intimately as to evil.  If it is empirically clear that good very frequently brings pain, if we have no rationale of their connection, and if, moreover, we give weight to a sound human instinct that good on the whole is the more widespread, we want little more to drive us into pessimism.  It is not so much that we genuinely observe pain to be predominant, as that we argue, "If pain attends upon the good, what is there that it will not attend upon ?"

So the answer to the theoretical difficulty about pain lies in seeing the ground of its necessity.  It *is*, we have seen, in principle an inherent hardship of finiteness and of soul-making.  Therefore, although *prima facie* it prohibits the satisfaction of our nature as a whole, yet we can, in principle, be theoretically satisfied, in so far as we are able to see contradiction as essential to the completeness of union—imperfection as essential to perfection.  We can see that it must be so, but we cannot see how, in all the detail of experience, it is so.  Our argument, however, gives us this much ; and it is the very necessity which it has exhibited that enables us, theoretically speaking, to set limits to our dissatisfaction.  If we did not understand the inherent ground of pain—if we held it to be a caprice of destiny—we should have no clue whatever to the total and possible extent of its prevalence.  But we know now both that it belongs, and in what sense it belongs, to the structure of reality.  And though we may fancy that the arrangements of a moral, benevolent, and omnipotent being would have been otherwise, yet we can more or less see, and have forced ourselves to confess, that the world's being a rough place, as for us it certainly

is, probably contributes to a greatness and perfection which would not be attained by the methods
that we should have preferred.[1]

Our attitude distinguished from apologetics of pain. 8. It will be well to distinguish the attitude which I have tried to defend from certain current types of what might be called the apologetics of pain. What I have said, in a word, amounts to this: that the root of our troubles is one with the root of our value, and if our value is unassailable, our troubles cannot preclude theoretical satisfaction. I am not flattering myself that there is anything new in this contention. All that I claim is to recognise the need for pushing it home, to the exclusion of weaker persuasions as to the mode of reconciling pain and satisfaction.

For this attitude is radically different from all attitudes which rest on the conception of pleasure and pain as plus and minus quantities to be brought into a single whole only by subtraction.

Reject theories of pain as hard opposite of pleasure, justified by moral ends i. Thus we reject all theories which treat pain as an opposite to be set in the balance against pleasure, furnished as a corrective, for moral purposes, in the scheme of the world. Doctrines of probation and discipline, according to which pain, in itself an evil, is permitted both as a test and as an education of character, have at least the merit of recognising that pain has some connection with value, and is not confined to the wrongdoer or to the consequences of wrongdoing. But they share the essential vice of treating it as a means, external and hostile to the character of perfection, an opposite of happiness, incapable of transformation, and therefore to be neutralised in the universe, but only by sub-

[1] See previous Lecture.

mergence under a balance of pleasure, which remains wholly heterogeneous from it. And this, of course, is not in principle a neutralisation at all, and we are back in the evasion which relies on inappreciable quantities. "The sufferings of this present time are not worthy to be compared" —"de minimis non curat lex."

On the other hand, in the doctrine of rewards and punishments we find the conception of pain still more arbitrary and external, involving the untenable idea of individualistic justice and apportionment which we criticised in the last lecture. It is inconsistent, we saw, with the fundamental fact of spiritual membership ; and as the restriction of pain to the wrongdoer would conflict with everyday observation, it is usual to supplement this doctrine by those of probation and discipline, involving compensation in this life or elsewhere.

In none of these conceptions has pain any organic place or inherent necessity. They leave it as an external means to moral ends, evil and censurable in itself, and therefore demanding to be justified, but justifiable only by neutralisation as an inappreciable quantity submerged under a huge overbalance of its opposite. And in principle, therefore, it is not justified, and no least amount of it could ever be justified.[1]

ii. No less we reject all theories which essentially

[1] But as a means by which a greater balance of pleasure is generated than could have been generated without it ? Is not this an organic function and a justification ? One can only say that it involves a terrific dualism, implying that the universe is so weak as to have to grasp at wholly heterogeneous means in order to accomplish its end. For, *ex hypothesi*, the means, thus considered, are in flat opposition to the end.

N

And theories of future evanescence of pain, except as some change which may throw light on whole reality.

found themselves on the probable disappearance of pain in the future. We hope, of course, for some degree of such disappearance, or rather for a certain kind of transformation, and we are bound to work for it. But our argument does not permit us to believe it possible in the main, and certainly not to think it the true ground on which the existence of pain is compatible with theoretical satisfaction.

We must carefully distinguish, indeed, between (*a*) the view that future experience may throw additional light, to be reconciled with that of the past, on the nature of the whole of reality, and (*β*) the view that a favourable change in the future may compensate for, that is, wipe out by a sheer overbalance, what we dislike in past and present.

(*a*) The former conception is obviously admissible, and it is impossible to limit dogmatically the extent of the modification which accepted theories may have to undergo. But to postulate so radical a future difference in the world's working as should revolutionise what now appear its fundamental conditions, and extinguish something like one-half of our experience, is a measure demanding very strong reasons. And I believe that such reasons are only present if we adopt the double conviction that the real is "good" excluding evil, and that pain is evil excluding good. Even then, and indeed because of this radical opposition, no change in the future could suffice to explain away in principle the evil that has apparently been.

But supposing that in the temporal world pain were actually to show signs of disappearing, it would no doubt become easier to conceive that it, which could thus disappear, could not have been a deeply inherent feature of reality, and might in some way be regarded if not as a pure illusion, yet at least as a relatively negligible character in the eternal whole. The argument draws its strength,[1] I believe, from an aspiration founded on the conviction above referred to; an aspiration that the real shall show itself in its supposed true character of goodness without evil. And if the conviction, as formulated, were well grounded, the conclusion would be hard to withstand for all who have at heart the unity of perfection with reality.

For us, however, the conviction that reality implies perfection does not carry the consequence of excluding or of minimising imperfection, and consequently it supplies no driving force in favour of the postulate before us. Our theoretical prepossession in some degree even leans the other way. It is part of the paradox of our finite-infinite being that we are bound to maintain the combat against evil, and no doubt in a great degree against pain, not merely without anticipating, but even without whole-heartedly desiring, their entire abolition in every possible shape with all their occasions and accessories. For we can hardly understand what of life would survive such an abolition.[2] And perfection itself, so far as we see, would lose some essentials of its being. The Utopian temper as a rule seems dull and inhuman; and, as I remarked above, there is something mediæval in the worst sense about the idea

---

[1] There is also a well-known argument which supports the evanescence of pain on purely evolutionary grounds. But this, I think, hardly demands attention to-day.

[2] Take, for instance, what we spoke of above, the pangs of creative travail, or the anxieties of love and work.

of a future in which—to take a typical instance —tragedy is to be enjoyed without any tragic experience.

(β) This brings us to the other and cruder attitude, for which a future annihilation of suffering will not operate merely by throwing a new light on the whole nature of reality, but will baldly and crudely overbalance and compensate for the sufferings of the past. Here we have again the absurdity of compensation for an admitted evil by sheer quantity of its opposite, and also the brutality which bases the happiness of some on the sufferings of others, and in fact, as would be inevitable, on the actual enjoyment of those sufferings. If pain is a wrong *per se*, untransformable, and incompatible with perfection, it is plain that no happier future can destroy the contradiction of its having existed. We may dismiss any view which suggests it as a thoughtless evasion.

iii. And yet in a certain sense, but not in that which we have been discussing, our own theory does prepossess us towards some belief in an alleviation of pain as the world goes on. What suggests itself to us is not the abolition of the finite-infinite conflict and tension, but rather its more conscious realisation, one might almost say, its intensification. As any race of finite self-conscious beings gains mastery over itself and its experience, there will be a tendency, we may hope and think we see, to convert brute agony and dumb endurance and despair into spiritual conflict and triumph ; to raise suffering, in a word, to the level of tragedy. The tragic element, it has been said, is the waste—the apparently objectless expense of spirit, as great characters

Though we think probable, in any finite world, progress towards a change from brute suffering towards tragedy.

destroy each other. It is a curious echo from a distant field of knowledge when we remind ourselves that in economics what is in one sense the waste— the direct or non-reproductive expenditure on the splendour and enjoyment of human life and social celebration—is in another the end or *raison d'être* of the whole arrangement. If to be a means to nothing is to be waste, then everything is waste which is an end in itself. So it may be with the tragic waste of spirit—the exhibition or realisation of the qualities that come nearest to perfection. All the empirical signs point to man's becoming more self-conscious, but wrestling at the same time —it is almost a tautology—with deeper and sharper problems. This is the direction in which it seems to me tolerably certain that suffering has been and is being transformed. The self-consciousness of labour in civilised countries, for example, is a commonplace of to-day. The full nature of reality will thus be brought nearer and made clearer, but not as a truncated perfection, or one with its characters dispersed through time—pain here and pleasure there—rather in a closer and closer concentration of experience, with tears made human by laughter, and laughter triumphant over tears.

It follows, I think, as we said in the last lecture, that we cannot pick and choose in estimating reality. We cannot judge our own possibilities or gauge our own nature. If we had our choice of pains, we should always rule out our own greatest opportunities. To the charge that if we may not pick and choose, may not say, this pain is fair and tolerable but that excessive, we should in logic have to be satisfied, though every being in the universe were in extremest misery, I believe that our argument has offered sufficient answer.

Organic
standpoint
as to pain
in issue of
optimism
and pes-
simism.
9. I hope that the reasoning of this lecture has reinforced a conclusion in the former volume,[1] to the effect that the issue of optimism and pessimism must not, and indeed cannot, be treated as a question of the quantitative balance between pain and pleasure, but rather from an organic standpoint as a problem of the function of pain in soul-making, and its transformation in the higher experiences, not its neutralisation or submergence by an overbalance of an opposite. In general we may say that this problem should be argued on the basis of value and not of pain and pleasure.

And I think our attitude explains why the challenge, "Would you willingly live your life again?" is irrelevant to the question whether life is worth living. We may wish to go on reading the *Aeneid*, without wishing to return to the Latin grammar. But, it will be rejoined, this is to assume a continuance beyond the life to which the question refers. It is a fair challenge to ask whether the experience we have had, with its actual proportion of grammar and *Aeneid*, is one which we should care to repeat. But I think our answer holds good. The idea of a repetition[2] is repugnant and meaningless in itself. Life, we believe, has a meaning and has values to realise which have their rank and place, such as it is, in the universe. Apart from theory, we all have this idea. We want to live out our life, to work out our self—a poor thing, but our own—and so all we have to give and to create. It is not much,

---

[1] *Principle*, Lect. VI.
[2] "All repetition is unspiritual," *De Profundis.*

but such as it is, no one else can give it. And in principle there would be the wishes of others to consider. Now, if you suggest a repetition, you cut us loose from this substantial basis. Repetition is stultification. Our life ceases to be a universal value, and is regarded as a game, to be played over again for our private amusement. Of course its interest is gone.

10. This is not the place to enter upon our main discussion of religion. It does not belong to the hazards and hardships of finite selfhood, but rather to its security and happiness. Yet in an account of the significance of pain and an estimate of its rank and rootedness in experience, it would be a grave omission not to touch upon the fact that the great religion of the Western world announces itself as a religion of suffering. By a religion of suffering I mean one which emphasises, and requires its disciples in some sense to share, the sufferings of its Founder. I do not enter upon problems of comparative religion, but I imagine that in most great religions a similar element is influential.[1]

*Rank assigned to pain in Christianity involves a universal and substantial reconciliation. Spiritual induction.*

In spite of all the sincerest efforts throughout the centuries of Christian development to apprehend the depths of this paradox, the fact that the cross is the banner of our religion and our civilisation[2] seems still to have far more meaning than we find it easy to grasp.

We ask in this place not what is the whole significance of religion, but what is the character

---

[1] Cf. Cornford, *From Religion to Philosophy*, on the Suffering God.

[2] For the sense in which our civilisation must be held to be Christian, see the essay "The Civilisation of Christendom" in my volume of that title.

of pain that gives it this pre-eminence—nominal at
least—in one of man's most conspicuous attempts to
realise the secret of peace.[1]  We have dismissed,
by implication, all such ideas as that pain can have a
value *in se* and *per se*, or, so taken, can contribute
to perfection and to complete satisfaction.   And yet
even here we must be cautious.   In science and
philosophy, for example, contradiction is *in se* and
*per se* a defect, but it may imply or carry along
with it a value, which its character as contradiction
indicates but yet detracts from.   A contradiction
may be better than a prejudice, for there cannot be
a contradiction without some complexity of considerations.   So, while thoroughly hostile to fanatical
or superstitious demands for meaningless torture of
body or mind, I am far from thinking that the very
deep-seated impulse towards such aberrations has
no shadow of justification in the truest needs of a
self-conscious being.   The impulse to make life
painful, especially at its critical moments,[2] seems to
be one side of the instinctive dissatisfaction which
pronounces unmodified nature inadequate to man.

But if, agreeing that the mere fact of contradiction is failure and not satisfaction, we ask what it is
in virtue of which such a failure may imply and
carry with it an essential factor of success, the
answer given by logic refers to the degree of
opposition between the discordant experiences.
Formally, indeed, there are no degrees of opposition ;

---

[1] The parallel of this to the development of tragedy in his
supreme attempt to find enjoyment is exceedingly striking.

[2] I am thinking, *e.g.*, of the initiatory ceremonies of many savage
tribes at the entrance upon manhood.   Mutilations, supposed to be
decorative, imply, as Goethe observed, the same feeling, that Nature
" will not do " as she is, and must be cut and carved to improve her.

a contradiction is a contradiction, neither more nor less.    But considering the systematic character which belongs to all organised experience, it is plain that one contradiction may only be removable by a complete remodelling of a system, while another may demand only a trifling readjustment within it. Contradictions of the former character may be considered as more radically contradictory than those of the latter, though it is perhaps truer to say that they are contradictions between more fundamental experiences than to say that they are more contradictory contradictions.    But however described, the contradictions which take more to reconcile them are the more significant contradictions.    The reason is, that what amounts to a new world must be experienced or conceived in order to bring their differences into harmony.    Such a contradiction in philosophy is that of freedom and necessity ; such, I suppose, in biology is that of preformation and epigenesis.    In such antithesis the one member *prima facie* excludes the whole system of experience to which the other belongs.    You cannot conceive them as united in a single whole except by complete recasting of the point of view from which their antagonistic systems are built up.

Now it is such a contradiction that is represented by the extreme of mental and bodily suffering. Finiteness seems here to reach its maximum.    Life and mind exist, only to support obstruction and be aware of impotence and isolation.    What would be *merely* finite would not even be finite, but would cancel and go out, as its root of vitality in the greater universe was cut.    And the extreme of suffering seems on the edge of this nothingness.

The contradiction is between fundamentals ; between the whole power and content of life and mind on the one side, and the whole obstructive and isolating reaction of a discordant externality on the other. And thus a contradiction arises which is *prima facie* a deadlock. The finite-infinite being retains only enough hold on infinity to realise its own finiteness in impotence and despair.

The value implied in such a contradiction, assuming it to be transcended, is twofold. The union or reconciliation which overcomes it must be (*a*) universal and (*β*) substantial.

(*a*) The contradiction has been driven to the extreme, as a mere contradiction. No possible case of pain, impotence, isolation, can go beyond it. In principle, therefore, it covers every example of the finite-infinite being. No one, who has life enough to be wretched, can be too wretched for the union to be asserted in him. Other forms of satisfaction or unity may be limited. But the satisfaction which involves a finiteness driven to its extreme, its extreme of extremes, indeed, for death is included, must be of a kind that is absolutely universal. And, of course, this is a commonplace of Christian teaching. I use it here merely to emphasise the significance of suffering, in forcing the problem of union with the infinite to complete universality. Of course, it seems to be only in principle that it covers every case. The awareness of reconciliation, it might be said, has never spread very far, and, according to the rule we have insisted on, the possibilities of the future afford no compensatory explanation for the past and present. But we are speaking of the nature and capacities of a finite-infinite or self-conscious being. We know that they seem never to be fully realised, and over an immense area hardly to be realised at all. But as imperfection is contributory to perfection, this is probably less the case than we think, and, so far as it is the case, matters less than we think. We have never been concerned to deny the actuality of suffering, but only to show its significance and its place in the logic of reconciliation.

And (β) the solution is substantial. It arises out of the apparent failure of the finite, its most hopeless contradiction.[1] And just because of this a new experience—a new world—is entered upon. The world of spiritual membership affirms itself; and the finite system, such a compromise, for instance, as the world of claims, is seen or felt in its imperfection.

The appeal to the experience of suffering has a curious analogy to what has been called the "method of difference" in Inductive Logic. What you can take away, and yet leave the substantive matter of the enquiry, is irrelevant and unessential. The solution of the contradiction of suffering is in this sense substantive. It shows us how much we can do without, and in what things strength really lies. Perfection, no doubt, demands the whole, and does not reside in any part alone. But some things have more of the nature of the whole, and some have less, and in finite life the gain is to discriminate rightly.

11. This we see more especially in cases which sum up the doctrine of suffering as a hazard and hardship of finite selfhood, the cases of accident and death.

*Illustration by accident and death. Their place in spiritual induction.*

---

[1] Cf. Lect. X., below.

Why no
religion
of pure
pleasure.
The tribute
of our
finite self.    By accident I do not mean all that in the logical
sense comes relatively from chance, but primarily
what we mean by it in colloquial language—an
injury to person or belongings that could not be
foreseen, or if foreseen, could not be provided against.
War or disasters due to nature are the principal
types.

As I disbelieve in the future evanescence of
pain, so I disbelieve in the future abolition of
accident.   Grant that the self-consciousness of finite
beings and their groups is to increase indefinitely,
and to play providence in a degree not now conceivable, still finite existence will remain finite, and in
the main at the mercy of accident.[1]   Accident,
injurious and disastrous hazard, is inherent in
finiteness, and has a part to play in that spiritual
induction to which I just now referred.[2]   Accident
is by the hypothesis external.   Externals are not
indifferent.   They are continuous with the spiritual
life, and their connection with it is a matter of
degree.   Still, the incursion of disaster into externals
is an instrument of emphasising their externality,
and making clear the distinction between particulars
of that kind and the roots of spiritual life.

[1] Indeed, this is ultimately indistinguishable from the general
course of nature so far as uncontrollable by finite beings, *e.g.* the
future of this globe.   For the temper which expects and demands to
exclude accident, cf. a newspaper after the loss of the *Titanic*.
" Until the way across the Atlantic is made safe, no liner shall sail."
Another journal well remarks, " That was indeed a great and tragic
catastrophe which has struck the imagination of the whole world,
and set it thinking about its own littleness in the grip of the forces
of nature.   But the dignity of it is lost when there rises up a great
clamour of people complaining that science and skill have not as
they thought made an end of the risks of the sea."—*Westminster
Gazette*, April 27, 1912.

[2] I do not say that war can never cease ; but we may illustrate
the place of accident in finite being by the effects of war.

So it is, finally, with death, the ultimate hazard, in which *prima facie* the very being of the finite self is cancelled.   We shall devote a special treatment below to ideas of the ultimate destiny of the finite self.   But it is plain in pure theory that to transcend the contradiction which death introduces into finite life means in some way to have hold of a world which, while including what is essential to the self, is not obstructed by physical death.[1]

Of course, either accident or death may be too lightly met.   The contradiction may be slurred over and not solved.   There may be a death, as Hegel says, which has no more significance than cutting off a cabbage head.   The contradiction, *i.e.* the apparent termination of all activities and interests, must be realised before it can be solved.

When we speak of what is untouched by death of the finite self, we do not mean merely that truth, for example, remains true.   We mean, for instance, the love and courage which make death seem a little thing, and which constitute a grasp of reality by which the finite being offers up its finiteness as a contribution to the true being of the universe. This will seem more intelligible when we have spoken of the nature of religion.

Why should there not be a religion of which the central experience should be pleasure?   I do not profess to know whether historically such an experience has been approached;[2] but there seems room to suggest it for the sake of illustration.   For pleasure, as we have seen, accompanies expansion

---

[1] Here again Spinoza's treatment seems the most suggestive.

[2] I believe that in Bacchic festivals and similar rites there was always a foundation at least of repeating the sufferings of the god or hero.   Cf. Cornford, *op. cit.*

or unobstructed activity of the self, and therefore ought to be a feature of any felt union with the infinite. And certainly in all religion there must be pleasure, or the element of pleasure within a fuller experience, as well as the element of pain. But in anything like a religion of pure pleasure the difficulty would be that a thoroughgoing expansion of the finite mind must be charged with a burden of contradiction or obstruction, and therefore it could not quite be the experience which we indicate under the name of pleasure. Religions of pleasure, I suspect, usually became savage or ascetic. There is something fierce and horrible about the lowest pleasures when fairly let go, and something severe and austere about the highest. The expansion of the self, as we said above, tears its way. Even if freely pursued, in the sense and intention of enjoyment, the ritual of such religions, I imagine, carried with it from the occasion of their origin some horrible or severe accessories. A mere service of pleasure would hardly give the sense of refuge and liberation, much less the guidance into the world of love and truth, which is ensured by the transcended contradiction of a religion centred in suffering.

Pain, then, with accident and death, belongs essentially to the hazards and hardships which are involved in the double nature of the finite-infinite being. And we do not believe that it is worth while to speculate philosophically upon the greater or less degree of these incidents of finitude. If we are prepared to quarrel with the scheme of things because finiteness is a factor in it, we are at least logical pessimists. But to say that we approve the hazards and hardships so far, but judge them a censurable feature of the universe when we think them more than we can bear, seems arbitrary in theory, and, as we have reiterated, and as experience constantly shows, would mean, if our choice had effect, the repudiation of our greatest chances.

What is important is to see that the incidents of our finiteness are more than finite incidents. They belong to the tension of our double being, in which it affirms its unity with the absolute. We have spoken of the spiritual induction to which the experience of suffering is instrumental,[1] and have indicated the direction in which to look for the pleasure that would be higher than pain, and not its co-ordinate opposite. Our pain, I repeat, has the same root as our value, that is to say, both lie in the tribute of our finite self which we bring, not rejected, but transformed through reconciled contradiction, to the absolute.

[1] Compare Francis Thompson's " Hound of Heaven."

# *B.* HAZARDS AND HARDSHIPS OF
## FINITE SELFHOOD—*Continued*

## LECTURE VII

### GOOD AND EVIL

Good and
Evil con-
trasted
with
Pleasure
and Pain,
as attitudes
of whole
beings.
Good in
what sense
definable. 1. WE have treated pleasure and pain as rooted in the nature of a finite being, necessarily self-transcendent, and, in its self-transcendence, which is also its self-maintenance, inherently liable to obstruction, yet capable of success. Pleasure and pain, we held, were the primary attendants of these hazards of finiteness. As commonly experienced, both are partial and *de facto*, we might almost say, indeed, incidental, and tell us little or nothing of the whole progress of the finite creature, and of its status in regard to perfection.

When we consider the further hazards of good and evil, also rooted in the finiteness of finite beings, whether natural or spiritual, we are dealing with a more fundamental opposition. We are taking account not merely of a partial superficial and *de facto* perfection and imperfection, but of an attitude, an idea, a desire; that is, a relation of the finite creature as a whole to perfection and to imperfection. The general character of good, by common consent, is that it satisfies desire. Absolute perfection may be held to exclude desire; or if, as I have argued, the character of desire is bound to survive in it, it must be in some form quite different from the unsatisfied desires which we know. But good is an element of finite experience, and it means not perfection as such, but perfection in so far as it appears in the dualism of finiteness, as involving a discord and a reconciliation of idea and existence. Thus the idea of good at once concerns the creature's whole being; it is not, like pain and pleasure, mere *de facto* experience of obstruction or unobstructedness. In its desire for good—its desire for an object which as desired is good—the creature as such takes a side, and pledges itself to the search for satisfaction as such, for complete satisfaction, for something in which its being will be at one with itself. It may seem that so much is not involved in the desire for this or that, which may be readily slurred over and forgotten. But this is only in so far as the creature is distracted between its objects of desire. Its nature, as self-conscious, is to aspire to unification. So far as it desires, it takes a side and assumes an attitude to this effect. In evil desire—there is, we shall argue, no desire for evil—in evil desire this taking sides, though confronted with hostility, is presupposed. Good involves an attitude to satisfaction, an approval on the whole. Evil is the reverse of this, the rebellion. It is the inclination to a satisfaction which is attended by dread or hostility against the threatening absorption in good; the self-assertion of some element which does not want—in which the self does not want—to be organised within the creature's satisfaction as desired. The point of

o

view of the whole, and opposition to it, are the characteristics of good and evil.

It has been maintained that good is undefinable. It is easy to see the difficulty on which this doctrine insists. Good is *ex hypothesi* not a content but a character. Definable, I should urge, is just what it is; describable, perhaps, is what it is not. We cannot describe perfection; that is, we cannot enumerate its components and state their form and connection in detail. But we can define its character as the harmony of all being. And good is perfection in its character of satisfactoriness; that which is considered as the end of conations and the fruition of desires. I have argued in the previous volume[1] that this is a character which can be reasoned upon and established in general, in accordance with the conception of degrees in being and trueness. And therefore I hold it in the true and systematic sense definable, not by external reference,[2] which is spurious definition, but by the law of its individuality, which is the only true definition. But it is not exhaustible by enumeration of its constituents; that would be indeed to construct the universe *a priori*, to deduce the detail of its components from the single fundamental character of satisfactoriness. Everything is good, so far as a constituent of perfection, which involves possessing the character of satisfactoriness or value. But we cannot deduce from this the detail of the universe; for example, the special nature of beauty or truth. "In order to be good, the other aspects of the universe must also be themselves "[3] (beauty,

---

[1] *Principle*, p. 298.　　　[2] As you define a yard to be 3 feet.
[3] Bradley's *Appearance*, p. 410.

truth, sensation, etc.). Therefore, if definition means enumeration of components, good is undefinable; if it means the exposition of the universal character of any whole, it is definable. Nothing which does not possess such a character, an individual or internal form and law, is in the true sense definable.[1]

Enough was said in the previous volume to determine our idea of perfection, as that which has the quality of satisfactoriness, as judged by the criticised[2] totality of conations or desires. What we are dealing with at this moment is the difference between good and evil on the one hand, and perfection and imperfection, and also, moreover, pleasure and pain, on the other hand. The difference in the first contrast, if we speak of the positive terms only, is between perfection as the complete experience, and good as its appearance in finite life as an object of desire; in the second contrast, between good as a line taken by the finite creature's aspiration, and pleasure as a *de facto* unobstructedness, sporadic throughout the activities of such a creature.

2. In conformity with these ideas I argued in the previous chapter that pleasure and pain were no reliable guides to the good and evil of our activities, being variously distributed consequences of the limitations of a finite being. Do we mean to say that, in themselves, pleasure need not be good and pain need not be evil?

*Can any pleasure then be evil, or any pain good, in se? As concerns partial pleasures or pains, reasons for affirmative.*

In the first place, the question is less important than might appear. For when we come to think of serious or total unobstructedness or obstruction,

[1] Author's *Logic*, ed. 2, ii. 261.
[2] See also Sympos. paper on "Mechanism and Purpose," *Arist. Proc.* 1912.

in the case of a finite creature or perhaps of a
society,[1] there is no doubt, from the definition, that
the one—*ex hypothesi* attended by pleasure—must
come to be considered as good, as approved and
desired, and the other as evil. The doubtful point
can only concern very partial exaltations and de-
pressions of vitality, where a partial exaltation may
be the condition of an all but total depression,[2] or a
partial depression of an all but total exaltation.

And even as regards these, it will be said, the
knot may be very simply cut by saying, "*So far* all
exaltation is good ; *so far* all depression is evil.
Their effects may overbalance their quality with
more of its opposite, but cannot modify it in itself."
I do not feel sure that this is satisfactory. According to Spinoza, I think, and also according to
Aristotle, it does not go to the root of the problem.
Good and evil really differ from pleasure and pain
by the attitude which they involve towards a whole.
So that a pleasure which involves all but total
depression may still be pleasurable in itself, but can
hardly, I think, be good even in itself.[3] For a
pleasure is not independent of its activity. It is
infected by it. If we follow Aristotle's doctrine,
surely the soundest, of the qualification of pleasures
by the nature of their accompanying activities, we
shall, I believe, call a pleasure evil which belongs to
an activity obstructive on the whole to life, and a
pain good which attaches to what destroys such a
pleasure, and so on the whole promotes vitality.

[1] This specification may be necessary to cover the case of self-
sacrifice in members of the group.

[2] That is to say, a depression total but for the exaltation in
question.

[3] I am aware that this sentence deviates from Spinoza.

The question is almost verbal.  But it is well to maintain the two points on which our answer turns : the infection or qualification of pleasure and pain by their activities, and the differentia of good and evil as bearing on satisfaction as a whole.  Thus a pleasure belonging to an activity hostile to satisfaction as a whole must be nuanced, infected, in itself, by the evil character attaching to such an activity.  And I am sure that in fact it is so.[1]

3. Wherever good is discussed, we shall find a curious problem intervening, though very frequently unrecognised.  There is, or seems to be, good in general, and also moral good.  All sorts of things are good, and among them is virtue, or moral excellence.  This is the *prima facie* impression.  But when serious discussion is entered on, there is a tendency for good to be narrowed down to moral good.  How can a thing be good, and moral beings—self-judging beings—not be bound to ensue it ?  And if we are bound to ensue it, how can it—the ensuing of it— fail to be a moral duty and a moral good ?  But then, on the other hand, if the attainment of it is a moral virtue or moral good, must not this moral good be pursued for its own sake rather than for any objective value outside the moral good of the pursuit ?  But then we have juggled ourselves out of the objective value of the thing—beauty, or truth, or love —whatever it may be, and have reduced good, the whole world of values, to goodness, which *prima facie* is one among them, and far from being the whole.

Nothing can save us here but to recognise that the difference between goodness and good in general is not the difference between the empty good will

The antithesis between moral good and good in general, as that between fundamentals of life and their corollaries.

and the values which it wills.   Moral virtues or the mere good will cannot be their own ends.   They are characters drawn out in the complete life of the moral organism, but without the objective filling of concrete values they are worthless or worse.[1]   To be brave for the sake of courage or kind for the sake of kindness is to lose all ground and standard in conduct and to approach a self-seeking hypocrisy.

Goodness as distinguished from good in general is not the good will or moral excellence as opposed to all concrete objective values.[2]   If this were so, those extremists would be right who have maintained that virtue and duty are valueless in themselves, and only have value as means to objective values beyond them.   But the question is really one of objective values throughout ; of constituents which enter into the total harmony and perfectness which in all its fragments we desire and approve.   The difference is merely that some of these are fundamental in all and any ordered life, in any permanent society or civilised grouping or pursuit of rational purposes.   These, being the conditions *par excellence*

---

[1] The point is familiar in criticism of Kant, but it needs reiteration, and is well insisted on by Green, *Prolegomena*, sect. 247, following a striking argument of Hume.

[2] Nettleship, *Remains*, i. 93.   " I suppose moral worth ought simply to mean whatever contributes in any way to whatever the person who is talking thinks the best thing or the thing most worth having in the world.   What I like in Greek philosophy is that it puts that point of view so simply.   It sickens one to hear the ordinary enlightened man talk about morality, whether he talks for or against it.   He almost never seems to realise that there can be only one standard of absolute value for things, and that ultimately the morally 'good' must either mean that (and then *everything* that is really worth having or being has moral value), or else must describe some special form of such absolute value (in which case 'moral' will be co-ordinate with, not supreme over, artistic, political, commercial, etc.)."

of all and any values, being the attainment of the
fundamental values on which all others depend, and
being readily recognised as akin, are traditionally
grouped together and called goodness or moral
excellence as one among other goods.  Other values
again are provincial or departmental, and are not
indispensable to every life, though they well may be
so to life as a whole.  These, though really of the
same kin, as forms of harmony and perfection in
mind and world, but lying apart from each other,
and often in apparently sharp contrast with the
former, come to be considered as in some inexplicable way independent gifts, excellences, values,
desirabilities of the world, which have nothing to do
with the central perfection of experience.  I have
urged this interpretation of the connection between
goodness and general goods in the previous volume,[1]
and need not insist upon it here.  All that makes
for perfection is good and has value; all of it is an
order and completeness in experience and in mind—
we may think, for example, of truth and beauty.
None of it can in principle be indifferent to the
finite creature for whom perfection is the inherent
aim, and good is what so far fulfils it.  And the
distinction between goodness and goods in general
is only the distinction between the fundamentals of
unified life and its outlying corollaries.

Thus the antithesis between good in general and
moral goodness is easily understood, on the lines
suggested in the previous volume.  It is in a great
measure a false and unwholesome antithesis, as when
we exclude from moral goodness the ordering of our
souls in respect of the sense of truth and of beauty,

---

[1] *Principle*, p. 346 ff.

or the capacity of dealing with the world. Goodness
is certainly wisdom ; and to draw a hard-and-fast line
between its simplest forms and its further developments is both illogical and ethically narrow-minded.
Thus, further, we cannot deny that in its degree all
wisdom is goodness.

Difficulty<br>in enlarg-<br>ing good-<br>ness to<br>include all<br>goods. It<br>comes to<br>include<br>" gifts."

4. And yet there is a difficulty—a very instructive
difficulty—in enlarging goodness to the compass of
all goods. We need not, indeed, think of goods
which are totally and in principle apart from experience, *e.g.* a world of beauty inaccessible to any and
every mind, finite or infinite. Such a world could
be neither beautiful nor a good. But it is true that
in considering the characters of perfection we are
driven more and more to recognise how far the
roots of a finite mind extend beyond itself; and
morality, goodness, the affirmation of fundamental
values, passes continuously into gifts and graces due
to nature or history. We should not like to make
health or good luck a part of moral goodness, though
they are certainly not unconnected with it. Yet if
we try to rule out from goodness all external gifts
and graces, physical endowments, education, age and
country, ability to learn and to act, we shall find that
we have ruled out moral excellence itself. The
conclusion is forced upon us that morality, even if
expanded to the compass of all mental and bodily
excellence, is still only a relative point of view,[1] one
which cannot be pushed to the point of conceiving
the finite creature, in, by, and of himself, as fully
equipped with the conditions and constituents of
goodness. Goodness passes continuously into goods,
and goods into gifts.

[1] *Principle*, Lect. VI.

The individual, though responsible, has nevertheless his roots deep in the universe beyond him.

5. Wholly apart from his attitude, on the other hand, it can hardly be said that we have what can count as good or evil. The relation of these to the antithesis of pleasure and pain has already been discussed. It is also customary to lend unconscious nature an attitude to perfection, and to see good and evil in her supposed failure and success. But all this, like much of our judgment of success and failure among mankind, rests upon an ascription of ends which is highly fallible, even if in any way justifiable in principle. To mention one elementary case, when the poet says, as an example of incompleteness permitted by nature,

> "And finding that of fifty seeds
> She often brings but one to bear,"

did he remember what *bread* is made of? No doubt, this is a human adaptation of a natural process. But if such an end is attainable through what, within nature strictly taken, is but arrest and failure, how can we lay stress on any ascription of ends to apparent organic purposiveness throughout? The fact is, it is neither nature nor finite mind that authoritatively recognises and prescribes the operative end of the universe. It is, so far as accessible to our judgment at all, the working of the whole, in which each in its place is an instrument. But good and evil are unintelligible expressions apart from the attitude of finite minds.

6. Thus it should not be counted strange that in spite of their fundamental importance for our life I should reckon good and evil among the perilous

*Yet apart from his attitude we hardly have good or evil. Conception of success and failure in Nature precarious.*

*Thus good and evil are rightly treated as incidents of*

finiteness ; but yet stability will attach through them.

incidents—the risks and difficulties—of finiteness. It may be objected that if we insist on thus emphasising the finiteness of the finite, we shall end by seeing in its whole experience nothing but hazard and hardship. And I admit that I am anxious to bring home this point of view. It is not in order to make life appear terrifying and chaotic. It is rather in order to point out that in all its risks and terrors there is, after all, nothing but what flows from the source of its strength and value; the continual passing of the finite beyond itself in the venture of achieving a fuller world. And under a later heading we shall gather up the suggestions on the positive side which have pervaded the whole argument, and shall insist, following the line of the previous volume,[1] on the note of completeness which permeates these very experiences of risk and obstruction and is actually sustained by them. This note of completeness, present throughout, has its own forms of expression, which are found imperfectly realised, but inherently implied, in all the phases we have considered.[2] When we turn to its characteristic shape, the religious consciousness, under a later heading, we shall not be sharply passing across an absolute distinction, from the discords to the harmonies of experience, as from opposite to opposite. In that case the briefer treatment of the latter would seem to concede that they are overbalanced by the former. And, moreover, it would suggest itself—and the suggestion would be one which we could not altogether repel—that even the religious conscious-

[1] *Principle*, Lect. VIII.
[2] See, *e.g.*, Lect. V. on the implication of organic morality in the world of claims.

ness is one among the risks and difficulties of finiteness. It is the invocation of a fundamental force, to which, as to the spell on the lips of the wizard's apprentice, terrible dangers are attached for the unthinking or the insincere. But all this only bears witness to the continuity of our double life through the forms which we are analysing. We shall only be drawing out to its explicit manifestation an element which has been present throughout as a spirit of vigour and inclusiveness, through which alone the risks and discrepancies we have indicated become endurable and significant.

7. With this explanation we may proceed to indicate the sense in which good must be counted a hazard, and evil both a hazard and a hardship. It would not, indeed, seem unnatural to extend the double title to good as well as to evil. But this would only mean that finite life is hard at best, and that point has been sufficiently illustrated. We will begin by noting the curious kinship and interdependence of the two experiences, in which both of them share the hazardous and adventurous character of finiteness resting on infinity.[1]

*In what sense good is a hazard, and evil both a hazard and a hardship.*

i. Both good and evil are formally self-transcendence of the finite mind. In both the finite creature throws himself forward, losing something that he is, and, formally at least, gaining something that he was not, if it were only a drunken hilarity. In both, therefore, and not in evil only, he is liable to contradiction and obstruction, and in a sense, which we drew out in discussing the kindred conditions of

*Good is liable to obstruction and made of the same stuff as evil— the distinction between them arises in the venture of making the self.*

[1] Cf. *Principle*, 242, on structure of reality and the kinship of good and evil in, *e.g.*, Green's theory.

pleasure and pain, is always confronted with them. This we might venture to designate as primary contradiction, meaning by that the elementary difficulty of adjusting the content of the finite creature with any degree of completeness to the demands of any situation, any case of union with the not-self, at all. All action, all living, has a side of difficulty, and formally involves self-sacrifice, evil as actually as good, though not in the same degree—to begin with less, and ultimately more.[1]

When we are told that it is a fatal dualism in the good to have two divergent paths of attainment, self-sacrifice and self-affirmation, that we approve of both, and cannot in principle determine ourselves to the preference of either, the answer is prepared by what has just been said. In principle every action combines the two; it is a single consequence of finiteness. The cost at which we achieve our ends varies in every instance, and in very many cases it would be impossible to say whether the element of self-affirmation or of self-sacrifice is predominant. Formally there are always both, and though they may seem to diverge as the one side or the other is the more prominent, yet they both spring from the single principle we are tracing.[2]

[1] I am merely pressing home an initial technical character of all finite action. I am not, I think, substantially in conflict with Mr. Bradley's conclusion (*Ethical Studies*, p. 277) that there cannot be in the strict sense self-sacrifice for the bad, *i.e.* for the bad reflectively known and considered *qua* bad.

[2] Here is an example, drawn from what I believe has not unfrequently occurred. A scholar abandons the notes and materials of his lifework, along with the moral monopoly or goodwill of it, to a younger man, who, he thinks, will accomplish it more efficiently. How far this is self-sacrifice as opposed to self-affirmation depends on the form of the end with which the self is identified. If the end is *my* achievement, we get one answer, if it is *the* achievement, another.

And in as far as the self can come, in the highest experience, to surrender itself without loss, a convergence between self-sacrifice and self-affirmation begins within finite life which in principle, we can see, must be completed beyond it.[1]

Again, both good and evil, like truth and error, are made of the same stuff. There is nothing else of which they can be made; desires, volitions, habits, ideas, these are what life consists in, and their mere positive nature is not stamped *ab initio* as either good or bad. Our evil desires are not desires for evil; our good desires are not desires for something heterogeneous from the objects of those which are bad.

What, then, makes things good or evil? How does good differ from evil, and evil from good? The first or formal answer, again, leaves them undistinguished and on the same level. Good is good because it is in contradiction to evil. Evil is evil because it is in contradiction to good. Of course this is not enough, for it does not tell us which is which, but it is so far true. Neither has or could have its character without the other; and if you could wipe out the one you would annihilate the other along with it. Each expresses, as we have seen, an attitude on the part of the finite being, and this attitude is in each determined by a contradiction, other than the mere liability to obstructedness common to all finite action and expression, though rooted in the same characteristics of finiteness. Good is primarily the conflict with evil and the triumph over it; evil is primarily the rebellion

[1] Cf. author's paper in *Ar. Proc.* for 1902 on " Recent Criticism of Green's *Ethics.*"

against good.   The purpose which is a root of evil in one self may be the spur to good in another; it is not the content of the object, but the side assigned to it in the contradiction of attitudes, that is decisive of its goodness or badness.

Thus we can understand how both good and evil are hazards of the finite self.   There is no simple general choice between rows of objects antecedently labelled as good and bad.   The whole positive material of life is in principle [1] before or within the finite self, and out of this it has to build up a symbol or relative world of perfection involving the repudiation of what conflicts with it.   To understand what makes one side good and the other side, inseparable from it, evil, we must look to a further characteristic, which, within the affinity we have noted, fundamentally differentiates them.

What makes evil evil, and a hardship? Its self-contradiction. Must take account of the organised world of good.ii.   Why do we call evil not merely a hazard but a hardship?   If hardship meant only what is hard, it would, we saw, be true in a great measure also or especially of good; χαλεπὰ τὰ καλά.   But we mean by it something more, something hostile to our fundamental nature, though in a way inherent in it; something in which the finite, though transcending itself, transcends itself towards ultimate dissatisfaction, and not towards harmony and completeness. The possibility of such hardship is rooted, we have to remember, in the possibility of satisfaction and harmony.

The answer is that besides the adventurousness which it shares with good, besides, moreover, the

---

[1] In principle, because, of course, it is not all in fact at the command of every finite self.   What is so in each case, and how related to the opportunities of good and evil, is part of the adventurousness which the finite must accept.

primary contradiction between good and evil in which both are on a level, the evil attitude involves a further or second contradiction. It is not merely interested to realise the self against a contradictory element, as good also is, but it is interested to realise it in and as a contradiction.

And here it is impossible to reason the matter further without reference to the realised or organic moral world, which was mentioned in contrast to the externality of the world of claims, and of which the world of claims itself was a very superficial aspect and anticipation. Any one who should insist on restricting the argument at this point to the apparent or finite individual would not be able effectually to distinguish between the good and evil attitude. For it is only possible to distinguish them by implicit or explicit reference to the world of spiritual membership in which the apparently finite creature comes to his reality. Apart from this, he is a chaos of impulses, all of which have their ends, and these ends, *pro tanto*, are goods. And if we find one of them contradicting another, by what possible standard can we determine which is right? The difficulties and irrational compromises of altruism and egoism, of asceticism and hedonism,[1] arise from the attempt to discriminate good and evil in the desires and volitions of the self without taking into account any totality to which it is relative by finding completion in it. No doubt, within every

---

[1] One may see a similar difficulty and its implied solution in Plato's account of the inward order which is the truth of justice, dissociated for the moment from the complement of the external world. The reader feels at once that there is nothing in this inward order to justify the rank or value of objects of desire, beyond an apparent tendency to intellectualism. Plato, of course, immediately, supplies the corrective in correspondence with the social organism.

self-conscious finite creature there is something of a formed system, which constitutes or indicates its attitude to perféction, and by contrast with which what opposes it is evil. But there is no standard or rationale for the identification and estimate of its structure unless we take it in connection with the spiritual organism in which the finite being finds to some extent completion and satisfaction. I do not mean simply the social whole or the general will, though that is an obvious part and instance of what is here in question. I mean the whole world of achievements, habits, institutions in which the apparent individual finds some clue to the reality which is the truth of himself. This, then, imperfectly as it is realised in connection with him, stands to him so far for the satisfaction and the foundation which his nature demands. And his attitude, so far as good, is to harmonise his being with it, while eliciting from the material of life a further harmony for both. This spiritual world, in its purpose and persistence, is the attainment, so far solid and real, in which self-transcendence is assured of the identification of the self with good, that is, with a something which is at once himself and greater than himself, and bears up to a certain point the coherent and satisfactory character of perfection.

Now, against this relatively solid achievement there is on the side of evil nothing—simply nothing —correlative to be set. There are, indeed, in the self-transcendence towards evil, positive ends and purposes which might have belonged to the good. But as evil, they have for their common bond and inclusive construction only the spirit of conflict and contradiction; of resentment and hostility as at a threatening absorption into the harmonious world of the good. Evil, one might say, is good in the wrong place, as dirt is matter in the wrong place. But being in the wrong place, it takes on the character of conscious contradiction. And being in contradiction against the unity in which the self is realised, and being affirmed by the self in such an attitude, it brings the self, so far as affirmed in it, into contradiction with itself. And it is into such contradiction that self-transcendence, so far as evil, passes out in the act which should constitute self-realisation. The act, of course, has a content. You cannot take up an attitude of bare contradiction and no more. But the point of the content is not in any whole which it subserves, but in hostility to the identification of the self with such a whole.[1]

8. Why do we represent evil as the inherent or adherent complement of good? The answer might be put in many forms.

We might say, for instance, that it is due to the inadequacy of finite good. If we could have all we want, without collision of ends, there would be no ground of discord and no motive for rebellion. But as finite good cannot satisfy a finite being as a whole, there is always some element of the finite creature which demands satisfaction outside the system identified with good, and consequently in direct or indirect conflict with it. And the self, being in this element as in all the rest, inevitably sets itself in rebellion, against itself as identified with the system of good. But if we ask why the finite good cannot satisfy the finite creature as a

*Why is evil adherent to good? Many forms of answer. "Inadequacy of finite good," which = "because finite being not a whole," i.e. "not adequate to perfection and perfection useless to it," i.e. "evil necessary to freedom," i.e. "moral standpoint involves conflict."*

---

[1] Of course I am following at a great distance Mr. Bradley's analysis of the good and bad self in *Ethical Studies*.

whole, by, so to speak, exactly fitting it, the answer must come back to this: that the finite creature, being only an apparent and not a real whole, cannot be satisfied except by being made into a real whole. And this means that it could not be satisfied by a good which, *per impossibile*, should just fit it as it is. For such a good would leave it in self-contradiction and inconsistency. Therefore the supposed good could not be more than a relative good, and to speak of its being a complete satisfaction would be a contradiction in terms.

So the fundamental answer is, that the contrast of good and evil, like the other hazards and hardships which beset the finite creature, depends upon its finite-infinite nature. For in consequence of this it perpetually transcends itself towards a perfection to which, as it stands, it is not adequate; and therefore the only perfection it can realise, its finite good, is in turn not adequate to it. Nothing, as we saw, can satisfy a self-contradictory being, except what will make it harmonious, which means a radical transformation. It takes the whole object—this is the moral of Plato's *Republic*—to satisfy the whole man. But then the man cannot receive the whole object, and therefore, *ex hypothesi*, cannot bring his whole nature into correspondence with any satisfaction. And thus his innate self-transcendence, his ineradicable passion for the whole, makes it inevitable that out of the superfluity which he cannot systematise under the good, he will form a secondary and negative self, a disinherited self, hostile to the imperative domination of the good which is, *ex hypothesi*, only partial. And this discord is actually necessary to the good; for it sets it its characteristic problem,

the conquest of the bad.   And the good is necessary
to the evil, for beyond rebellion against the good,
the would-be totality of the disinherited self can
find no other unity.

A shorter form of the answer would be, that evil
is necessary to freedom.   I do not mean that tempta-
tion is necessary to prove and train the empty free
will.   The ego has a content before it is a moral
agent.   But I mean, what I take to be the truth
underlying this doctrine, that a spirit which has its
being in transforming the external into the absolute
must proceed by trial and error, and so by setting
itself against itself.   Its business, we have seen,[1] is
to initiate, to fuse and concentrate externality into
elements of perfection.   Now this origination presupposes a perpetual struggle with misdirected desire
and endeavour.   The constructive spirit rises upon
its own failures, and in advancing loses itself often
in blind alleys.   If it could not go wrong, its creation
would not be its own.

In a word, the world of hazard and hardship
arises over the whole arena where finite individualism battles with spiritual individuality ; and in this
arena good and evil form the central conflict.   Their
import is an antithesis to be fought out on finite
ground, which is as much as to say, there is an
insuperable antithesis to be overcome.   Thus, as
in the world of claims, so, though in a lesser degree,
in the world of organised and realised morality,
moral faith is found looking to the future, to progress
and modification of the finite, in short, to an infinite
advance in which the insuperable opposition may
be overcome.   This is, as we have seen more

[1] *Principle*, Lect. IX.

generally, the typical moral attitude, the fundamental individualistic attitude to which the antithesis of good and evil belongs.   Each being has his work to do ; he is responsible for the future of the world ; he looks to do his part in modifying and reforming the universe.

In drawing to a conclusion of this attempt to exhibit the rationale of the risks and buffets which are inseparable from finite selfhood, we are bound to say a word on the question how far these hazards and hardships characterise the absolute.   Let evil stand as the typical case.   How far is evil a character of the Absolute?

*These hazards, etc., how far charac-ters of the Absolute ? Evil, e.g. a sub-ordinate aspect in good, and good itself hardly a character of the Absolute. Evil and error are in it but not of it.*

9. There is a very important consideration of principle which affects this question in regard to all the forms of imperfection.   All of them, we have seen, spring from the general source of satisfaction and value, the self-transcendence or finite-infinite nature of finite beings.   Each of the imperfections, moreover, is relative and subordinate to a certain aspect of completeness and perfection, which belongs (as a hazard, we have maintained) to the tension of finite being in its transformation towards the Absolute.

Now, in the first place, the Absolute cannot be fully characterised by any one of these subordinate excellences itself.   As the perfect experience it is more than beautiful, more than pleasant, more than true and than good.   We have seen this from a general argument in the case of all particular perfections,[1] and more especially we have seen it in the previous lecture in the case of pleasure, and in the present lecture in the case of good.   It is plain

[1] *Principle*, Lect. VII.

that a perfection which reconciles all these characteristics must be more than each of them. It cannot
be a conjunction; it must, as we have argued
throughout, be a transformation.

Much less, then, can the Absolute be characterised by any one of the imperfections which are
relative to each of these several forms of perfection,
each to each. Thus the Absolute certainly contains
error, as it contains everything. But we cannot
say that it is characterised by error, *i.e.* that when
we think of it as the perfection which transcends
and completes the nature of truth, we can think of it
as, in this completeness, having error as a constituent
member. The same argument applies throughout,
to error as to ugliness, to evil as to pain. Error is
made through and through of the same stuff as
truth. It is affirmed as truth. It is an arrangement in the same world as truth and deals with the
same realities. The very same judgments are true
or erroneous according to the purpose, conditions,
and context which we supply to them. It is false to
say that water boils at 200° Fahrenheit. That is to
say, it is false if you understand it to mean, under
normal conditions, viz. at sea-level. But if you
supply the condition "at a certain height above sea-
level" it becomes true. You may, of course, specify
conditions which wholly and utterly conflict with
the possibility affirmed to be real. But still you are
only dealing with a confusion between realities—
with the assertion of one alternative under the
condition belonging to another.[1] By rearranging
and readjusting the condition the error can always
be transformed into truth.

[1] See Author's *Logic*, ed. 2, vol. i. p. 383.

Thus error differs from truth simply in systematic distinction and completeness. Its character of falsity is a matter of degree, normally reducible to exaggerated emphasis on some one element in a whole.[1] And I suppose there is no finite truth— and all truth is finite—which has not such ex- aggerated emphasis, "partiality" in the most pregnant sense.

Error thus shows no characteristic irreducible to truth. The perfection which finite mind implies as its only ultimate reality involves the absorption of error into a coherent and "impartial" system of truth, and consequently of values. That is to say, in as far as truth becomes complete, error must be absorbed and disappear. There is nothing to keep it alive, except the incompleteness of truth. If truth, in becoming complete, ceases to be truth and becomes, say, reality, that transformation none the less involves the disappearance of error. Error is what stands out and refuses to come into the system, though of one substance and texture with it. If the system is completed, in itself or as something else, that is to say that error is absorbed.

If, then, we consider the absolute, the perfect experience, from the standpoint of truth and error, we must say though it contains error, this is a subordinate aspect of its character as truth, and can only belong to the ultimate experience so far as imperfect truth belongs to it. But that can only be

[1] Take the simplest and most definite blunder. "The lady in blue is Mrs. A.," when she really is Mrs. B. The judgment is a confusion of identities, due to some fact or mark about Mrs. B. which suggests Mrs. A., and which the percipient overestimates, neglecting all the other facts and marks. The mistake may or may not be a bad one. The two ladies may be "identical twins."

as an element absorbed in it, so that all varieties
of relative points of view and one-sided emphasis
come together in the one experience of reality
and value.

So with evil, taken in the sense which gives it a
distinctive meaning apart from mere natural facts of
pain and of what we take to be failure in external
nature; that is, as anything which is or implies an
attitude opposed to good.

The stuff of which evil is made is one with the
stuff of which good is made. No tendency or desire
could be pointed out in the worst of lives or of
actions which is incapable of being, with addition
and readjustment, incorporated in a good self.[1]
There would not be the contradiction of good and
evil if there were not this community of nature as
in pain and pleasure, or in error and truth. The
essence of the evil attitude is the self-maintenance
of some factor in a self both as good and also as
against the good system. It is, as we saw above,
good in the wrong place, and therefore wrenches
the whole nature of the soul out of gear. It is, to
employ an old definition, " when we use what we
ought to enjoy, and when we enjoy what we ought
to use." [2] No doubt, we cannot easily see how it is
psychologically possible to will or approve something as good, while recognising it as in conflict
with the good system. It is as if one asserted error
not merely as truth, and *de facto* against the system

[1] I do not believe, *e.g.*, in disinterested cruelty. I take the
appearance of it to be due to certain forms of self-assertion which are
capable of finding perfectly legitimate objects. They become cruel
by their narrowness, just as " virtuous " fanaticism may.

[2] The classical account of evil, from this point of view, is in Plato's
*Republic.*

of truth, but as truth, and yet consciously against the system we hold to be truth,[1] which seems strictly impossible. And in the case of evil it will perhaps be necessary to go back to Socrates, and to admit that in the moment of evil volition the inherent contradiction is blunted, and the system willed and recognised as good (if not willed it is not recognised) is modified by self-deception so as apparently to accept for the moment the evil attitude.[2]

However this may be, on the main point there is no doubt. The evil attitude is an incident of the good, asserting the same sort of aims, and asserting them as good; and only asserting them against the acknowledged good system because the acknowledged finite good and the finite creature are unable to adjust themselves to each other in an all-inclusive system. The evil, it is sometimes said, is superseded good, good of the past; as heresy has been said to be the orthodoxy of the past. At any rate this doctrine illustrates our point.

Supposing, then, the good to become an adequate system in which some being could fully affirm itself—and in the absolute it must be so, even if in becoming so it transforms itself—there can be no difficulty in thinking of evil as absorbed in it. There is room in good for the character of all evil, redistributed and resystematised, just as there is in truth for the elements of all error. In the case of

---

[1] We can very nearly do this, and the limiting case throws a good deal of light on the evil attitude. We can say, "I know that all experience and authority, except a very little, are against me; but I cannot see my way out of that little, and I must defy the whole social and scientific world." If there is temper in such a position, it passes into evil. [2] See Bradley in *Mind*, xliii. 306.

good the transformation, instead of being specially difficult, is singularly easy to conceive. The ampler judgment of the world and of practical life tells more on the good than on the true, because it is a more widespread and a more indispensable experience. The world is wiser than the abstract moralist. It knows that no qualities are wholly valueless. How constantly we hear it said, "They will do capital work together ; A's failing will counteract B's," or, "if A and B could be shaken up in a bag together, they would make a perfect man." The Absolute is a limiting case of such a process. John Brown at Harper's Ferry showed himself what might be called a cold-blooded murderer ; but a good which could not include the spirit of his will would be a wretchedly poor one. This was recognised by all plain men who came in contact with him.

There is evil, then, within the Absolute, but the Absolute is not characterised by evil. That is to say, there is nothing in evil which cannot be absorbed in good and contributory to it ; and it springs from the same source as good and value. If we think of good as a character of a perfect experience, we cannot help thinking of evil as transcended and subordinated in it. It is true, good as good involves evil, but good as absorbed in perfection only involves evil as absorbed within good. And so, if we think of judging the universe, we should remember that our highest form of judgment is not the judgment of good and evil ; not even if we take good to imply an attitude to all that has value, the widest meaning of morality. Our highest judgment is the judgment of perfection, and raises a different problem from the judgment of moral good and evil in their widest sense. The universe may be perfect owing to the very fact, among others, that it includes, as conditions of finite life, both moral good and evil.

Borderland of this and previous lecture— objection to a world both suffer- ing and contempt- ible. Our object, to clear up relation of pain and value. Must choose whether to argue from pain or moral badness.

10. Before concluding this lecture I will try in a few words to clear up a point on the frontier between its subject and that of the previous one.

It is all very well, we may be told, to take things thus in detail, and to find an exalted source first for pain and then for the evil attitude. But this does not meet the overwhelming impression of the whole. It is not mere pain and it is not mere moral failure. It is the mass of combined misery and worthlessness in the world. We could stand, it might be argued, continual pleasure along with brilliant wickedness, or high values very widely distributed along with a good share of pain. But what shocks us is the general low level of life, accompanied with misery ; the mass of heathendom with its wars and sensuality ; the oppression and ignorance of the dark ages, or the wretchedness and vice of a very large part of our life in the height of civilisation. If everybody was like our noble selves, cultivated, peaceful, and living in moderate comfort and refinement, it would all be much easier to understand. And some day, we hope, they will be so.

Disclaiming, as throughout, all attempts at a *théodicée*, because we do not regard the universe as ruled by an omnipotent moral person, we must attempt to consider the connection and real facts of things with an open mind, and we must insist, to begin with, that the critic should elect with which horse he means to win.

If he means to found his complaint on suffering as such, then he must go to the facts of suffering as such, as actually felt by the sufferers, and must not bring in our moral ideals to eke out the sense of failure. He must analyse the actual life of heathendom or of Europe in the dark ages or of the poor in our great cities, or any other type of life he chooses on which to rest his case. He must rebut the presumption drawn[1] from the inherent relation of pleasure and pain, that where the capacity of pain is actualised, that of pleasure must be so at least in the same measure, and he must deal with the improbability that life should be sustained at the precise point at which it can support suffering without an overbalance of vitality for unobstructed activity. For if that point were not precisely kept, then if life fell below it, it must soon end; if it rose above it, pleasure, which is attached to all life as such, must on the whole be predominant.

    I do not love this mode of argument, but the critic who insists on the brute facts of suffering condemns himself and others to it. I should have said that *prima facie* the poor and the benighted heathen were more light-hearted—we are now speaking of facts and not of "oughts"—than the well-to-do, cultivated, and respectable Christian. Light-heartedness is not mere pleasure; but then I believe the argument on the basis of mere pleasure-pain to be inadequate. If, however, you go, without moral prejudices, to pleasure merely, you must remember that, say, a savage or barbarian chief, whose life, if I had to live it, would be to me prolonged hardship, terror, and remorse, probably enjoys his existence as much as I do mine, or more. And he would certainly prefer to be

---

[1] Lect. VI.

shot a dozen times rather than, well warmed and well fed, to sit in my arm-chair and try to read Hegel.

If, on the other hand, we are to go upon moral or cultural failure, then we *ipso facto* acknowledge a certain moral or cultural development in the creature we are criticising, and the question becomes one of particular kind and degree. And it is very far more difficult than most pessimists have for a moment conceived. The popular revolt against "intellectualism," dating at least from Rousseau, has done good in this direction. Self-conscious civilised life and self-culture are no doubt fine things in their way, but very largely because they presuppose and reveal such great fundamental values as love,[1] and courage, and self-sacrifice. The notion that the supreme values lie all, as it were, up above and beyond us, on a road which has yet to be traversed, and at some higher pitch of civilisation, contains, I should suggest, only a very moderate amount of truth.[2] Values are distributed all over the temporal revelation of the Absolute, not reserved for a climax.

And if any one speaks of "slum-life" as a whole and treats it as not worth living, he writes himself down

[1] Compare, *e.g.*, the function of sacred art as a revelation of the fundamental experience of the family through its treatment of the Holy Family, and also of heroism and self-sacrifice in the saints and martyrs. Such, too, is the function of tragedy, which we have often insisted on.

[2] Cf. Wallace, *Lectures and Essays*, p. 200. "Non-moral, *i.e.* non-social, and non-civilised man, we know not. Morality, sociality, civility, is his *proprium*. His morality, indeed, may be quaint and untasteful as judged by later specimens more familiar to us ; yet that is a judgment which the lowest savage, as we complacently call the savages of another type than ours, can easily retort."

as a victim of class prejudice and conventional superstition.[1]

11. In regard to the general problem of the censure of the universe, I may repeat in other words what I said in the last lecture. The test is the satisfaction of our criticised desires. We obviously can require no other satisfaction. Criticism means reducing their object to a self-consistent ideal of perfection or proving the reduction in principle impossible. And therefore it is hardly conceivable that we should ever possess the basis from which we could go forward confidently to an estimate of the universe. Except by possessing perfection, that is, we are unable to grasp in detail the nature of the satisfaction it would offer, and therefore, *ex hypothesi*, some elements of our nature must always, for finite creatures, seem likely to stand out unsatisfied, just as they would if perfection were theoretically inconceivable. It is an instance and illustration of this that our moral judgment, if that means our estimate of things as determined by the antithesis of good and evil, and the consequent yearning for infinite progress and for compensation or poetic justice, is plainly not our highest form of judgment. Even if we take it in the widest sense, in which it practically is never taken, that is, as including all finite values in the conception of moral good, this remains true. The judgment which conceives the

In regard to general censure of universe, test is satisfaction of our *criticised desires*, and to possess this almost involves possessing perfection. And we cannot limit our own nature antecedently.

---

[1] There is a curious illustration of a parallel limitation of judgment to that which we have been discussing in the arguments of some at least of those who think that Bacon must have written "Shakespeare." It comes out quite plainly in some of the treatises that the true motive of the contention is the idea that no one but a cultured man of letters could possibly have written the plays. It does not occur to the writers that a man of letters in their sense is the last sort of person to whom these works should be attributed.

universe as a perfection within which good and evil arise and conflict is the highest expression of our underlying or real self, and the only one which attempts to do justice even in the abstract to the demands of perfection.

And I must urge once more in reference to criticism which restricts itself to the degree of evil, what I urged with reference to similar criticism dealing with the degree of pain.  So long as we can experience the general nature of satisfaction and solution, revealing to us the clue to all problems in our finite-infinite nature as their root, we cannot pick and choose among the hazards and hardships which empirically confront us.  We cannot say, so much of evil would be all very well, but this which we find is more than we can put up with.  We have seen it to be evidently essential to the logic of our station in the universe that its dealings with us should transcend in detail our finite discretion.[1] If not, we should be placing antecedent limits, drawn from our ignorance and impotence, upon the communication to us of our own nature, which we have called "Soul-making."  As with pain, so with evil ; if we might rule out what we think excessive, it is clear that our best experience would be lost.  What finite creature, in drawing his schedule of permissible evil, would not have ruled out the crucifixion? If we are going to rebel, and repudiate pain and evil, we must begin at the beginning, and go to the root, by repudiating our finite-infinite nature, with the frightful strain, amounting to dissolution and recasting, which it necessarily involves.

In the considerations of this and the two previous

[1] *Principle*, Lect. I., *ante* Lect. VI.

lectures, I hope that we have fairly exhibited in action that double nature of finite creatures which makes them inherently the prey of hazard and hardship. For accident and disturbance are, we may say, their own nature in disguise. This is why they come in pairs, so strangely opposite yet akin, according as the strain and friction or the satisfaction and solution predominate in the self-transcendence of the finite-infinite being, which inevitably lends itself to both. This is why, again, as has been pointed out above, there persists, within and by means of accident and disturbance, a recognition implicit or explicit of an underlying real in which the two aspects of our being become one and their contradiction rises into a satisfaction which it deepens. This recognition, we saw, accompanies the whole series of our development, but it is enough to take it in a single explicit form as typical of all.

And therefore I will pass from the hazards and hardships of finite selfhood to exhibit in the ~~two~~ three next lectures the principle of its stability and security ; in other words, the recognition which constitutes religion—we may call it the stability and security of the finite self.

# C. THE STABILITY AND SECURITY
## OF FINITE SELFHOOD

## LECTURE VIII

### THE RELIGIOUS CONSCIOUSNESS

The Religious Consciousness as typical of stability and security in contrast with the two previous headings.

1. THROUGHOUT this second course of lectures, down to the present point, we have been treating of the finite being, the Individual commonly so called. We have spoken of his origin and formation, as a self to whom on the one side his own nature is communicated by the world, and who, on the other side, in eliciting that nature from the world, reveals himself as a creative force, and as a copula raising externality towards the Absolute. We regarded him so far as being moulded by nature, though in being moulded he reveals the power of eliciting its secret, a secret even from itself.

Thus the finite being was considered as identified with a range of natural circumstance, whose meaning is embodied in him through a severe formative discipline, analogous to what operates in lower nature as "natural selection." As a consequence of this position he has for his apparent destiny to be the plaything of hazard and the prey of hardship. For he is a unit engaged by a process of self-adjust-ment—necessarily more or less obstructed—in

forming a link through which a *prima facie* confusion is absorbed in and transformed into the
underlying harmony.    The technical formula for
this position of his we found in some such expression
as "a finite-infinite" or "self-transcendent" creature.
This is to say that his nature is in contradiction
with his existence, and in the adjustment of this
contradiction at once by remoulding circumstance
and by recasting the self he has to deal with the
chances offering *prima facie* now satisfaction and
now obstruction, which we discussed as the hazards
and hardships of finite selfhood.    We emphasised
the point that the chapter of accidents is necessary.
It belongs to finiteness.    It is just the appearance
of externality, by overcoming which in its degree,
the finite self makes its contribution to the Absolute.

Now I turn to insist on the other side, implied
throughout in this conception of the finite self-
conscious being, and present throughout in the facts
of his existence.    What I have in mind is most
simply and adequately indicated by the title of this
lecture, " The Religious Consciousness."    If we wish
to consider what our third general sub-heading
postulates, " The Stability and Security of the
Finite Self"—a characteristic correlative to its
hazards and hardships, and, like its value, rooted in
the nature which gives rise to them—if we wish to
complete our treatment by considering this foundation of all our experience, it is to the religious
consciousness, however broadly interpreted, that we
must have recourse.    Its general formula, in the
wide sense here in question, is simply the completion or recognition of the finite-infinite or self-
transcendent nature which we have attributed to the

"individual." It is the surrender or completion of finite selfhood in the world of spiritual membership. It is the full opposite, therefore, of the world of claims, which was the typical case of that insistence on finite isolation, mitigated by relations, in the contrast of which with the spirit of self-transcendence we found the source of all hazard and hardship. The finite being tends to fix and rely upon rules, incidents, characteristics, which his own nature, always aiming at unity with the whole which inspires it, as constantly repudiates.[1] But if the finite-infinite nature asserts itself with any approach to completeness, then we have not merely the constant self-transcendence of the finite, but a recognition, implicit or explicit, of what lies beneath it; and therefore, in principle, a present realisation of the perfect satisfaction. The perfect satisfaction would be the possession of the Absolute as such, in short, to be the Absolute. But the present realisation of the perfect satisfaction, which in its degree the religious consciousness offers, is just the recognition by the finite being of its own impotence, as finite, for such an attainment, and the insistence, in spite of this, on its own unity in principle, through recognition, with perfection as opposed to the evil which persists in its finite being, i.e. with perfection in the form of good. Thus we must not say that every satisfaction, every sense of attainment or self-transcendence by the conquest of externality, is religious. On the contrary, the sense of satisfaction

---

[1] How as to moral goodness? Moral goodness, strictly taken, is something the self attempts in its own strength, and insists upon as its own. And this is a possession which its ultimate nature repudi-ates, and even tends to identify with evil. But there cannot really be a healthy working morality apart from religion, as we shall see.

and achievement, in our own strength (taking no note of what is implied in the self-transcendence which all achievement actually involves), may well become the self-sufficiency which is the essence of irreligion.[1]   But every satisfaction and achievement —every self-transcendence in which we become united with something which was beyond us—may be religiously felt, if it is taken as involving recognition of a higher perfection, that is, as coming to us not in our own strength, but as a pledge of our absorption in the greater world.

In this consciousness, then, which amounts to the recognition of its own nature by a finite-infinite creature, we have the justification of the general heading under which I propose to speak of religion. There are two preliminary points on which a word of explanation may be of use ; first, the reconciliation of this heading with the two previous headings, "The Moulding of Souls" and "The Hazards and Hardships of Finite Selfhood"; and secondly, the question whether this recognition involves the possession of a reflective metaphysical doctrine, or how far it may be an experience even of a naïve consciousness.

*a.* In the first place, then, if we broke off our treatment at the point we have reached, we might be held, in spite of our protests, to have done little

*Reconciliation of the third sub-heading with the two previous.*

---

[1] We have not to go to Christianity to learn this.

" εἰ μάλα καρτερός ἐσσι, θεός που σοὶ τό γ᾿ ἔδωκεν."—*Il.* i. 178.

" If thou hast strength, 'twas Heaven that strength bestowed.
    For know, proud man, thy valour is from God."—POPE.

Fluellen, I always supposed, does not see the point of the king's recognition that the victory was God's giving, but tries courteously to meet it by assigning God *some* merit. " Yes, by my conscience, he did us great good."

but lay a foundation for pessimism. We have insisted throughout that the troubles of the finite being spring from the same source as his value. But what has been explicitly set out belongs in the main to the accidents, the obstructions, the contradictions of finite living. All this is involved in what we might call the particularity of finiteness, in its contrast with the true individuality or completeness which underlies and inspires the finite being. That is to say, it belongs to the *prima facie* position of the finite being as an external among externals, a one exclusive of others, while at the same time in various degrees disowning this exclusiveness and reaching out after completeness or individuality. Thus it is from and through this particularity that its participation in individuality has to emerge. In other words, it is out of finite particulars, and more than that, it is by their instrumentality, that the grasp of completeness has to be created.

Thus the value of the unit, the enrichment it brings to the perfect whole, is only the other of the selection which, along with the miracle of will, has moulded and recast it, of its own continual toil and trouble in partly obstructed self-adaptation to environment, and of its spiritual education under the influence of the chapter of accidents. And in turning to the " Stability and Security of Finite Selfhood " we are not abandoning our insight into the world's roughness and hazardousness. We are merely completing it by indicating the spirit and impulse of reality which lives throughout all these troubles—in fact, as we have seen, producing them —and implicitly or explicitly carries with it the recognition of a whole which they can only intensify and enrich.

In a word, when besides experiencing finiteness we take hold of the real which it reveals as something more than the finite, then, in principle, the troubles and hazards pass into stability and security. In letting go his false, *prima facie*, fragmentary individuality and accepting its value only as contributory to the true individuality manifested through it, the finite creature replaces the world of chance and disaster by one of stability and security. For perfection is stable and secure ; it possesses, as we saw,[1] the full character of satisfactoriness—of non-contradiction[2] or of trueness and reality. And by identifying the private self not with its own achievement, but with the perfection divined as its true individuality, the finite creature attains what he cannot attain in his own right, the character of perfection. His partial satisfactions, full of friction and obstruction, then become simply enrichments, matters which contribute their significance to the fundamental individuality of the whole. If you claim nothing for your finiteness but to repose on the perfection of the whole through your recognition of your spiritual membership, you have a position which is secure with the security of the whole itself.

β. Secondly, we asked whether this recognition involved a grasp of metaphysical theory, and whether, therefore, the religious consciousness is only to be had through philosophy. The answer to this question seems plain. Philosophy depends on

*Is the religious conscious-ness only to be had through philo-sophy?*

---

[1] *Principle*, Lect. VIII.

[2] We must bear in mind the discussion in *Principle*, Lect. II., which showed, as I hope, that the only genuine non-contradiction belongs to a positive and inclusive system.

the religious consciousness; the religious consciousness does not depend on philosophy. This is not to
deny that in considering the religious consciousness,
as in considering the essence of art or the foundations
of science, much assistance may be given by philosophy in separating the essential from the unessential.

But, primarily, philosophy is the theoretical interpretation of experience as a whole, and thus, no
doubt, the forms of experience which come nearest
to the whole—which have the most of trueness and
reality, or the highest logical stability[1]—are obviously
for its purpose of the highest significance. And in
as far as the religious consciousness at its climax
comes to include the vision of all that has value,
united in a type of perfection,[2] metaphysic comes
to be little more than the theoretical interpretation
of it alone. In this case, observing the limits of
religious and philosophical subject-matter to be
pretty much coincident, we may probably fail in
noting the difference between their respective
attitudes. We may forget that religion is largely
practical, or rather inherently unites the attitudes of
practice and of conviction, while philosophy is in
the first instance a purely theoretical activity. And
therefore we may find ourselves maintaining that
philosophy is religion in a higher form, or even
that reflective theory is essential to all forms of
religious experience.

---

[1] Bradley, *Appearance*, ed. 2, 449. "We can see at once that
there is nothing more real than what comes in religion. To compare
facts such as these with what comes to us in outward existence
would be to trifle with the subject. The man who demands a reality
more solid than that of the religious consciousness knows not what
he seeks."

[2] See *Principle*, Lect. VII., on Dante's religion. *And the same
is true of all religious consciousness in its reference or intention.*

Of course there is nothing to prevent the two from coming together in the same person, and heightening one another, as in Plato, or Dante, or Spinoza. But the distinction between them may be simply pointed out by the observation that neither, strictly taken, can supply the place of the other. No doubt, a philosopher should understand a thing if he is to philosophise rightly about it, and one might argue that a man cannot understand religion if he has not experienced it, nor experience it if he does not possess it in himself. But this argument would prove far too much and yet too little. It would require the philosopher to be the Stoic's perfect man, and yet would not show the two attitudes in question as the same. In fact, the power of thought is the power of apprehension and appreciation on a foundation of direct experience which may be relatively very slight; [1] and it is very differently distributed from the actual possession of special experiences. The religious consciousness, like the perception of beauty or goodness, or the belief in the uniformity of nature, permeates the whole of life. It is the business of philosophy to understand it, like any other leading characteristic of life. To understand it is in some degree to liberate it from accidental accretions, and, so far, indirectly, to reinforce it and promote its maintenance. And we may say, if we are careful to limit our meaning, that philosophy is the same thing as religion in another form; and this, though it is true

[1] Shakespeare's power of understanding things from what must have been in each case a small experience relatively to that of a specialist, is what has misled uncritical thinkers into attributing to him in turn pretty nearly every profession or vocation under the sun.

of all facts and their interpretation, would be rather more true in the case of philosophy and religion than in the case of, say, logic and the details of natural science. For the two former, at their highest pitch, do represent, because of the near identity of their subject-matter, very closely kindred interests of the mind; whereas for one interested in philosophical logic it is conceivable that the detail of natural knowledge might have the value of example for his theory and no more.[1]

Still, in strict method the above answer holds good. Religion is at least half practical; philosophy is *prima facie* pure theory. Religion, being a very full experience, is a subject-matter highly essential to philosophy, but philosophy, as the theoretical interpretation, is not necessary to religion, nor any component of it. The religious consciousness stands on its own foundation, and needs no support from philosophical theory, except in the way above mentioned, by disengaging its essentials. And, of course, in the end and in general, all facts and theories which harmonise reinforce each other.

---

[1] This does not in the least represent the writer's attitude, but it seems quite a possible one. It may be asked whether the observation in the text would apply, say, to Hume, and if not, whether it is denied that he is a great philosopher, and, if he is, whether this is not a disproof of the view that religion and great philosophy are akin. I should answer, first, the view of the text is an *obiter dictum*, a concession by way of departure from the strict and main contention; but, secondly, the writer remembers to have been greatly impressed with the observation of a very competent friend that "Hume's thoughts must have burned within him." I believe that his cool and careful manner often betrays a white-hot passion for truth, traceable perhaps, as has been said *mutatis mutandis* of Virgil's love of natural beauty, mainly in the special strength and attentiveness of his style in certain passages. And a devoted passion for truth is certainly in the region of religion.

2. We may now speak in a more general sense, other than that which is traditional, of the significance of religion, and apply our account to the fundamental characters of stability and security in the nature of the finite self.

In a striking discussion of what is meant by religion[1] it has been observed that a name in the first instance expresses what the outsider sees and marks, and is not given by a race or persuasion, or the intimate possessors of anything, to themselves or their belongings. So the name "religion," in its Latin etymology, in whatever form we accept it, utters more especially the feeling of those who looked from the outside on the "religious" man. He attracted observation, we must suppose, as being in some way more bound, more attentive, than others. "Religiosi = qui omnia quae ad cultum deorum pertinent diligenter retractant" (Cic. *De natura deorum*, ii. 28), "superioris cuiusdam naturae (religio) . . . curam ceremoniamque affert" (*De inv.* ii. 53). The religious man produced the impression of being peculiarly careful in certain matters, of being under a law, or bond.

And long after Roman times this characteristic has continued to attract notice. "And so Calvin says (*Instit.* 66), 'J'estime que cet mot est opposé à la trop grande licence et excessive que la plupart de monde s'est permise. . . . Religion donc comporte autant comme une retraite et discrétion mûre et bien fondée.' It is the same disciplinary consciousness of being ever in the great taskmaster's eye that made Frenchmen speak of the Huguenots as 'messieurs de

Marginal note: "Religion" in broadest sense includes *all* devotion, *e.g.* to truth and beauty. "Ethical" and "natural" only distinction of degree. *Some* social solidarity in it all.

[1] Wallace, *Lectures and Essays*, p. 52 ff. I am largely indebted to Wallace in this lecture.

la religion.' Religion is the sense of a covenant obligation, a binding tie. It need not surprise us, therefore, that in *Parsifal* and the *Nibelungen Lied* the word for religion and its sanctity is *Ê* (the modern *Ehe*, now only used of marriage); *e.g. in Kristenlicher Ê*, or *den touf, und Kristen Ê*. And so in Shakespeare the commonest sense involves this emphasis on conscientious obligation, strict fidelity, loyal obedience, *e.g.* 'Keep your promise with no less religion' (*As You Like It*, iv. 1. 201), 'When the devout religion of mine eye' (*Rom.* i. 2. 97), 'How many a holy and obsequious tear hath dear religious love stolen from mine eye' (Sonnet 31)." [To which I add, "A coward, a most devout coward, religious in it," *i.e.* he keeps his "rule" (*Twelfth Night*, iii. 4. 424).]

Luther in effect deepened rather than overthrew this traditional impression. But he started from the other extreme. "For the outward ordinance, the minute and accurate performance of measured duties,[1] it (the Lutheran reform) substituted the inward feeling, the subjective attitude of faith. The word for true religion in the Lutheran language is Glaube, 'Du muss bei dir selbst im Gewissen fühlen Christum selbst, und unbeweglich empfinden, dass es Gottes Wort sei.' "

And so the term "religieux," descended from the older tradition, "has no English equivalent."[2]

Still we cannot dismiss the original impression. "It hardly needed Schleiermacher to repeat that the

---

[1] The ordinary reader, for example, of Cardinal Newman's life, is struck at once by the fact that the first requirement of a religious house is its "rule," given, it appears, by some external authority.

[2] Bradley, *Ethical Studies*, p. 300. And I suppose the nearest German equivalent is "Geistlicher," a remarkable contrast.

essence of religious life is the sense of utter and all-round dependency."[1]

When we turn to consider religion in its widest bearing upon life, the impression thus left by the specialised tradition, though broadened, is confirmed. In this sense the religious consciousness has no special or exclusive connection with the super-natural, the other world, or even the divine. It is essentially the attitude in which the finite being stands to whatever he at once fears and approves, in a word, to what he worships. It is impossible to draw the line at any point between the simplest experiences of this kind and those completest forms of devotion to which the term religion has been exclusively applied. Whatever makes us seem to ourselves worthless in our mere private selves, although or because attaching ourselves in the spirit to a reality of transcendent value, cannot be distinguished from religion. The Shakesperian passages cited above, for example, although, perhaps, echoes of a conventional language, yet point to a continuity which is undeniable. It is, indeed, explicitly set forth in the phases of Dante's adoration of Beatrice.

Whenever, then, we find a devotion which makes the finite self seem as nothing, and some reality to which it attaches itself seem as all, we have the essentially religious attitude. Thus there may be false religions,[2] conflicting religions, partial and

[1] Wallace, *op. cit.* 58.

[2] I suppose the attitude of the whole-hearted worshipper of wealth and power must be called a religion. There cannot be a religious attitude towards an object recognised as bad (Bradley, *Appearance*, p. 440), but there may be any degree of defectiveness in the object taken as good. Of course the stability connected with it is greatly decreased by such defects.

hesitating religions. But a finite self-conscious life without religion is hardly to be found.[1] As we saw in the Introduction to the previous volume, there is always death. Its significance as a negation of the finite may vary from the fullest to the cheapest. But, in form, it is always there to realise the suppression of the finite which is inherent in the finite's own nature.

From this widest point of view most of the distinctions drawn by the positive science of religions appear as matters of degree. There is, for example, no really fundamental difference between "natural" and "ethical" religions.[2] In the crudest forms of worship directed to external objects there seems to be the sense of something, however capriciously selected, which is of value and importance to a community, and the ritual in honour of which, therefore, takes the individual worshipper out of himself, and places his centre of gravity, so to speak —his sense of value and importance—in the concerns of a group extending beyond his private self. Where such a common interest is recognised, it cannot be

---

[1] What of the brute creation? It has been said that man is the god of the brutes; and when the religious attitude is described as above, it is hard to avoid finding some kinship to it in, *e.g.*, the dog's attitude to his master. I suppose the technical question would be whether the dog has a self and self-transcendence at all.

[2] "We may . . . assert that in the very beginnings of religion there was morality. Non-moral, *i.e.* non-social, and non-civilised man, we know not. Morality, sociality, civility, is his *proprium*. His morality, indeed, may be quaint and untasteful as judged by later specimens more familiar to us; yet that is a judgment which the lowest savage, as we complacently call the savages of another type than ours, can easily retort. But the rudest savage has a life only because he lives in others, for others, by others; because his life is determined and formed by rules, customs, observances, painfully numerous and apparently onerous" (Wallace, *Lectures and Essays*, p. 200).

said that the ethical consciousness is lacking.   The truth is that its fuller and truer form, the religious attitude, comprehends it from the beginning as it transcends it in the end.   The strictly moral attitude, in its self-consciousness and self-isolation, is a phase within and dependent upon the religious attitude, as the economic world, to which we have so often compared it, is a phase within and dependent on the normal social tissue.[1]

If a difference of kind is to be found in early religious phenomena, it would probably lie in the contrast between a social and an anti-social application of supernatural resources.   The latter seems to involve an outlawed and rebel consciousness, hostile to the simple recognition and good faith of service to the social whole.[2]   The identification of the religious spirit with rules of the common life is a fine feature of early religions which later spiritual refinement has too much thrown aside.   " They (the Jews) knew some things which it would have been well if the later ages had not lost sight of. They knew that even if religion is not a matter of meats and drinks, meat and drink are no trifles which religion may ignore.   They knew that religion is intimately wrapped up with the tillage of the field, the pasture of the flocks, the rules and

---

[1] All this is strikingly illustrated by the unity of the primitive collective consciousness, as described in Cornford, *From Religion to Philosophy*.

[2] The prominence of the common interest in the crudest forms of cultus is emphasised by Caird's suggestion that ancestor-worship is the effect and not the cause of importance attached to external objects as concerning the common weal.   They are held to be ancestors because they are important, not held important because of a misinterpreted tradition that they are ancestors (Caird, *Evolution of Religion*, i. 239).

modes of wedlock, the customs of the market, with
sanitary rules, with the treatment of disease. They
may have been mistaken in some of their views,
but they were certainly right in their main thesis;
and the whole bent of modern progress is towards
doing what they did in a completer way." [1]

Throughout this attitude, whether directed to
the so-called natural or the so-called supernatural,
we see the essence of the power conferred by the
religious absorption in a reality worshipped by the
finite self. I will venture to permit myself one
more quotation from the volume which I have
already exploited so freely. " It is usual in these
days to regard everything under the conditions of
the struggle for existence, and as a weapon for use
therein. Of material weapons man has invented or
appropriated many. He has wrested from the
creatures their own tusks, claws, bones, and used
them to subdue others ; he has chipped and shaped
stones, and finally hammered and fused metals into
his tools. But all these implements are slight in
importance if compared with the metaphysical ally,
the supernatural aid, which he has secured in his
contest. All the ranges of nature, animate and
inanimate, may regard as they like his efforts to
subdue them ; but man has a weapon in his possession
stronger than anything they can possibly bring
against him. By an instinct earlier than any history
can trace, he sets the power in and behind phenomena
on his side. He is naturally a *theogonic* being ;
he has at the very root of all his actions an instinct,
the instinct of reason, which grows and becomes
more determinate, that he is, as it were, backed by

---

[1] Wallace, *op. cit.* 162.

great powers to the extent of which he can and will fix no limits. He projects his own self to be, into the nature he seeks to conquer. Like an assailant who should succeed in throwing his standard into the strong central keep of the enemy's fortress, and fight his way thereto with assured victory in his eyes of hope, so man, with the vision of the soul, prognosticates his final triumph."[1]

Thus the religious attitude, if we judge by what is *in* the mind, and not merely by what is explicitly before it, permeates, at least, the whole of finite self-conscious life. In the broadest sense, wherever man is devout—wherever he places his value in something beyond his private self, and that something taken to be real—there he has set his foot on ground which so far emancipates him from the hazards, the hardships, the discipline, of finiteness; or rather, emancipates him not so much from these incidents as actually through them. Like the beings of folk-lore whose life is hidden elsewhere than in their own bodies, his worth and his interest are laid up where accidents affecting his temporal self cannot reach them, and in the complete and typical case, where no accident or injury can do anything but intensify them.

It is, I suppose, a question of degree how far the true tribal or social consciousness involves a religious spirit, though we have seen that religion in its most naïve and early forms certainly involves the social consciousness.[2] The true social consciousness, such

---

[1] Wallace, *op. cit.* 192-3. On the words "final triumph," compare the comment, p. 326, below, on the expression "ultimate triumph" as employed by Caird.

[2] In a late and reflective development of religion, it may seem to be a relation between the individual and God alone, independent of

as it is described by Mr. Bradley in his well-known essay on "My Station and its Duties,"[1] seems to me to possess the essential feature of religion. It has the value of the self placed in a real whole in which it is absorbed and with which the will is identified. It is true that in society it is not the whole ideal of perfection which is taken as realised. The social religion, taking religion to imply a real object, must be a partial religion only, more especially in the higher grades of civilisation, when so much of life has been apparently separated from it. But we have seen that we must take note of partial religions; and, moreover, the view drawn from earlier phases when interests seem less subdivided, is fundamentally sound even in later times when the social whole has become in appearance an accidental condition only.[2]

In short, then, wherever man fairly and loyally throws the seat of his value outside his immediate self into something else which he worships, with which he identifies his will, and which he takes as an object solid and secure at least relatively to his private existence—as an artist in his attitude to beauty or as a man of science to truth—there we have in its degree the experience of religion, and, also in its degree, the stability and security of the finite self. I am careful not to say its happiness. The whole argument has been directed to show

---

society. But this is one of those forms of independence which are only possible when the condition, taken as superfluous, has been so absolutely secured that it is tacitly presupposed.

[1] *Ethical Studies*, 1876.

[2] See *Philosophical Theory of State*, ed. 2, Introduction, on the relation of the higher experiences to the social whole, and cf. *Principle*, Appendix II. to Lect. X.

that happiness in the current sense of the word[1] is
not secured to the finite creature by any goodness,
or by any religion, or according to any doctrine
involved in religion. We are least of all implying compensation in this life or in another.
We are speaking of the consciousness inherent in
the finite-infinite being, so far as his full nature
affirms itself, that he is one with something
which cannot be shaken or destroyed, and the
value of which is the source and standard of
values.

3. It is certain that in some sense the existence
of evil is recognised by the religious consciousness.
Nothing, it might be said, is more characteristic of
religion than the sense of sin. Religion is largely
practical, and therefore the contradiction of good
and evil is essential to it as truly as to morality.
How are we to think of evil from the religious
point of view, seeing that it does not interfere with
the stability and security of the self?

*Evil from the religious point of view.*

i. The answer is given in the nature of religion
as already explained, and is emphasised by its contrast with morality, that is, with the reflective and
individualistic morality of the world of claims. In
this reflective morality the contradiction of what is
and what ought to be is brought to an extreme. It
is almost held that nothing which is, ought to be,
and therefore that nothing which ought to be, is.
Thus, one might say, it rests on the conviction that
evil is real, and good is a mere thought. In the
concrete morality of social observance the good is

*Opposite attitudes in religion and sheer morality. Evil recog- nised only to be disowned in the simplest example of devotion.*

---

[1] And it is not worth while to argue about the right to understand
the word otherwise. But I have no doubt that it carries a compound
meaning, and that the security, the stability, which I speak of, is a
large part of what it indicates even in everyday usage.

at least partially realised, and ethical faith takes the shape of holding the good to be a reality in which the individual finds himself sustained and affirmed against the evil which is less real.   In religion the attitude of abstract morality is reversed, and that of concrete morality is intensified.   The characteristic faith of religion is not merely that the good is real, but that nothing else than the good is real.   I quote[1] "the vehement expression of mysticism. When reason tells thee ' Thou art outside God ' then answer thou ' No, I am in God, I am in heaven, in it, in him, and for eternity will never leave him.   The devil may keep my sins, and the world my flesh ; I live in God's will, his life shall be my life, his will my will ; I will be dead in my reason that.he may live in me, and all my deeds shall be his deeds.' "   This tells us more . than volumes of argument directed to prove, *e.g.*, the "existence" of God.   The primary point in the religious consciousness, then, is that the finite-infinite self, implicitly or explicitly conscious of the secret of its own nature, holds the evil of the world and of its own finiteness to be absorbed in the whole of which it is a spiritual member.   It takes for its own, for its ideal self, the character of what it worships, and repudiates everything in itself which conflicts with that character.   The theory, as we have urged, is common and inherent throughout finite life.   One man's career, for example, may be summed up in a sentence by those who knew him best.   " He faithfully served King Charles I. from Edgehill fight to the end of the unhappy

---

[1] From Bradley's *Ethical Studies*, p. 293, note.   I presume from the previous note that J. Böhme is the author cited.

war." [1] There, we may suppose, he set his stake and his value, "there took his station and degree." All he asked was to be allowed to serve what he took to be the best. Failure cannot touch the essence of such a life, even though expended in a cause which seems to some of us so poor. " 'Tis better to have loved and lost Than never to have loved at all." I will speak below of the relation of religious faith to factual truth. But the first thing is to understand the experience itself, and to grasp it as in one form or another the commonest of experiences—one, perhaps, of which no human life is devoid, and possibly not all lives of the higher brute creation. It is, in principle, the self-surrender to some perfection taken as good and so as to be realised, though having itself the power and rank of a dominant reality. Thus there is thrown into it the whole will, and the whole attribution of value. It may be asked what identification with a higher will there can be in a devotion to something which is not obviously a cause or general principle of action ; what will, for instance, is presupposed in truth or beauty with which the will of their devotee can be identified. The question answers itself if we reflect on the example from which we started—the devotion to a cause. The cause which a man takes to claim his devotion is for him the type and centre of a real perfection and he wills it as such. He finds in the aspiration which it realises the content, or the main content, which for him constitutes the value of

[1] Epitaph in a country church known to the writer. We may urge that knowing nothing of the man in question, we cannot tell that his consciousness was such as the text proceeds to postulate. But it does not greatly matter. The sentence has its full meaning in many cases, if not in this.

life, and his will to give it visible and total victory is one with his belief that in truth it is absolutely founded among the very roots of things. Truth and Beauty are thus each of them, to its devotees, a cause, and one in its own nature triumphant, against which falsehood and ugliness have no true hold on the real, and which only need to have made evident the triumph which they possess in their inherent nature. It is true that they are not in themselves of the nature of will, and the religious attitude towards them is therefore not so simple and natural as that in which the central fact is the surrender of the will to the aim of some self-conscious group or being. But the will towards perfection is involved in devotion to them, and in souls of a certain type this forms a sufficient basis for a religious attitude.

As in the highest experiences of religious genius. ii. In the case, however, of an experience recognised as religious in the full sense, the surrender of will, in its identification with the higher will, is the central and predominant fact. We are on the same track which we traversed in dealing with the world of claims, but we see it more clearly. There the supreme will was treated as that of a being self-contained, external to the universe of nature and finite souls, the typical god of Theism.[1]

But after completing the discussion of finiteness, which has brought us within sight of its complement, the true religious experience, it becomes inevitable that we should recognise the true human-divine nature in its completeness. This recognition was anticipated by the repudiation of the strict Theistic

[1] Lect. V. It was recognised that modern Theism would not admit this isolation of the Deity. But it seemed, nevertheless, to be the logical consequence of any view which refuses to recognise the unity of the human-divine will.

position which was found essential to the reality of human freedom.[1] There cannot be freedom, we saw, unless the divine will is genuinely one with that of finite beings, in a single personality.[2] The creation of creators is a mere self-contradiction.

Thus, then, what we have in religion is the practical recognition of the absorption of the finite will in the will for perfection, that is, in the will for good, as the real and actual will dominant in the universe. It would not be suitable to the tone of these theoretical reflections to enlarge upon the utterances, in this sense, of great minds who have had a genius for religion. But I will venture to remark that, whereas in commonplace orthodoxy and current theology, we meet with perhaps the acme of super-stition and unreason, in the actual convictions and experiences of religious genius in all religions we find, with few exceptions, an insight in the fullest harmony with philosophy; from which, indeed, it has only to learn. We may take Plato, St. Paul, and Dante, not to say Jesus himself, as typical instances. The stability and security of the finite self, which is felt, as we have urged, sporadically over the whole area of human life, reaches its climax in these great minds. It here reveals to us in luminous experiences what is everywhere true in principle. The finite mind so far as religious accepts as its true self an actual perfection, which alone is real, and in which evil is absorbed and annihilated. With this perfection it identifies itself by faith, that is to say, in the will to be, allied with the judgment

---

[1] See citation from Vatke, Lect. V. p. 136.

[2] Unless, of course, the supreme Being is taken as finite, and one among others. In that case he has no such relation to other spirits as is typified by inclusion or creation.

of what is, disowning its finite imperfections and those of the world, and treating them as nothing—but, it must be added, not as non-existent. This is the secret of the stability and security of the finite self so far as religiously minded, in spite of, and even by means of, the discipline of its moulding and the hazards of its finite existence. "So far as religiously minded"—and here, perhaps, philosophy can be of some use. For, by comparison and analysis, which the religious temper will not undertake for itself, it is able to point out that at least self-conscious finite mind is always religious in its nature and structure, and, one way or another, has always a religious side in actual empirical fact.

The Paradox of Religion. Its double make-believe. The two aspects and the necessity of their fusion.

iii. "Treating its finite imperfections as nothing, but not as non-existent." This is the paradox which survives in religion, because it is practical, and therefore "good" in it, although perfection, is perfection as the object of an attitude which inherently contrasts it with evil. Evil, or finiteness, so far as still self-assertive and not wholly subordinated to the perfect will, is sin. That is to say, it is the acutest conceivable contradiction of the self, as identified with perfection, against itself. It is something which is in the self, but does not belong to it, and while existent, is yet repudiated with the whole ardour of the self. The self, aware of itself as rebellious, and as asserting itself in its finiteness,[1] nevertheless as identified with the higher

---

[1] There is a technical point here which might cause difficulty. *All* volition, we have argued throughout, is technically self-transcendence, *i.e.* the self in it asserts itself in something new, and sacrifices something old. How, then, can some volition affirm finiteness against the infinite whole, and some affirm identification with the infinite whole? The answer is drawn from the theory of

will repudiates and rejects the self which it is thus aware of.   It will not admit that it *really* is what it is *in fact*.

This complexity of the religious attitude is the explanation of the extraordinary combinations of habit and conviction which are found in persons the genuineness of whose religion up to a certain point can hardly be disputed.   Probably, in principle, all religious persons exhibit such phenomena, but in some cases they appear beyond measure paradoxical. · Many preachers, whose honesty and devoutness there is no reason to deny, have invoked the blessing of God upon the cause of negro slavery. And perhaps there is no practice, however vicious, which has not in some stage of civilisation been hallowed by a religious temper which could not justly be called insincere.   If the whole complex attitude fails to cohere, if repudiation of sin as our true belonging fails to be fused both with a wide appreciation of what perfection must mean and with a complete subordination of the personal will to the will taken as perfect,[1] it is obvious that such a repudiation may develop, as it has been known to develop, into the most fatal antinomianism.

In religion, then, as in morality, good is still loaded with the inherent contrast to evil ; and if evil

---

the good and evil self, and, strictly and rightly, emphasises the point that in *all* volition the finite-infinite or self-transcendent nature is in play, but in some volition negates its own infinity by affirming a very partial end against the infinite whole with which the good self is identified.   It is the same point as that of partial satisfaction, in which immediate obstruction may be evaded at the cost of inconsistency with the system of self as a whole.   See Lect. VI. p. 68.

[1] Cf., *e.g.*, J. Böhme's language, cited above, p. 242.   We have here the essence of the controversy about faith and works.

were entirely to disappear, the practical attitude, which depends upon its presence, would vanish, and with it would go the attitude to perfection as a good; as something to be realised. For in religion—this is the other side of the paradox of evil—perfection is the good, necessarily to be realised, because it is the sole reality. It has been said, therefore, that religion is doubly and contradictorily a make-believe.[1] It is a make-believe as if good were all reality, and again as if it were not, but demanded to be realised. If the first side of this paradox falls out, the stability and security of the religious consciousness falls with it. If the second side is omitted, the practicality of religion —the sense of sin and the devotion of will to the good as its opposite—disappears. In either case the nature of religion loses its characteristic completeness, and to fail in holding the two together is to be arrested by the central problem of all philosophy.[2]

The inherence of evil as sin within the religious consciousness, combined with the essential doctrine of the unity of the divine and finite will, raises the inevitable problem of the presence of sin or evil in the consciousness of God.

For the general and technical answer, it is enough to refer to the previous discussion of the absorption of evil by inclusion and rearrangement. Evil, we saw, is only in the contradiction of good; it is any aim which excludes the good system and is excluded by it. If this contradiction is adjusted, so that inclusion becomes possible, the content of the evil

[1] Bradley, *Appearance*, p. 443.
[2] For the inclusion of these sides in a single attitude, see *Principle*, Lect. VII. p. 272 ff.

attitude passes as a positive factor into the good. *What is evil* in the finite will, then, and its very contradiction with the good—the heat of opposition and rebellion—is, for religion, *in* the divine will, but not *as* evil.   It has undergone transformation.

But this answer, acquiesced in by itself, would destroy, as we saw, the practical attitude essential to religion, which depends on the preservation of the good in the character of what is opposite to evil.   The contradiction of the world of claims, of the "ought" which is not real, and the real which clashes with the "ought," recurs, if only as a vanishing factor, so long as the practical attitude survives, and with it the contradiction of good and evil.   God, conceived as identified with the finite struggle against evil, cannot be the perfection— the Absolute—in which all evil is absorbed.

4. The fact that the religious attitude is largely practical, and the fact that religious tradition, with one voice, admits that it contemplates God in imaginative shapes,[1] are thus obviously in agreement.   Father, Son, Holy Spirit, Lord Omnipotent, Creator, Providence—none of these terms can apply to a Universe or an Absolute which has nothing outside it.   The practical attitude means that the contradiction between good and evil survives, and the survival of this contradiction necessarily implies that God as worshipped in religion is not a being

*Practicality of Religion agrees with the fact that its doctrines express God's nature imaginatively, and not as the Absolute.*

---

[1] Cf. Dante, *Paradiso*, iv. 43.

> " Per questo la Scrittura condiscende
> A vostra facultate, e piedi e mano
> Attribuisce a Dio, ed altro intende :
> E santa Chiesa con aspetto umano
> Gabriel e Michel vi rappresenta,
> E l'a ltro, che Tobbia rifece sano."

for whom evil is annihilated. Granting that evil as evil is not in him, yet evil as essential to finite freedom produces itself in beings continuous with him. And a being who had no concern for the triumph of good, that is, who was not a moral being, would not be the God who is worshipped in religion, and so stands in relation to finite minds as their Lord, Father, or Creator. It is true that we do not with Theism assume specific and miraculous communications of grace to the finite mind. We have held that the divine intercourse with man is mediated by nature and society,[1] and the means of grace are the same as the disciplining and exalting influences of the world. At the same time, the God who is worshipped in religion is the will for good as against evil, and a universe in which this antithesis is absorbed in perfection cannot be one with a God whom the religious consciousness thus presents to itself. We saw in the previous volume that the universe as a whole must rather be the theatre of good and evil than good or evil in itself, and thus the God who is the object of religious adoration is rather the representative of the universe when considered as overcoming evil by good, than the universe in its totality which absorbs good and evil in perfection.[2]

In thus conceiving the matter, it may be remarked, we recover something of the unity and concentration which are aimed at by Theism. God,

---

[1] Green, *Prolegomena*, sect. 110.

[2] This ought to be clear, the moment it is carefully considered. If, as we hold, good and evil are relative to each other, and depend on the contradiction between them, it is quite impossible that the universe as a whole should be either one or the other. They must inevitably be features or characters within it.

we might say, is for us the world-consciousness, to which all consciousnesses are contributory, in respect only of a certain nisus or characteristic, viz. its attitude to or in the genesis and absorption of evil. And it is for this reason that he is always represented by religion in imaginative forms, which could not be applied to the totality of things as a totality. The genesis of evil is the condition of finite life; its absorption or suppression as evil is the condition of the contribution made by the finite to the whole. The whole considered as a perfection in which the antagonism of good and evil is unnoted, is not what religion means by God, and must rather be taken as the Absolute.

5. I have now to explain, perhaps in presence of an impatience in my hearers which at the same point in the argument I have in past years myself strongly experienced, the relation of such conceptions as we have been advancing to objective truth and fact. Do we mean that "religion is true" or not? Is there or is there not a God? Does he in fact exist or does he not?

*The Relation of Religion to objective truth. Does it not involve the existence of God as a fact? The religious consciousness is not concerned with a separate Being's existence. It is an insight into the human-divine nature of the self.*

In other words, does the religious consciousness *prove* anything? May it not be—is it not, *prima facie*, if we accept the sort of thing we have been saying—either an arbitrary fancy of the individual mind about facts which it cannot prove, or, if other than that, a practical attitude adopted towards the universe, independently of any assignable state of facts or realities which can in reason sustain it?

I will say at once that the latter is the difficulty which, if any, threatens our view. The former issue is irrelevant to it, because, if we keep to terms in their ordinary sense, it cannot be alleged that we are professing to affirm any facts at all. It is not here asserted that the reality of the religious consciousness establishes the fact of human happiness, as the word is currently understood, for past, present, or future, nor the fact of the future visible triumph of the good in this world or another, in any mode in which it has not been triumphant hitherto; nor of personal survival beyond our present life, nor of a supreme being existing as a consciousness external to finite mind, personal in the sense of being a magnified man. The religious consciousness is self-contained, and stands on its own basis, although it must be remembered that in our view that basis is exceedingly broad, and includes indeed the greater part of our most vital experience.

We may put the matter in this way. The truth of religion, as we conceive it, does not come to us as something forced upon us, by metaphysical or theological argument, through which we are to be driven to conclusions about matter of fact, beyond our normal beliefs. But this does not mean that it rests upon an arbitrary or *a priori* conviction, derived only from private fancy, and devoid of roots in the working of intelligence. It is, as we understand it, a leading characteristic of experience. Its outward aspect, in itself a mere fact, is guaranteed first by the naïve unity of human beings within it, and in later and reflective ages by the comparative sciences which recognise it as a phenomenon co-extensive with humanity.[1] Its value and its inter-

---

[1] I am aware that there is danger in this line of argument. The extensive occurrence of a fact is a very different matter from its value. Some facts, of extensive occurrence in some ages, disappear in others. Still, reserving the right of interpretation, we may treat very extensive occurrence as emphasising a problem.

pretation are primarily self-contained, and are part of the experience itself. But, like everything in human consciousness, they can be supported, in the sense of being analysed and connected, by critical and philosophical reflection. And, as has been said, the essential in it can in some degree be separated from the unessential.

But it may be asked—and here we confront what we called the more serious problem—is there not one great fact at any rate to which this treatment of religion will not apply? Is not the assertion that God exists either true or not true, and how can any appeal to an attitude of finite experience, unless it is relied on as a metaphysical proof of something beyond it, establish the fact of that existence, which is needed for the *raison d'être* of the attitude itself?

I may set forth the whole difficulty which confronts us at this point by referring for the sake of illustration to an extreme doctrine of the orthodox tradition, which I have in the past uncompromisingly rejected, and which, as understood by its adherents, I still uncompromisingly reject. I will borrow the statement from an authority whose learning and sincerity are unquestionable.

"Christianity therefore as the absolute religion of man assumes as its foundation the existence of an Infinite Personal God and a finite human will. This antithesis is assumed and not proved. No arguments can establish it. It is a primary intuition and not a deduction. It is capable of illustration from what we observe around us; but if either term is denied no reasoning can establish its truth. Each man for himself is supposed to be conscious of the existence of God and of his own existence. We

254 THE RELIGIOUS CONSCIOUSNESS LECT.

can go no further.   If he has not, or says he has
not, this consciousness, he must be regarded as one
whose powers are imperfect."[1]

Now, taken as a description of the religious
consciousness in its complete and characteristic
shape, I believe this passage on the whole to express
truth, allowing for the reservation to which the
author calls attention in the following paragraph.
The epithets "infinite" and "personal," he points out,
involve a contradiction.   Obviously, then, a statement which contains them cannot be read either as
a statement of simple fact or as one of ultimate truth.
The term existence, as of two separate finite things
or persons, must be a misnomer for what is meant
to be affirmed.   And indeed the existence of a
supreme being, as a person external to ourselves
and to the world, like a magnified human creature,
is not affirmed by the religious consciousness, and
if it were known to be fact, would have no bearing
on religion.   But the truth of the experience, in
which we are aware implicitly[2] or explicitly of the
finite-infinite nature of the finite spirit — this is
actually present and contained within the religious
consciousness itself.   It is plainly the same which
the statements above cited are intended to describe ;
but by throwing it into external and relational
language they mutilate its nature and transform it
into an assertion of an independent and isolable
existence, which would need a special demonstration,

[1] Westcott, *Gospel of the Resurrection*, pp. 15-16.   Similar
language is of course constantly held by J. H. Newman, *e.g. Apologia*,
ed. of 1865, p. 4, "two and two only absolutely and luminously self-
evident beings, myself and my Creator."

[2] I call our awareness implicit when the devotion which expresses
it is directed to a partial object, say, to a woman.

and would not, if so demonstrated, harmonise with the essence of the experience itself.[1]

Thus the religious attitude, being at bottom a recognition of the nature of the finite and of an underlying reality which inseparably belongs to it, is, as recognised by the doctrine just mentioned, an inherent character of experience. But it neither needs nor establishes any external or isolable fact or existence. It rather bears witness to a character or nisus of the world of spiritual membership which is inseparable from the finite self - consciousness. We are not, however, to say that religion thus taken is an arbitrary attitude of the finite mind, resting on no reality beyond it. This might be true of the above-mentioned theological doctrine in respect of the assertions which it grounds upon the recognition of the finite-infinite nature. But the recognition itself, so far from being unsupported by experience, is the sum and substance of what it is when it is most solid. And the reservation which we noted the orthodox doctrine to make, in respect of the self-contradiction in its language, along with the imaginative nature of the phrases which throughout history have been employed in the description of the supreme being, thoroughly support our analysis.

The conclusion is, in a word, that the God of religion, inherent in the completest experience, is an appearance of reality, as distinct from being the whole and ultimate reality ; a rank which religion

1 Much of the introductory argument of Westcott's book above cited is of extreme interest for our purpose, *e.g.* such a sentence as that "pure Theism is unable to form a living religion," which I believe to be perfectly true ; or the idea that for some great men "faith in a thought," as opposed to a historical fact, is possible, and that it is only for the masses that some outward pledge and outward fact is necessary (*op. cit.* pp. 9 and 10).

cannot consistently claim for the supreme being as it must conceive him. But this conception, which finds him in the greater self recognised by us as present within the finite spirit, and as one with it in love and will, assigns him a higher reality, than any view which stakes everything on finding him to exist as a separate being after the model of a man. Religion establishes the infinite spirit because it is continuous with and present in the finite—in love and in the will for perfection. It does not need to appeal to facts of separate being, or to endeavour to demonstrate them. It is an experience of God, not a proof of him.

Here, then, I trust, the stability and security of finite selfhood, as its inherence in the whole of reality and value, and its contribution to it through the birth-pangs of soul-making and the hazards of self-transcendence, have been in principle elucidated. In the following lecture I hope to apply this doctrine to the difficult questions affecting the continuance of the finite self after what we call death.

# C. THE STABILITY AND SECURITY OF FINITE SELFHOOD—*Continued*

## LECTURE IX

### THE DESTINY OF THE FINITE SELF

1. IT is the idea of Transformation, which has governed our argument up to this point, that alone gives hope of any clearness in considering the destiny of the finite self. That the ultimate reality of persons, like that of everything else, is in the Absolute, and that the Absolute is non-temporal, are conclusions which seem inevitable from the idea of completeness or perfection. Therefore the only remaining questions, as regards the destiny of persons, are, in the first place, whether we can form any conception of the degree of transformation compatible with what we desire in the way of personal continuance; and, in the second place, whether we can see any reason for expecting one degree of transformation rather than another. *The Idea of Transformation.*

2. The latter is the direct question to which we should all welcome a direct answer. There is but little that I can say about it; and it will be best to say this little at once. *We hardly possess reasons for expecting any special degree of Transformation.*

The whole problem is governed for us by the principle that the finite self, like everything in the universe, is now and here beyond escape an element in the Absolute.[1]   Thus, if we desire to affirm that its destiny involves becoming more fully one with the absolute experience than it is in the world we know, this must be established on special and relevant grounds.   We must not fall into the habit of equating the Absolute with heaven, and assuming that to be "in" the Absolute is a new thing and a sequel compared with our present degree of finiteness, as heaven is for the ordinary Christian compared with life on earth.   We are here and now participants in it, and if a change in the kind or degree of our participation is to be expected, definite cause for this expectation must be shown.

We have even seen that finiteness is an element essential to the infinite real; and this doctrine, if sound, does seem to militate against any conception, according to which it should be, even apparently, the law of the inferior appearances to lead up in time to a perfection which should in principle supersede and abolish them.   That is to say that it is an inconceivable abstraction to place eternity, or heaven, or perfection as such, in a future beyond all time and finitude.[2]   Of course such a presumption determines nothing about the possibility of future experiences much more perfect in degree than anything

---

[1] I do not say "a member of" the Absolute.   Such an expression might imply that it is, separately and with relative independence, a standing differentiation of the Absolute.   And that question must not be prejudged.

[2] See McTaggart on the relation of Time and Eternity, *Mind*, lxxi. 343.   Of course he does not say that Eternity is future ; only that it may be the law of appearances that it should seem so.   It is the same question as whether Hegel's Absolute involves in its nature the process which generates it.   See the same author's *Commentary on Hegel's Logic* and the present writer's review, *Mind*, Jan. 1911.

we know, on the part of finite selves in a continued existence. It must be remembered, however, that the deeper view of religion itself[1] has usually insisted on the idea of eternal life as something to which the contrast of present and future is indifferent.

On the other hand, our conception of a representative nature or origin of the self does not essentially involve its transitoriness in time. Historical and natural conditions, such as we have supposed to be focussed in finite selves, are *prima facie* transitory appearances. But there seems to be no necessary limit to the power to constitute a centre of experience that the being in which they are focussed may elicit and reveal within them. And this power, which is their value for the whole, and which in any case cannot pass away, might for all we know express itself in a temporal continuance of that spiritual being, just as again it might express itself merely in the contribution of some modifying element to the experiences which come together in the Absolute.

But when the question of man's destiny is stated in this the only reasonable form, it inevitably refers us away from the second to the first of the two questions which we propounded. We cannot determine what period or degree of recognisable continuance may be appropriate to different orders of finite spirits.[2] But we can, by consideration, to some extent introduce order into our own desires, and determine how far the reasons which seem

---

[1] Certainly in St. John's Gospel.

[2] To illustrate by a very old suggestion. Is it clear that if all human spirits are such as to continue, no spirits of the brute creation are so? If we are to go by our wishes, I take it there is much in these spirits that the world would not willingly let die.

operative in our longing for continuance are consistent with one another; and what sort of destiny, therefore, we do recognise, and ought in reason to recognise, as a genuine and also desirable continuance of our self. This self-criticism of our desires may show that our faith in their satisfaction is less dependent on unanswerable questions than is commonly supposed. And it seems worth while, therefore, to lay some stress upon it.

What Destiny we can consistently desire.

3. And first, it is inconceivable to me that the truth which for us is now established, of the reality and perfection of the Absolute, can fail to carry with it a fundamental value in its bearing on the continuance of the self. We have seen in a previous lecture what positive elements we believe the self mainly to consist in, apart from the impotence and bodily limitation which, interpreted in a negative fashion, are the rationale of its formal or repellent distinctness. No one will much object to an identification of the self in the main with the things we mainly care for. Now when we are sure that the things which we care for are valued in the universe on the whole as they are for us, and are by the very nature of the universe guaranteed as characters of the Reality [1] throughout its appearances, it seems to me a mere want of considerateness to deny that the main problem of our continuance is in principle solved. If our main interests are guaranteed as enduring, then surely that for which we desire our own endurance is in principle safeguarded. Common sense recognises, and a sound psychology sustains the recognition, that we can and habitually do desire and delight in a future

[1] Cf. citation from *Appearance and Reality* in *Principle*, p. 269.

prosperity of interests which, in desiring it, we do not expect that "we" shall live to see.   It is true that for common sense such interests are naturally of a kind closely concerning ourselves, and readily realised in imagination.   But when the principle is admitted, it will carry us all the way.   The self can and ultimately must identify itself with what transcends its direct personal experiences, provided it is of a qualitative texture to unite with the main web-tissue of our being.   This, we have amply seen, is secured to us in the Absolute.   We are at worst in a general position corresponding to such particular positions as that of a patriot who dies knowing that his country's freedom is secure, or that of a man of science who passes away, confidently assured that the truth for which he has spent himself is victorious.   Our assurance is less particularised than theirs, but is fundamental and has a universal range.[1]   In general, we know that what we care for, in so far as it is really what we care for, is safe through its continuity with the Eternal.   In this assurance there is comprised, in principle, all that we long for in the desire for our own survival. After illustrating this point by some extreme examples of belief in what would naturally be called impersonal continuance, which, I shall suggest, derive their power from this general truth, I will

---

[1] This non-particularity of assurance—the belief that whatever comes is the true fulfilment—is always the characteristic of the highest religious faith, as we see it from the central petition of the Lord's Prayer downwards.   It is distinct and emphatic in William James's examples of assurance, collected in his *Varieties of Religious Belief*, p. 285.   These are precisely of the type of a belief in the Absolute, and the sharp separation between them and conviction in intellectual form is seen, after the explanation of *Principle*, Lect. II., to be illusory.

return to a closer consideration of its relation to the common wish for personal immortality.

Of those extreme forms of belief I will select three for remark—the "subjective immortality" of the Comtist, with which we may rank the causal perpetuation insisted on by the scientific mind; continuance by way of metempsychosis or transmigration, which is impersonal or nearly so in its transitions; and the views which may be typified by the conception of Nirwana, according to which, however the ultimate being may be conceived, the absorption of what common sense understands by personal consciousness is not only complete, but is illustrated by contrast with the activities and values of our experience, and not by a self-transcendence in the same direction as theirs. I take these views as three typical cases of tendencies of the mind, and do not pledge myself that they are stated with historical exhaustiveness and precision.

Subjective Immortality and Causal Continuance.

*a.* I cannot think that any considerate person can reject the kindred ideas of subjective immortality and causal continuance as wholly worthless and negligible. We survive, these doctrines tell us, in the memories we leave behind us, and in the effects of our lives and actions. No one who looks at the question attentively will brush aside this solution on the ground that enduring fame, and obvious causal influence on the future, are granted to very few indeed among the human race. It is true that the memory left behind by individuals is fugitive, and that the effects of their lives very soon become indistinguishably blended with the innumerable other influences operative in the course of events. Yet we may note that the remembrance of common persons is not really annihilated when it ceases to record them by name. It is absorbed in and blended with the tradition of character and achievement in all the great groupings and interests of humanity— the family, the nation, the religions, the trades,[1] the arts and sciences. All of these things we recognise as the quintessence distilled from human lives, and our reverence for them is inextricably interwoven with the praise of ancient men and our fathers that begat us. If their names are forgotten, while we understand their deeds, does it greatly matter? Do the authors of the *Iliad* and *Odyssey*, or of the early books of the Old Testament, gain much in honour and remembrance if we call them Homer and Moses? Or do the cathedral-builders, or, even greater than these, the generations who have built up racial and national character and religion, lose much in honour and remembrance if we have no distinct vocable by which to call them over one by one?[2] On the contrary, we seem here to have a lesson on the expansion and absorption of the self, which, when we look precisely at the problem of survival, sets before us inevitable conditions of its solution. The suggestion is that the self which

[1] We may take this as the limiting case, in which remembrance of individuals is at a minimum, and reflect upon our consciousness of what we owe to the generations of "tradesmen" (craftsmen). Cf. Goethe's lines—

> "The mason's ways are
> A type of existence,
> And his persistence
> Is as the days are
> Of men in the world."

[2] "Those perfect in their little parts,
> Whose work is all their prize;
> Without them how could laws or arts
> Or towered cities rise?"

does much for the universe must blend with the universe in proportion to its achievement.   And so, in a sense, absorption is inevitable at both extremes ; the multitude bequeath no name to posterity, which nevertheless reverences them in their tradition ; the greatest men leave little more than a name, because their work has blended with cosmic forces, from which it cannot be separated for estimation.[1]

Thus, from speaking of remembrance, we have passed into the region of continuance through causation.   Conscious tradition passes gradually into unconscious, and unconscious tradition into the effects of causes.   " A man touches me with his hand, looks at me, speaks to me.   All this is called ' personal ' communication.   He writes a letter to me.   This, too, would be called by some ' personal.'   He builds a house, makes a picture, founds an institution, passes a law ; I live in his house, enjoy his picture, am maintained by his institution, am put in prison or protected by his law.   Is this personal or not?   If not, why not?"[2]   It is not personal, the author continues in effect, so far, and only so far, as men come short of the power to recognise that it is.   Only, I add, we have to remember that this want of power extends to the finite personality whose action is being considered. He does not know or contemplate the full destiny of his picture or his law, any more than we are able to restore contact with the full personality out of

---

[1] Note the remark that Jesus and Socrates left no written records or doctrines.   We know them only from the " movements " they initiated.   So it is, too, with great poets and statesmen, from the enormous cosmic material which they embody.   You cannot estimate their " persons " apart from their " worlds."

[2] Nettleship, *Remains*, i. 5.

which they sprang. This is a self-transcendence, in the world of finite context, which does not carry the main character of the self as conscious beyond itself, but only fragments of it. But it puts the problem of self-transcendence in a very striking light.[1] We shall have to suggest below that there may be a self-transcendence which carries the self, even as a conscious whole, beyond its own powers of recognition.

Thus it is needless to labour the point that these two kindred forms of survival are fragmentary and contingent, partaking of the transitoriness and impotence of the human race. Yet, though insufficient to constitute a personality, unquestionably they are integral parts of one. Unquestionably the being of any person would be diminished by the annihilation of his share in remembrance, in tradition, and in causation. You cannot conceive the part played by one person in the experience of others to be diminished, without conceiving his personality *pro tanto* to undergo diminution. We may say, then, that these are not adequate accounts of personal survival; but it would be irrational to say that they amount to nothing, or do not count at all in the problem of continuance. And in suggesting the conception of a personality expanded beyond its own recognition they raise a question which will return upon us below.

---

[1] Jesus, for example, if merely human, could not conceivably have any idea of the range which his own personality was destined to attain. Cf. Clough's poem, "The Shadow"—

    " And the Shade answered, ' What ye say, I know not ;
         But this is true,
         I am that Jesus whom they slew,
    Whom ye have preached, but in what way, I know not.' "

But, while we admit the value and profound suggestiveness of these two ideas, it seems plain that nothing can have caused them even for a moment to seem satisfactory solutions, except an instinctive reliance on the reality of the whole.   If they are at bottom recognised as symbols and manifestations of a reality beyond time and contingency, then they may pass muster well enough as favourite forms of belief with this or that mind, deeply interested in matters to which such beliefs are specially relevant.[1]   But when we come to think of the complete and ultimate persistence of persons, it is plain that ideas bound up with the future of the human race and of our globe, and dealing only with fragments of the personality, can give us no final satisfaction.[2]

Metem-
psychosis.
β. In the above conceptions of continuance—*prima facie* impersonal continuance—the content of personality survived and might be immensely expanded, while the subjective centre remained as it were disconnected from its circumference—a characteristic of all who builded better than they knew,

---

[1] I mean, minds not busied with ultimate problems, but deeply absorbed in progressive human interests, from the family upwards and outwards.   They may throw their instinct of perpetuity into the shapes in question ; and these, because incarnations of the fundamental truth, may serve them well enough.

[2] It may be well here to mention the idea that the continuity of the germ-plasm in human beings annihilates the individual's causal influence on the future.   There are two points mainly to bear in mind.   One is the nature of the tradition in which civilisation consists, which is such that on it the individual exercises full causal influence.   The second is that through his own action and his influence upon others he operates as a cause on the selective process itself.   In many stages of society and to many persons in all known stages, continuance in children seems a satisfactory survival of the self.   It is a peculiar case, neither merely traditional nor merely causal.   The very basis of the self is passed on.

and thus perhaps ultimately of all finite spirits. And in this type of persistence we recognised a real value for personality.

In the doctrine of metempsychosis, when taken in bitter earnest, *i.e.* giving full weight to the absence of conscious personality connecting any one life with its successor, we have a precisely complementary conception. Here, the bare subject or ego, the naked form of personality, the soul-thing, is supposed to persist; but no content of the personality goes with it. We are offered chains of personalities linked together by impersonal transitions. We need only point out in passing the difficulty, which Aristotle put his finger on, in the conception of an identical soul animating wholly different bodies in succession. Our question at present is simply how far and in what sense any such doctrine appears to satisfy our desire of immortality. It has been, of course, of enormous influence in the history of philosophy and religion. It readily lends itself to pessimism, and has roots perhaps in very primitive beliefs;[1] but it is, I am convinced, the form which Plato preferred to give to his working conceptions of human survival, and, in shapes largely borrowed and spiritualised from Oriental tradition, it is exceedingly popular to-day.[2]

---

[1] Such, I mean, as the kinship of man and the brute creation. Cf. also Cornford, *From Religion*, p. 162 ff.

[2] Dr. McTaggart's advocacy of it on strict philosophical grounds is familiar to students (*Studies in Hegelian Cosmology*, sect. 41 ff.). I may draw attention here to a difficulty which Mr. Bradley mentions, nearly following Plato, *Rep.* 611 A. "A constant supply of new souls, none of which ever perished, would obviously land us in an insoluble difficulty" (the universe being held incapable of increase) (*Appearance*, ed. 2, 502). It would follow that some souls must perish, or be used over again as in metempsychosis.

The satisfaction which it unquestionably affords to many minds is founded, I imagine, on one specific and one general presumption.

The specific presumption, on which Plato, for example, insists, lies just in not taking the doctrine in bitter earnest according to the views of common sense. Life is separated from life, according to one form of his story, not only by a period of reward and punishment, but by the draught of the water of forgetfulness. But you can drink of it more or less, according to your self-restraint, and it matters to the future how much or how little you drink. That is to say, somehow, though not through a self-conscious continuity, the character of each individual's life makes more or less difference to the lives of those other individuals (" other " as we commonly name and regard them) who are his successors in the chain of existence. Advocates of this conception point to the fact that character and the principles of knowledge can persist in the soul through intervals of oblivion and unconsciousness, wholly apart from specific memories of the incidents of their acquisition. Why, it is asked, should they not persist from life to life, as they persist from day to day, and from youth to age, unimpaired by intervals of unconsciousness and by the loss of particular memories? Such a conception affords, to minds of any elevation, a motive for self-improvement which for them is all the stronger that it is wholly divorced from ideas of personal self-satisfaction in a future world.[1]

---

[1] It is perhaps hardly necessary now to point out that Plato's colloquial reference to a second existence (*Rep.* 498 D) concerns a second terrestrial life.

The difficulty is to accept this transition through an impersonal phase. Probability suggests that as there is bodily transmission of qualities, it is superfluous to imagine any other. Then a soul would carry nothing with it, and if the conception of a soul's character is completely abandoned the satisfaction afforded by this kind of belief in continuance is less easy to account for. It then comes to be fairly represented by Leibniz's comparison of the " King of China."[1] It is taken in bitter earnest, and we can hardly see how continuity, so construed, even if referred to a continuous substance,[2] has any element of personal immortality.

Yet it is unquestionable that this mere name, as we may think it, of continued identity, does convey to many minds a certain reassurance, and I do not doubt that the only possible explanation of the fact lies in the general presumption to which I referred above.

This I take to consist in the underlying conviction that such identity is the pledge and symbol that the values of our life are one with those of the world, and that therefore what we have set our hearts on is continued from and beyond our life into the future of the universe. " I shall live on

---

[1] Leibniz criticising Descartes, cit. in Latta's *Leibniz* (*The Monadology*, etc.), 225 note. " This immortality without recollection is ethically quite useless; for it is inconsistent with reward and punishment. [This reason surprises us.] What good, sir, would it do you to become King of China, on condition that you forget what you have been? Would it not be the same as if God at the moment He destroyed you were to create a king in China? " Not that Leibniz himself believed that a mind could entirely forget (*op. cit.* p. 258).

[2] See Dr. McTaggart, *Hegelian Cosmology*, sect. 41 ff. But Dr. McTaggart endows the substance with those persistent characters referred to above.

in another," so many seem to feel, and though I, as I am, shall never know it, yet it will be myself, for what is being accomplished in me will be carried on in that other.[1] This amounts to that belief in an eternal real, which on the whole sustains our valuations,[2] to which I referred above, and I submit that at least all the doctrines of survival which we have so far discussed acquire their reassuring force from being concrete cases in which this belief is incarnate.

Nirwana and absorption in God. γ. In the conception of Nirwana, whatever may be its precise formulation in Oriental Divinity, we can hardly fail to recognise an absorption of the finite self incompatible with its self-conscious continuance. Yet the enormous range and influence of doctrines which deny a conscious personal survival show that they correspond to some fundamental need of human nature. "If you ask," the writer has heard an experienced Anglo-Indian say, "if you ask any native of India, from the most ignorant to the most highly cultured, what he expects from his religion, he will answer with the same word, 'Liberation.'" Thus we are still in presence of our main presumption. The fundamental need of human nature is to be assured of its continuity, at its best, with an analogous best of the universe. Nirwana, indeed, however positively it may be construed, remains a very different thing from our Absolute with its appearances. Yet there can be

---

[1] See footnote above, p. 266, on the sense of continuance in children. The conception seems to me better fulfilled in spiritual heirship, as in inheritance of a work or of ideas, than in any form of metempsychosis.

[2] The conservation of values. To identify this with the survival of persons seems to me quite unjustifiable.

little doubt as to its logical nature.    It is an attempt
to conceive the highest identification with the
Absolute, rejecting as pure illusion all its appearances.    Now if the best has been thus defectively
interpreted, that is an error in ethical and logical
insight, which cannot destroy, and never has been
found to destroy, the force of the central conviction.
The demand, we saw, in this, its negative form,
is still for Liberation ; for the ideal and complete
satisfaction of unmixed and unconditional affirmation of the self.    And this, it is confidently believed
by the supporters of such a doctrine, the universe
has to bestow, although in many influential forms
of the creed the liberation becomes not an absorption of the self in the more concrete, but the
annihilation of it in an abstraction.

It is easy to criticise the logic and ethics of such
a doctrine.    But the fact remains unshaken that a
large portion of the human race ask no better
destiny than to be lost in the Universe or in God.
Their real desire clashes with their nominal self,
and for the sake of their real desire they are willing
to abandon what they are accustomed to call their
personality.

4. We have now passed in review certain wide- The ques-
spread beliefs, in each of which considerable groups tion of 3
of mankind have held, and still or even increasingly further
hold, that they can satisfy their yearning for what considered.
is beyond their present self.

It appeared to us that, literally taken, none of
them were genuinely commensurate with the desire
which all of them recognise, but that their strength
really lay in being incarnations of a fundamental
instinct towards the identification of the self with

ultimate reality. This discussion was to serve as an introduction to the explicit treatment of the former of the two questions raised at the beginning of this chapter, viz. whether we can frame any idea what degree of transformation of the self is compatible with what we should recognise as our own continuance; or, in a word, what immortality can we desire if we make our desires self-consistent? [1]

The question is not one of mere data, to be answered by the collection of opinions, and its interest is not one of mere curiosity. It is a metaphysical issue; whether the elements that enter into our longing for personal immortality are consistent with each other, and whether or in what form the desire, therefore, is consistent with itself. It may be that if it is to be justified by criticism—that is, by being exhibited as an inevitable outcome of our nature as a whole—it must undergo a modification of its current shape. Even when so modified it is not by itself an infallible argument for the reality of its satisfaction. But without being so modified, it is self-destructive, and goes no way to prove any satisfaction of it at all. [2]

Simple prolongation— reduces itself to chain of lives?
*a.* In the first place, should we accept as a satisfaction of our longing for immortality a certainty of the unending prolongation of our present existence? Here two difficulties stand in the way of an answer.

---

[1] Always bearing in mind that we are sure to begin with of our eternal reality as an element—I do not say a member—in the Absolute, and of the recognition of values, on the whole agreeing with ours, throughout its appearances. The question of "immortality" is a question about a further temporal appearance more or less intimately related to our present self, but in no way affects our present or our eternal reality in the Absolute.

[2] Cf. Mr. Bradley's well-known note on the argument from the affections, *Appearance*, ed. 2, p. 509.

The first is the question of the conditions implied in the offer. Are we to be guaranteed happiness, or are we to take our chance in the ups and downs of human destiny, or even to experience the prolongation of some one among the most miserable of human lives? Again, how are the phases of life, infancy, youth, and age to be dealt with? Are they not something more than a biological accident? Are they not a logical necessity? And if so, how are they to be adjusted to an unending existence?[1]

As to the former difficulty, there may be minds which think that they would welcome an endless prolongation of commonplace comfort, or, more reasonably, of the natural progress of an energetic spirit, following the changes of the centuries. But we must remember that any such conditions of prolongation are themselves of the nature of a bargain, by which something is offered which in ordinary experience cannot be counted secure. Even they, I mean, involve more security of progress than ordinary existence affords. And when we turn to the conspectus of everyday life, we find that its *prima facie* unhappiness and insecurity have been the very mainspring of the desire for something beyond. Compensation for misery, or at least a sure refuge from it, the cure and ending of sin, even when misconceived as retribution, and in minds which see their want more clearly the nearer approach to God, or, by a logical error, a self-affirmation pure from appearances, and so from everything— these are the principal shapes adopted by the

---

[1] A deathlessness which involves unending senility has been adequately treated, I presume, by Swift and Tennyson. Homer, in the wish or promise of deathlessness, is careful to exclude old age.

instinct of perpetuity.  And surely they betray its
ultimate nature.  The question is metaphysically
the old one of satisfaction in the unending series
contrasted with that in the self-contained whole;
and the philosophical answer is given in Plato's
*Symposium* and Hegel's *Category of Life.*  The
longing for continuance is at bottom the longing
for the satisfactory whole; and we have seen, I
think, that this character is verifiable in it when we
come to criticise the commonest desire for a further
life.  What we want is never merely something
more, but always something better, if only in its
greater security.

The second difficulty is at least a matter of
curiosity, and also, I think, has philosophical
significance.  Is not the chain of lives, which we
have already discussed, the only conceivable form
for an unending temporal existence?  Must we not
suppose the finite being to be finite in its power of
reception and development, and to pass through
phases, of the type which we know as infancy, youth,
and age, appropriate to the degree of the burden
which experience progressively lays upon it?  And
although we may imagine *ad libitum* the phases of
youth and growth to be lengthened out, yet must
we not conceive in the end an arrest of development
and an overburdened state, such as we call senility?
It is this that the chain of lives, with the periodical
fresh start in an advancing environment, seems
successfully to avoid.  It secures not indeed perpetual but periodic youth, and also a periodic fresh
look at the world, or new departure.  The old, however great and familiar his experience, can never
again acquire a first impression from its totality.

If this suggestion were sound, we might rely here on our previous discussions of the chain of lives, and on our conclusion that satisfaction in such a conception rests either on the special presumption of spiritual progress from life to life, or else on the general presumption that such an arrangement guarantees an open chance at least of approximation to the ultimate satisfaction.   The latter, as well as the former, is definitely stated by Plato, as well as in Oriental religion.[1]   If a chain of lives is the only logical mode of conceiving a highly prolonged existence analogous to our own, we may apply these conclusions directly to all our desires for such an existence.   But even if this latter speculation were ill-founded, the truth which has always been recognised stands fast.   What we really care about is not a simple prolongation of our " personal " existence, but, whether accompanying prolongation or in the direct form of liberation, some affirmation of our main interests, or some refuge from the perpetual failure of satisfaction.

β. The problem, how far such a desire can be consistent with the desire for what we call personal immortality, is, as we said, the problem of transformation.   How far is the desire for complete self-affirmation compatible with the desire for the continuance of what we call the self—what we indicate to ourselves and others by our proper name?[2]   Any suggestion of an answer must hinge upon the consideration that personal identity—the

The demand for a *better* state. Conflict of identity and perfection.

---

[1] I mean in as far as the succession of lives is regarded as capable of leading up to a goal beyond the succession.

[2] *In Memoriam* includes a study of this question, though not in philosophical form.   See Professor A. C. Bradley's *Commentary*, pp. 47-48.

continuity of the self—is a matter of degree, and is conditioned by the stages of the personality which we are calling upon it to connect. Therefore when we raise the question of personal continuance in a further existence, it is arbitrary to limit the amount of change which we are ready to accept by our current judgment of what constitutes personal identity under the conditions of existence which we know. We have noted[1] the current tendency to exaggerate the claims of negative or exclusive elements in the self. We observed a difference between the formal distinctness, or apparent individuality, and the material or substantial stuff and content of unity, the element of true individuality, which to some extent conflict in the normal self.[2] It is the same contrast which was referred to in the previous section when we contrasted our self with our best.

Now if we accept the current estimate of the normal person as to what his personal continuance involves, we are at the mercy of a demand which rests mainly on his exclusive self-feeling or formal individuality. It is true that his best, his real self, lies elsewhere. But, as we saw, the best and the self are often felt to conflict, and even those who have the instinct to throw in their lot with their best do not in all cases realise that in doing so they are at one with their substantial self.

Thus, then, our desire for a high perfection of the substantive individuality is pretty certain to conflict with the desire to maintain the current and

---

[1] Lect. II., above.

[2] The formal or exclusive self has its proper place in the substantial self. But that place is not the place which it is most apt to claim.

average relations of the formal or exclusive self. In a critical reconciliation of the claims of our nature, how are the two to be brought together? There can be no doubt, according to our previous analysis,[1] that the exclusive self really falls within the substantive self, consisting in elements of the latter which tend to fix and exaggerate the necessary practical distinction between you and me. The substantive self is the entire self-maintaining content or living world which alone gives significance either to our exclusiveness or to our universality. Thus we conclude that in a criticised whole of desire our current postulate of the exclusive personal identity which we yearn to see maintained cannot hold its ground against the self-transcendent impulse of individuality to complete itself and to include what belongs to it. Perhaps we never know quite where our satisfaction lies until we have achieved it. And here we have an obvious instance of that principle. In claiming a continued and better existence for ourselves, as we think we are, we are seeking our satisfaction where a criticism of our claims reveals that it is not to be found.

γ. We may both test and further explain this line of argument by comparing it with the discussion of continued personality in a writer most anxious to maintain no doctrine of ultimate satisfaction which is not most definitely supported by spiritual experience.[2] *Discussion of Green's doctrine of the conservation of personality.*

The whole discussion of man's ultimate destiny is conducted by him in subordination to the principles that "all other values are relative to

---

[1] Lect. II., above.

[2] T. H. Green, *Prolegomena to Ethics*, bk. iii. ch. ii. init.

value for, of, or in a person,"[1] and "a capacity, which is nothing except as personal, cannot be realised in any impersonal modes of being."[2]  And further, "a capacity consisting in a self-conscious personality cannot be supposed so to pass away" [as, *e.g.*, the capacities of myriads of animals may]. " We cannot believe in there being a real fulfilment of such a capacity in an end which should involve its extinction, because the conviction of there being an end in which our capacities are fulfilled is founded on our self-conscious personality—on the idea of an absolute value in a spirit which we ourselves are."[3] And again, such a fulfilment involves a society. "Without society, no persons."  The statement is as clear and strong as any believer in personal immortality could demand.

But there is another side.  Membership of a society "implies confinement in our individual realisation of the idea." . . . " No one so confined, it would seem, can exhibit all that the Spirit, working in and through him, properly and potentially is.  Yet is not such confinement the condition of the only personality that we know ? "[4]

The author here fully emphasises the discrepancy between a given personality in human society and the complete realisation of spiritual capacity. But throughout the discussion he has in mind, chiefly though not exclusively, the contrast between any speculation on a perfected condition of the human race in what is called civilisation, and the real spiritual gain of character and developed capacity in the human individuals who compose the

---

[1] *L.c.* sect. 184.       [2] *Ibid.* sect. 185.
[3] Sect. 189.       [4] Sect. 183.

race or people in question. He is dwelling on the danger that by a want of clearness in conception the former, which is valueless *per se*, may be mistaken for the latter, which alone has value. This is so far a question of the contrast between impersonal conditions below self-consciousness, and a self-conscious personality. This is quite a different thing from the contrast between personality as limited in an earthly society, and an experience which may be conceived in various degrees to transcend the limitations of such a personality. The latter distinction has grave importance for the moral and religious consciousness, because it enables us to deal finally both with the hostile reproach of Agnosticism and the crude insistence on "personal" identity which condemns as Agnosticism everything but itself.

And this latter contrast was not unnoticed by the author I am quoting. To make his position and our inference plain, I will cite two passages at length.

"There may be reason to hold," he writes,[1] "that there are capacities of the human spirit not realisable in persons under the conditions of any human society that we know, or can positively conceive, or that may be capable of existing on the earth. Such a belief may be warranted by the consideration on the one hand of the promise which the spirit gives of itself, both in its actual occasional achievement and in the aspirations of which we are individually conscious, on the other hand of the limitations which the necessity of confinement to a particular social function seems to impose on

[1] Sect. 185.

individual attainment. We may in consequence justify the supposition that the personal life, which historically or on earth is lived under conditions which thwart its development, is continued in a society, with which we have no means of communication through the senses, but which shares in and carries further every measure of perfection attained by men under the conditions of life that we know. Or we may content ourselves with saying that the personal self-conscious being, which comes from God, is for ever continued in God." And then follows the sentence previously cited—the negative assurance at any rate must remain—that "a capacity, which is nothing except as personal, cannot be realised in any impersonal modes of being." In this case the exclusion of impersonality expresses the nature of the highest conceivable forms of being, and not merely excludes those forms which are below self-consciousness.

Here, I think, we begin to see that the fulfilment of the personal conscious being may lie rather in that which it would most wish to be assured of— its fundamental interests—being eternally real in an ultimate being and in the universe of appearances, than in itself, with the formal personality which belonged to its proper name, being consciously perpetuated in a prolonged existence.

So in a further passage. The idea of human development, as a demand involved in self-consciousness, implies the eternal realisation for or in the eternal mind of the capacities gradually revealed in time. "When that which is being developed is itself a self-conscious subject, the end of its becoming must really exist not merely *for*, but *in* or *as*, a self-conscious subject. There must be eternally such a subject which is all that the self-conscious subject, as developed in time, has the possibility of becoming; in which the idea of the human spirit, or all that it has in itself to become, is completely realised. This consideration may suggest the true notion of the spiritual relation in which we stand to God; that He is not merely a Being who has made us, in the sense that we exist as an object of the divine consciousness in the same way in which we must suppose the system of nature so to exist, but that He is a Being in whom we exist; with whom we are in principle one; with whom the human spirit is identical, in the sense that He *is* all which the human spirit is capable of becoming." [1]

The important point for our argument lies in the conception that the ultimate being can be conceived as comprehending in itself the human spirit and all that it is capable of becoming. [2]

The necessity insisted on throughout that the goal of development shall be nothing short of a personal self-consciousness, does not, I think, signify for the author in the last resort an emphasis on the conscious continuance of you or me, with unbroken identity, keeping us one with an earthly past, within or into the ultimate being. In the last resort I believe that it means simply and solely this: that the contents, the interests, the qualitative experience and focussing of externality, which are our best —*i.e.* our whole in its fullest adjustment—and the

---

[1] Sect. 187.

[2] Cf. sect. 189. It is clearly repugnant to Green to think of "persons—agents who are ends to themselves"—being "extinguished." But the question is, what sort of destiny is held to imply extinction?

centre of our being, for which so far as we understand ourselves we would readily sacrifice our
nominal self—that all these things find their full
development in the ultimate being, and in a form
of experience not lower, but higher than what we
call personality.   In a word, then, what is held
essential is not primarily that the goal of development should be *our* personality, but that it shall be
*a* personality ; and the doctrine has nothing against
its being more than a personality, so long as in it
all that constituted ourself can have fuller justice
done to it than in our given self it ever could have.
We, both our form—I mean, our peculiarly qualified individual self-consciousness—and our content
—I mean, our interests and experiences—are thus
real and eternal in the ultimate being.   And this
satisfies the condition which the author lays down,
and is, I think, what he means to treat as the
ultimate necessity when he speaks of the personal
self-consciousness that came from God being for
ever continued in God.   The terms of the sentence
are *prima facie* in some degree conflicting.   Their
combination needs some interpreting ; and I believe
that our conclusion gives the right and inevitable
interpretation.   I will now try to justify it further.

Details
illustrating
transcend-
ence of
given per-
sonality.    δ. In the first place, there is every reason to
suppose, and common sense fully admits, that we
do not know with any approach to completeness
even what we ourselves, in our present finite being,
actually are.   As it was suggested above, if Shakespeare were to depict us truly to ourselves, we
might hardly recognise the portrait.   *A fortiori*,
when we had come to know ourselves far more
truly, and that not as we are now, but in a more

perfect being, our present state, then our past, would not appear to us in the least as it does to-day. Even within actual life our past may appear to us a hostile not-self; and it would be so still more if we assume a progress towards perfection. We should know that there had been a creature with such and such a history, but we should only recognise a very imperfect continuity between its particular features and our surviving self.

This argument may be driven further. I have suggested elsewhere that in a total or partial completion of our being, which would necessarily be desired in desiring a progressive satisfaction of its nature, elements would have to be included which now appear to belong solely to the minds of others. Obviously, the separation on which suffering and despondency so largely depend, between labour and effort in one mind and its recognition and effect in other minds, would tend to pass away, as it does in part within our common experience, by every diminution of the impotence which constitutes our finiteness. But this being so, the mere formal link with our past formal personality would be progressively weakened. We should include much more material, and lose something of our exclusiveness. This is an effect which we know very well by the name of spiritual heirship and the second birth. My present self was not born, we feel, of my actual parents at such and such a date and place. It was born when I met such a friend or was taught by such a teacher, or was awakened by such an experience. Suppose us now free of our original body, and uttering ourselves through a new arrangement of qualities, admitting of a wholly

new distribution and apportionment of experiences.[1]
The psychological basis of continued identity on its
formal side, the mere continuity of feeling, would
be gone with the body.  The overweight of the
material, the content, the interests and experiences,
as against the mere identity, would become more
and more emphatic.  And, in a word, the very
fulfilment of the self would be favourable indeed to
personality, but unfavourable to its formal identity.
I am not saying, it should be observed, that our
true personality lies in our defects, and that with
their removal it must be annihilated.[2]  I am trying
to give the true meaning of the considerations
pointing in this direction, on which commonplace
mysticism relies,[3] and which will certainly force us
to abandon the higher personality if they are not
confronted with a fuller interpretation.  What I
am urging is rather that our true personality lies in
our concrete best, and that in desiring its development and satisfaction we are desiring an increase of
our real individuality, though a diminution of our
formal exclusiveness.[4]

And on this follows a further conclusion.  Because we wish our self to be developed to its fullest,

---

[1] Cf. *Appearance*, p. 529, on readjustment and supplementation
of the self.

[2] See on question whether Self-Consciousness is a defect, *Principle*, Lect. VI.

[3] " Earth, these solid stars, this weight of body and limb,
    Are they not sign and symbol of thy division from Him ? "
                    TENNYSON'S *Higher Pantheism.*

[4] It will be rejoined that true individuality—greatness of range
and organisation—augments personal distinction as well as comprehensiveness.  Undoubtedly ; but it decreases exclusiveness.  The
great world-men are not born simply of their earthly parents.  Whole
ages and countries are focussed in them.  Schiller—I think Goethe has
said—in a brief time "grew so that you would hardly know him again."

and to draw into it from without all that belongs to its satisfaction, the temporal and spatial incidents by which simple or so-called numerical identity might seem to be guaranteed, actually lose their applicability to the fulfilment of what we long for. Details of place and time cannot be predicated of a being developed as we demand that our self shall develop. When we think out what would satisfy us as the perfected being of Dante or Wordsworth, we see that their proper names and private histories would no longer be true of it. Dante's own treatment of Beatrice may serve to illustrate. The historical figure is submerged in the meaning. The detailed determinations are not lost or abstracted from, but they are absorbed in significance, just as we saw to be the case with the features of the landscape which animates Dante's poem.[1] In desiring a highly developed perfection we are desiring to be something which can no longer be identified either with or by the incidents of the terrestrial life.

ε. It at once suggests itself that the relations of finite individuals in love and duty form perhaps the most valuable constituent of our "best"; and it will be asked if we suggest that, for desires which involve the readjustment and expansion of personality, these are to cease to have a meaning. But, on the contrary, it seems clear that a desire for the perfection— the harmony and self-consistency—of these relations themselves is the most obvious case of desire for an experience which cannot at a higher level stand as it is given. The case put by the Sadducees to Jesus, along with his answer, remains typical.[2] The

Argument from the Affections.

---

[1] *Principle*, Lect. VII.
[2] See Bradley, *Appearance*, p. 509, referred to above.

mother, again, does not long to meet once more the child she has lost, as a complete and perfected personality.  What she longs for is the child.  Yet we cannot consistently desire that for her sake the infant should remain an infant to all eternity.  In a word, our conflicting duties and affections form a splendid content for our finite life of self-discipline and self-sacrifice.  But if we demand a fuller completeness and satisfaction, then it would seem that the limited self-identity, out of which the complications of affection arise, must be modified, and there must be a system which can include the whole of our experiences without failure or waste.  " The whole of our experiences "; it is easy to base a partial view of a future destiny on idealised cases of non-conflicting affection ; but we have to include the instances which are the prey of accident, conflicting tendencies, and isolation.  Our desire for the solution of all these seems inconsistent with a desire that we should remain what we are.  We are bound to aim, in our longings, at some sort of system in which the whole affections of every being should be harmonised with each other, and discrepancies and repulsions should be not merely omitted, but transmuted into forms of harmony.  But if this is to be what we desire, again it follows that personalities must undergo material readjustment, and their adequacy to one another must involve a new type of completeness.[1]

It is needless to labour the point further.  It is perfectly plain that the desire for the attainment

[1] Cf. Aristotle on the friendship of the good.  Note the extraordinarily narrow limitations involved in a demand which, on first hearing, seems precisely to voice our need, as in Lockhart's lines, p. 289.

even of a relative best, and the desire for the continuance of the given self, are *prima facie* at variance. But it is all-important to be clear what conclusion we draw. It will consist first in a negative proposition, and secondly in a positive one, to which a corollary of the highest importance must be attached.

5. First, then, we do not conclude that the desire for the attainment of the best, of perfect satisfaction, can only be self-consistent as a desire for the absorption and annihilation of the positive and concrete self.[1]

*Conclusion : what is certainly preserved is the content of the self, which is secure in the Absolute.*

But, secondly, we do conclude that such a desire is only self-consistent in as far as it consents to accentuate the true positive self of content, at the expense of formal distinctness, or what I call under protest numerical identity, that is, the identity with myself as a bodily being, externally described by name and terrestrial history. I cannot desire my continuance as what would seem *to my present consciousness* the same personality, while also desiring completeness and stability in my experience, due to comprehension of all relevant elements. More than this, I cannot desire, along with a relative perfection, even such a prominence of my terrestrial individuality as would enable the higher self to look back and say, " I am he that was born in such an island at such a date." For, as we have seen, no such temporal and spatial characters could remain true of the expanded being. They remain but very scantily true on this earth through three-score years and ten.

---

[1] Cf. Professor A. C. Bradley, *Commentary on In Memoriam*, pp. 47-48.

And lastly, from this latter statement it is a corollary that in desiring a future which will realise our best, we are truly ready to be content, if we understand our own meaning, with the being of the absolute Reality. For our formal self, our self as given to-day, is not that of which we mainly and imperatively demand the continuance. We demand what we care for; and what we care for are interests and affections which carry us beyond our formal and exclusive self. And thus we are and must be prepared, if we in the least consider our own meaning, to regard as the satisfaction and perpetuation of our self something which for common sense is separated by a gap from what we indicate when we name our proper name. Common sense itself, as we saw, will admit that we can care for what transcends us, more than for our self. And it is no great step to urge that only our impotence hinders us from recognising that what we thus care for most is in deed and in truth the essence of our self.

It is thus no juggle, no "faith as vague as all unsweet," to offer the eternal reality of the Absolute as that realisation of our self which we instinctively demand and desire. It is impossible to deny that there may be future gradations of experience continuous with our finite selves; we know them in our present existence, and no one can disprove the possibility that there are others beyond it. But in any case it is not in principle the bare continuance of what we now seem to ourselves to be, which our heart is set upon. It is not the unbrokenness of the link of personal recollection. It is the security, the certainty, of the realisation of what we care for most, in the Absolute; and this does not mean in a remote and supernatural world, but in the fullest experience and throughout the universe of its appearances. Whether "we" are to be aware of it, that is, how far what is or possesses the realisation is to be consciously identified with our present self, is really a question of degree, of the importance of the distinctiveness of our present self within the whole in which it is an element. The fundamental truth is that it *is* an element, and instinctively regards the eternal whole as its reality and its satisfaction.[1]

[1] I subjoin here Lockhart's lines, referred to on p. 286, note. The last couplet, intended to ask for more than we now possess, plainly asks for much less—one only of many beauties and phases. Clearly we demand *either* all our phases, *or* more than all.

> " But 'tis an old belief,
>    That on some solemn shore,
> Beyond the sphere of grief,
>    Dear friends will meet once more
>
> " Beyond the sphere of time,
>    And sin, and fate's control,
> Serene in changeless prime,
>    Of body and of soul.
>
> "That creed I fain would keep
>    That hope I'll not forego
> Eternal be the sleep,
>    Unless to waken so."

# C. THE STABILITY AND SECURITY OF FINITE SELFHOOD—*Continued*

## LECTURE X

### THE GATES OF THE FUTURE

"Un plan est un terme assigné à un travail ; il clôt l'avenir dont il dessine la forme. Devant l'évolution de la vie, au contraire, les portes de l'avenir restent grandes ouvertes."

BERGSON, *Évolution créatrice*, p. 114.

". . . da quel punto
Che del futuro fia chiusa la porta."

DANTE, *Inferno*, x. 108.

Theories which make drafts upon the future.

1. In the previous lecture we did our best to ascertain what the demand for continuance after death amounts to, if we reduce to self-consistency the finite being's desires as we find them in ourselves. We hoped that the result was such as to coincide on the whole with what the nature of finiteness inherently presupposes and demands.

And now it seems desirable, in concluding our argument, to consider what attitude our theory seems to warrant towards the kindred problem of the future of finite beings in general, but primarily in what we are accustomed to call "this life." Yet as there is a view which holds that "this life" may altogether and universally pass into something different, we must not omit this alternative in

290

speaking of the earthly future, though it partly takes us back over the ground of the previous lecture.

In theorising about the future of finite beings, my object is clear and limited. I am very far from believing that philosophy confers the gift of prophecy. Hegel's famous disclaimer expresses my doctrine on this point.[1] Philosophy comes after the fact, and interprets it. It neither preaches nor predicts. But yet a philosophical position is definitely characterised by the attitude adopted to the course of time. There are theories which in one way or another manage to gain much support by making heavy drafts upon the future. I am thoroughly convinced that all such theories are in the eye of logic discredited *ab initio*.[2] Having recourse to what is in principle unverifiable, they cannot be tested,[3] and, what is worse, they obstruct genuine insight and appreciation of values. It is a view of finite life as substantially rooted in an all-pervading reality, and opposed to the thinness and external motivation attendant upon such theories, that I desire in this final lecture to elucidate. My hope is thus to complete an outline of a philosophy which might express the reasonable faith of resolute and open-minded men, as suggested in the beginning of the previous series.[4]

I take the passages which stand at the head of

---

[1] *Rechts-Philosophie*, p. 20.

[2] See the same criticism applied to theories of inappreciable quantity, *Principle*, Lect. V. p. 172.

[3] Hdt. ii. 23 ἐς ἀφανὲς τὸν μῦθον ἀνενείκας οὐκ ἔχει ἔλεγχον. I am aware of Mr. Bradley's comment on the use of the term "verifiable," *Eth. Studies*, p. 283. I mean by unverifiable a fact of the historical order, alleged as future.

[4] *Principle*, p. 30.

this lecture as typical of the current antagonistic attitudes towards the future, that is, towards time.

The Gates of the Future open. Time a reality.

i. On the one side,[1] time is treated as going on for ever. There can be no plan, preconceived or preconceivable, for a plan involves an end. In going on, time not merely expresses, but is, the movement of the real, that is to say, of the universe. It may be conceived, indeed, not as a mathematical abstraction, but as a concrete super - intellectual experience, a creative growth. It is so far, *qua* more concrete than the object of discursive knowledge, akin to the Absolute as we conceive it. But not only is it not, as manifested, a whole, but there *is* no whole for it to manifest. The Universe *is* creative progress *ad infinitum*. Unity, if anywhere, was at the beginning, in the primal impulse. It may or may not, so I understand the doctrine, be recovered—"in the end" I had almost said; but there is no end, and no completeness. I should have said, therefore, it may or may not be asymptotically approachable. Divergence, novelty, free originativeness, and a certain degree of indetermination are the principal laws of things. And this is the very source of our freedom and of our inspiration. The open gates of the future make the interest and excitement of life.

> "It may be that the gulfs will wash us down:
> It may be we shall touch the happy isles."

There is nothing fixed. "Tout est donné" is the

---

[1] The particular text cited from Bergson refers directly to evolution in the organic world, including man. I use it, *meo periculo*, as typical of a general view which is widely prevalent to-day, according to which the development of the real, the universe itself, is plastic and progressive *ad infinitum*.

principle most abhorred. Our destiny and that of the universe is really and effectively in our own hands, with no reservation except that the universe has many other members besides us. Time, in the sense of duration, is at the very heart of things.

ii. On the other side, it is postulated that time will one day cease. The plan of the universe will be fulfilled. Time will pass into eternity. Either the number of the elect will be accomplished, or "good shall fall" The Gates<br>to close<br>one day.<br>Time to<br>cease.

> "At last, far off, at last to all,
> And every winter change to spring."

The difficulty that eternity must be inclusive, and cannot have a place after time, nor can anything subsequent in a mere series of facts really and strictly compensate for or overbalance anything that is past, is overcome by the suggestion that time may be in truth an appearance of an eternal real, but may be such as one day to be absorbed into the reality which always underlay it. It may then not so much overbalance the past as transform it in the light of the whole. It is only a modernised form of this theory which suggests that the kingdom is to come on earth as an everlasting millennium. Under this whole theory, as under the former, our hopes are dependent on future events. If the good time is coming, either on earth or in heaven, then "the sufferings of this present time are not worthy to be compared——" We may give up the past and present, or confidently expect their transformation under a light new in principle, and not merely an intensification of what we possess. The golden age in the future will make good the heaviest drafts.

These are the two extremist views, both representing *prima facie* demands of human nature. Let
time be the most real of realities, and give us a
fighting chance of making over the universe into
something nearer to what we take to be our heart's
desire. Or let time be a minor incident or phenomenon in a whole, planned with certainty to bring
us in the end to our heart's desire, whether on earth
or in heaven.

These views agree in a facile reliance on future. iii. In the broadest sense these two opposite
doctrines have a common attitude to the future.[1]
Both of them use it as a counterbalance which they
can rely on to turn the scales against any conceivable amount of past and present evil. Either "the
world may be as bad as you please; we can re-
model it *ad libitum*"; or "the world may be as bad
as you please; the sufferings of this present time are
not worthy to be compared."

If, indeed, the passing suggestion were seriously
relied on, that we may expect a future which will
not overbalance nor re-create in principle this world
as we experience it, but will cast a very considerable
new light upon its nature—that doctrine implies
a serious consideration and appreciation of the
world as we have it, and so far forms a transition to
the point of view we shall adopt.

But looking to the main logical motive of the
two doctrines, I am convinced that it is as we have

---

[1] The difficulty attaching to the term "we" or "us" as denoting
the subjects of the future experience is fundamental for both these
views. If the succession is to be a reality, we should have the
happiness of some based on the misery of others (*Principle*, p. 18).
If it is not to be a reality, but finite beings are all to continue, or to
be phases of one individual, then we get into an order of ideas for
which the "future" has little meaning.

represented it. I do not hold that we have nothing
to gain from either. I admit that much is to be
learned from the idea of a relative wholeness of the
self, postulated in the doctrine of "duration," on the
one side, and that we have no right to rule out the
possibility of changes in finite life, beyond what we
can now imagine, on the other. But granting to
both sets of ideas this relative significance, I am
still convinced that by postulating unlimited resources
of a facile kind they enter into irresistible temptations to neglect the arduous scrutiny of what actual
experience reveals. I believe what is thus offered
us[1] to be both what we cannot prove and what
we do not want. Our attitude to the open
secret of existence is thus, as I hold, seriously
distorted and superficialised, because such facile
resources pauperise us, so to speak, and obstruct us
in grasping the arduousness of reality, and therefore,
what is the same thing, its value. In what may be
called our literature of happiness—serious fiction
and popular philosophy—the reliance on the future
has become, it seems to me, an actual disease.
There is much recognition of the higher values,
which the best of such literature itself reveals by
an analysis of our daily experiences, but it seems
as if the effort to concentrate such recognition into
the straightforward philosophical doctrine which it
suggests were too difficult to be made. Or is it
perhaps too obvious? The story of Naaman the
Syrian often appears to me to carry the moral most
needed for our civilisation.

2. We repudiate, then, both of these extreme
standpoints. We consider time as an appearance

---

[1] See *Principle*, Preface.

Our ques-
tion is the
rank and
value of
progress
according
to our
theory. only, a position which the former doctrine denies, but, in opposition to the latter doctrine, as an appearance inseparable from the membership of finiteness in infinity, and therefore from the self-revelation of a reality which as a whole is timeless. We have thus to assign a place to progress within such a whole, and as its manifestation. The test of a philosophy in dealing with progress is, I am convinced, to reconcile the sense of creative achievement in the self as promotion of the good cause, with its recognition and acceptance of a perfection which is not won by its own finite activity, though represented in it—in shorter phrase, to reconcile the attitudes and postulates of morality and of religion.

I will recapitulate, so far as possible in positive and non-controversial form, the main characteristics which I have tried to establish as belonging to the perfect real. And from this statement it will be possible, I believe, to see convincingly how the attitude and demand of moral progress necessarily belongs to the members of such a whole, but not as an ultimate attitude.

How a non-
temporal
real can
express
itself in
an infinite
temporal
series. i. We are compelled to ask how a perfect whole can contain the material of a progress *ad infinitum*, and all its steps. The infinite real, which, according to our argument, manifests itself through a temporal series, is but little akin to numerical infinity, even if that could be established as a given reality. The real cannot be conceived as a series or succession. It is, as we have seen, not numerable.[1] A succession or even a duration—for a duration implies a succession, though a succession *per se* is not a dura-

[1] *Principle*, Lect. X. App. I.

tion—a succession or duration is an appearance which can only be presented to a consciousness relatively split in two.[1]  And that must be a finite consciousness, a consciousness incapable of entering wholly into one experience, that is, again, of having an experience which can occupy it as a whole.  Any analysis[2] of the sense of time will establish the necessity of two concurrent lines or streams of experience for its apprehension.  A mind that was perfectly present to itself, that is to say, that was complete in a complete experience, could not be aware of succession except by a relative impotence through which its rounded whole should reduce itself to discriminated and comparable lines.  The full and rounded whole might be compared—if we bear in mind that we are not likely to possess so complete a mastery except in comparative trivialities —with the profound and inclusive feeling which may rest, for example, on the innumerable events of the history and achievement of a great family, and which may be qualified and enriched even by the architectural details of the house which has been throughout its centre and symbol.[3]  Such a feeling could be expressed or analysed in serial or spatial form only by the acts and events which constituted the history, and by the spatial details of the fabric which constituted the symbol and the focus.  And if it were not so actually expressed, there could be no such experience as the feeling itself, which is the

---

[1] Nettleship, *Remains*, vol. i. p. 10.

[2] *E.g.* the author's *Knowledge and Reality*, p. 330.

[3] Cf. the illustration from Dante's *Divine Comedy* in *Principle*, Lect. VII.  I have here especially in mind, of course as a mere hint and analogue, the family feeling portrayed in Baroness von Hütten's striking novel *Sharrow*.

concentration and quintessence of the spatio-temporal series.

We saw [1] that an infinite series could not as such be given, but that a problem could be set in a given experience such that its expression in serial form— just because the serial form is inadequate—could only be a series *ad infinitum*. This characteristic might represent the relation of the spatio-temporal unendingness to the perfection which it continually endeavours and fails to express, but to which, nevertheless, its members belong, and are aware that they belong, and have their true hold of perfection only through this awareness.

It was pointed out in the previous course of lectures in what sense a true infinite is self-representative.[2] This is a character which the recent theory of infinity may be taken to emphasise. In every true part—hence in every member—of an infinite whole there is something corresponding to every feature of such a whole, though not repeating it. The part, living with the life of the whole and claiming its perfection, may be said in a general sense not to be less than the whole—to have, that is to say, a feature for every feature of the whole. It is, in truth, something more than a part; it is a member, or an aspect; and if its character is to be expressed in the language of whole and part, perhaps it demands some such expression as that it contains no fewer elements than the whole. It would certainly be true of a genuine infinite that if we speak of whole and parts at all, the whole represents itself within every part. This helps us towards our view of the place in perfection which

[1] *Principle*, Lect. X. App. I.    [2] Lect. II. p. 38, note.

belongs to the finite-infinite being, and his creative achievement and self-realisation.

ii. When finite illustrations—the only kind at our disposal—are used to elucidate the nature of a time-less experience, certain typical objections are raised against them. In what sense infinite progress can be contained in a perfect reality.

I will refer to two of these, which, I believe, exhaust the real significance of such criticism.

If we say that there is a difference in the ampli-tude of experiences, and that this indicates a scale of degrees upon which we might extend our views to the conception of an experience which is all-inclusive, the answer comes that we are confusing memory and direct apprehension. It is true, the critic urges, that the past can be presented to us in memory, and that one man has much more memory than another. But this does not mean that one man's experience has, more or less than another's, the character of succession. You might even argue that for the man of ampler memory the successive-ness of time is more emphatically given.

This criticism does not appear to me to deal with the point. To live in a larger world is not reducible to having either the longer or the fuller memory. I have indeed refused to appeal to the doctrine of the specious present[1] as an adequate account of the all-inclusive experience; but the specious present insists on a truth which the reduction of our present experience of the past to memory ignores. And if this doctrine admitted, what I understand it to deny, the principle of transformation, it would help us towards conceiving both the perfect and the partial timeless experience. When a man's whole world is

---

[1] *Principle*, Lect. X. App. I.

modified and penetrated throughout by the influence of things and events which are living and essential to him, though to another they are a blank both for thought and feeling, this is not a mere affair of memory—of course, indeed, memory could at most only touch the factor of personal past experience. It is a question of the depth and width of the world in which we live. Memory may have contributed to its formation, but it is not constituted by memory, but by the whole constructive work of thought, envisaging the objects of conations and interests. A great scholar, whose mind is dyed and shaped by the thought and feeling of ancient Greece, possesses so far an ampler immediate experience than others in whom that factor is wanting. He is a denizen, so far, of a larger world; and time does not touch the mode of his dwelling in it. He has more in him that is independent of serial experiences. The fabric of his being has, so far, more of trueness and of reality. I submit that an ampler life in such a sense as this, a life in which the self approaches nearer to possessing itself (its complete or ideal self, of course, must be the standard), is a fair example of a life in which time so far ceases to prevail.

And then there is the case in which serial apprehension seems of the essence—the familiar case of, *e.g.*, a piece of music. We are told, and it is true, that if the apprehension of it were not serial, the whole would become a mere chaos. The serial order is inherent. Now this is not met by suggesting that the music can be repeated in memory just as it was performed. A series repeated in memory is no less temporal than a series when first heard. We get nearer the point by observing that a whole can be apprehended or remembered as a whole, without apprehension or memory of its detail as such. As in the last case, so in this, transformation, or rather apprehension as a more perfect real, of which the serial form is an imperfect rendering, gives the clue to the familiar experience. Take the musician's whole frame of mind—the significance of the piece as one with that general form and impression of it which can be apprehended as a whole—and you get something like what we may conceive to be the complete real, which for a being that apprehends successively through sensation must be so drawn out in time. It must be remembered that we hold the temporal succession to be essential to the non-temporal experience. The notes must be a series, but the impression of the piece is not; and the notes are only an attempt to render or convey the impression. Of course it is not suggested that a timeless experience is confined to what would be a point of time to a temporal consciousness. No contrast of simultaneity and succession is here relevant. The essential is the totality which forbids the split into parallel series,[1] not a consciousness of simultaneity.

Logic affords another clue.[2] Causation in time, for example, can only be understood as the manifestation of an underlying system, itself not temporal. The apparent temporal relation of present to past is the same with its relation to future, in so far as both are negative, and neither pair can be real together. It is as unreasonable to say that the real present is caused by a past no longer real, as by a future not

[1] P. 297, above. Simultaneity is a case of succession.
[2] Author's *Logic*, ed. 2, i. 250, 258.

yet real.    The genuine reality must lie in a system
to which all three belong together, though in finite
appearance they are transformed.    "Duration,"
indeed, is meant to supply a continuity which is
both real and in time.    But this, as it seems to me,
is a half-measure.    The continuity is incomplete.
Some of the past is abandoned, some of the future
is deferred.    If not, the distinction of past and future
would vanish.    The distinction, being maintained,
means finiteness, and is all very well in an appearance; but what sort of ultimate reality is it that is
thus, even if only in degree, external to itself?    It
is the essence of *durée* that "nous ne nous tenons
jamais tout entiers."    We are obliged to treat the
future as springing from past events, because we
have *prima facie* nothing of the past, except past
events, to serve as a guide to the future.    But we
know that nothing really springs from past events
as separate and successive, but only from a real
totality that underlies them.    And in all sound
logical procedure it is our conception of this system,
and not a transition from a series of particulars to a
further particular, that engages our attention.[1]

Thus we find on all sides that the difference
between a finite life and apprehension on the one
hand, and reality on the other, is not adequately
expressed by the difference between part and whole
or between completeness and incompleteness.    It
is a difference rather of kind; something which
we might remotely liken to the difference between
a great mind and a little one, or between a man's

[1] Cf. author's *Logic*, ii. 220, note and reff.  *E.g.*, you cannot go
straight from an enumeration of actual cases to a statement of chances.
You must consider what sort of system the enumeration indicates.
Cf. Sigwart, *Logic*, Eng. Tr. ii. 227.

mind and that of a lower animal. The efforts of the finite creature to achieve the infinite experience naturally fall into series. But it is not the cumulative events of this series, but a character to be won or developed by their means, that can bring the finite mind in any way nearer the perfection which attracts it. These considerations are all-important for the problem of progress to which we shall return directly.

iii. But one more point must first be considered. It sounds fine to say that the gates of the future, of creative evolution, are wide open. Yet in saying it, do we not plainly say that the gates of perfection are absolutely closed? There is one road, and one road only, we have held, by which the finite creature can identify itself with perfection, and that begins by accepting perfection as real, while admitting that he cannot attain it in his own right. Our seemingly innocent boast about the gates of the future, interpreted as we above thought fair to interpret it, appears to annihilate both these simple postulates. If the real is an infinite series, there is no perfection. And, paradoxically, this is the consequence of the false assumption that we can attain it in our own right. Now that the finite-infinite being must be able to realise his nature by self-identification with perfection, we hold to admit of no doubt at all. But no less we are certain that this necessity, which overthrows the former of the two extreme views above referred to, will not justify the latter. We cannot entrust the fulfilment of our postulate to a miracle of the future. We must find it within the limits of that very universal fact which suggests and demands it. We have seen in principle how the fulfilment comes, and we have just now con-

*If the ultimate real is progress to infinity, the gates are closed against perfection.*

trasted this principle with the two extremist views, the one of which denies it, while the other, we might say, no less incredibly, pretends to achieve it by a *salto mortale*, but in doing so denies it none the less.

iv. It remains to explain the rank and value of the attractive demand for a modifiable universe, really changeable as a whole, and through the achievement of its members. This view, we have seen, necessarily denies a real perfection.

The explanation does not seem difficult. The finite-infinite creature, as we have repeatedly observed, is always in a condition of self-transcendence. This is the same as saying that he is always endeavouring to pass beyond himself in achievement. That there is always scope for this, his membership of the universe, as we have analysed it, guarantees. He is always a fragmentary being, inspired by an infinite whole, which he is for ever striving to express in terms of his limited range of externality. In this, *ex hypothesi*, he can never succeed. But this effort of his is not wasted or futile. It is a factor of the self-maintenance of the Universe, and so far is a real achievement; and it constitutes, as we have seen, an element in the Absolute—an element through which the detailed conflict of good and evil is sustained, and the relative triumph of good, within this conflict, is made possible.

Thus the only question of attainment which can be raised about this progressive endeavour is whether or no the finite being recognises, it may be implicitly or explicitly, the full significance of his own nature. It is this that determines the relation of his progress to its aim.

*a.* So far as his recognition is one-sided, or rather The one-sided self-recognition or purely moral standpoint —progress an absolute demand. (for a double recognition is quite inevitable) so far as the reflective recognition of one side is in advance of the implied recognition of the other, he remains in the general atmosphere of the world of claims. The fundamental characteristic of this, as we saw, is the externality of the members to one another, counting among them the creator and supreme will. Harmony or perfection, it follows, is taken to be attainable only by an infinite progression; because it is a bringing to harmony of things which are independent, and which act out of natures which they do not share with each other and the whole. Thinking of himself thus according to one side of his *prima facie* appearance, as a self-contained substance, he holds the progression which he is aware of to be an advance originated by himself and others, each by himself, out of himself, and in his own strength, except in so far as a theological doctrine may suggest a miraculous grace, to repair the defective recognition of the being's inherent nature. The changes that are brought about seem therefore to be the creation of new things, bringing into being what ought to be and therefore is not, and annihilating what is and therefore ought not to be. This latter antithesis, though barred from its full effect by our inherent recognition in experience of the world in which all are at one, is involved in principle in the doctrine of each for himself and no real solidarity.[1] This antagonism, and the consequent demand for a modification of

---

[1] It is a complication if you hold that there was a solidarity at starting, that this is lost as "individuals" develop, and, perhaps, may be re-created in the end. But it only prefixes a phase, and makes no essential difference.

the whole reality, actual in time, from what is to what ought to be, is the necessary consequence of the individual's failure to appreciate reflectively his own nature and the meaning of his self-transcendence. This failure is never completely experienced within actual life, for the gulf which it sets between the "is" and the "ought," between the conditions and the action, would make actual life impossible. As we have amply seen, an implicit recognition of man's nature, an implicit religious attitude, is the inherent condition of all actual living.[1] But reflectively noted and made the basis of a theory, the misunderstood awareness of self-transcendence may give rise to the demand for a progress of the universe in time. And because of the incompatibility presupposed in its factors, it must be an infinite progression.

The inclusive self-recognition : real perfection a condition of the value of progress. β. When, on the other hand, the finite being's implied recognition of its own full nature is trusted, as it is by all mankind in the current affairs of life, or in any degree made explicit through religious symbolism and reflection, we have the inclusive attitude which was analysed in the former course of lectures.[2] The fact and the duty of self-transcendence remain where they were. But instead of dealing with a machinery of external wills to be reconciled, as in the world of claims, they now symbolise the absorption of the self by will and conviction in the perfection which inspires it and

[1] We asked if the lower animals have religion. It might be said that so far as they live in unconscious dependence and without doubt or suspicion—how far this is so, I suppose, is questionable—they possess an essential of the religious attitude, which, however, can only become religion when it is held against more conscious antagonism than can exist for them.

[2] *Principle*, p. 277.

belongs to it, but which, in its character as a
finite self or aggregate of such selves, it can never
realise.

The true rank and value of the demand for
progress is thus inherently secure.  There can be
no fear that a self, identified in will and conviction
with the transcendent perfection, will be lacking
either in the spirit or in the detailed occasions
for fuller expression of that which inspires it in
the actual modification of its world.  The Absolute,
we have seen, is all-inclusive by transmutation,
and is thus no mere aggregate, which might be
exhaustible, but supreme in kind.  Therefore it
cannot be adequately expressed in any mere partial
appearance, though all its being lies in the tension
towards self-expression.  The conflict of good and
evil is inherent in it.  But if the fundamental
perfection, maintained throughout imperfect appearance, were not real, the conflict of good and evil,
that is, of perfection as the object of a positive
and of a negative attitude respectively, would
have vanished *in toto*, and the inspiration of progress, and the value of its contribution to the real,
would inevitably be gone.

Thus, finally, a view which rules out real perfection, rules out the whole content and inspiration
of progress.  For it is the spirit of perfection,
working within the finite self, which at once
demands perfection, and secures it in the only way
open to finite beings.  The infinite actual progression, and the progression which is to cease
at a future point with the abolition of finiteness—
the open gates and the shut—are both of them
self-destructive ideas.  The former has thrown

away its inspiration; the latter its concrete actuality. Nothing but the infinite perfection, working as that which inspires the imperfect, can fulfil the concrete need for the conflict and the victory. Both are certain and secure, for both are of the essence of the finite-infinite self. And we have seen that the analysis of life—of the forms which must be held in principle akin to religion—show beyond any doubt in what way this doctrine is universally true.

What attitude to man's future in time conforms to our argument?

3. At this point it will be well to make some explanation of our own attitude to the future, seeing that we do not expect it to bring any special and unprecedented contribution to the solution of our speculative problems. It is plain that we have an interest in it. If not, we should not continue to live. It is on the very ground of our interest that we object to the conception of change in the ultimate real, which seems to destroy what we care for. It may be said, "Your question is wrongly put. You do not continue to live because you are interested in the future. You are interested in the future because you and the race have to continue living, unless you take violent steps to prevent it." But even so, continuance in living is not a bare fact. We are bound to think of it as bringing us something. The finite being is, as we have constantly reiterated, essentially self-transcendent, and this means that he is bound to have something before him, at least symbolic of the satisfaction which he inherently pursues. We cannot continue living unless the continuance implies something like hope. Now we do not hope for a new and ultimate experience, which will solve all problems

and end all discontents. There is such an experience; but no finite self—no self in time—can possess it.

Therefore, as we reject traditional views of a future climax of being, and their modern equivalents of a millenary type, as also the alteration of the ultimate real, it seems well to say what sort of future, should it be realised, would be compatible with our ideas. The answer, as has been indicated, will not be a prediction for its own sake. The hypothetical prediction, so far as that proves necessary, will be for the sake of the philosophical answer; that is, for the sake of explaining what sort of future our philosophical views would welcome as bringing the type of satisfaction which they suggest.

i. In principle, then, I think it is fair to press upon us the question, "What sort of thing do you hope?" Theoretical satisfaction is impossible, we saw,[1] without satisfaction of criticised desire. So from a theoretical point of view we are bound to have some idea of what such a satisfaction might demand and bring. As regards the destiny of the "individual," the finite being by himself, we have already confronted the question. But there is still the question of the spatio-temporal life of the race, and of any kindred races within the universe.

*What sort of thing can we hope? A fair question. In the main, an increasing sense of true values.*

And our answer in principle is simple and direct. Where the question speaks of the future, we speak of the whole. That the mastery and realisation of it for us lies largely in the future is in one sense a mere consequence of our finiteness. The

[1] Lect. VII., above.

future in this sense means any experience which we do not already possess, and must therefore acquire hereafter, if at all. But that the object of such an experience lies in events subsequent to a certain point of time, is quite a different implication, is by no means universally true, and perhaps in strict principle is not true at all.

That our mastery of the whole must in some sense be "further" and not merely "continued," that is, that it must be relatively and within our connected course of history progressive, is guaranteed by the nature of the self-conscious being, whose "duration"[1] or affinity with the timeless lies in his accumulating a past which he carries along with him, adding to it what comes after. On the whole, this is so, and in some degree is true of the race. But that what he keeps and gains always exceeds in value what he lets go, would be a bold assumption for which I can see no justification.

In general, however, this is our answer. What is left that our probably limited future, the future of the race, can do for us, when we discard what I call miraculous expectations, is to increase our grasp of the whole, both in practice and theory, and more especially, in consequence of this fuller grasp and also as a contribution to it, to aid us in a very profound and considerable transvaluation of values.

The frame of mind which corresponds to the recognition of the Absolute whole, as beyond religion.

ii. It will repay us at this point to consider for a moment a question which we may seem to have treated too cavalierly, deserving as it is at least of a little curiosity. If the standpoint of religion is, as we held, not ultimate ; if it is possible and necessary to conceive of the Absolute as something of which

[1] See *Principle*, p. 355, on affinity of *durée* and timelessness.

religion itself, with the conflict of good and evil, is not a complete account, to what attitude or mode of recognition on our part does such a conception correspond? We have definitely rejected the idea that philosophy is superior to religion. But there is something more to be said. There is always, I suppose, a normal and general mode of consciousness, an awareness of a certain kind of object, corresponding to every reflective attitude which really proves distinct and well-grounded ; and to this philosophy, as the theory of the Absolute, is no exception. We feel throughout — as I have frequently urged in these lectures—a general rise and fall of life, a pervading greatness and amplitude and coherence which in the higher tides of vitality seems to blend all finite individuals and to leave nothing outside it.[1]  Now religion, as it takes definite shape through adoration of an object and community of will with its will, tends to become engaged in the specific conflict between good and evil, and though it transcends this, yet remains determined by this particular transcendence. But our sense of wholeness is aware of something that does not precisely fit into such a *cadre*. We are aware, as I said, of a strength and amplitude of the world, which even the contrast of good and evil as it definitely takes shape for us under the determinate pressure of practice, does not exhaust. The universe, we feel, though it is a rough place, and not exactly fitting into the frame of good as against evil, is great and splendid in ways that are to us inexhaustible. . If we interpreted our "good" with sufficient breadth, it might almost fit this experience.

> *Our awareness of an inclusive totality.*

---

[1] See *Principle* on multiplicism as opposed to pluralism, pp. 372-3.

Certainly the greatness and the goodness are on the whole akin. But the stress of practice forbids our reducing them to one and the same thing from our standpoint. The universe is the magnificent theatre of all the wealth of life, and good and evil are within it. This, I think, we are aware of when at our best ; and this awareness corresponds to the sense of the Absolute whole within which religion itself is a feature or characteristic, putting a point, for our special needs, upon the general recognition of a transcendent amplitude.

Here, in passing, we have elucidated our common sense of the Absolute, the real awareness of an inclusive world to which philosophy as a reflective theory corresponds, and which widens and sweetens our religious consciousness by forbidding its components to harden into mere antagonistic factors. And here, too, we have seen how the whole, the inclusive and all-permeating world, is the ultimate watchword of our theory.

Now, preserving the standpoint of the whole, we return to the question, what the future might bring.

Distinguish interest in the future from interest in the whole, to be satisfied in the future.
iii. We may note again, with reference to what was said just above, how deeply our hopes for the " future " [1] are entangled with what concerns the " past." Great part of our pride in the present, and our hope for what is to come, turn upon such matters as unravelling the laws of evolution and the history of man, the real significance of documents and events belonging to the first century of our era,

---

[1] Cf. the question of the true formulation of the principle of natural uniformity as opposed to the expression " will the future resemble the past " ; and the nature of so-called scientific " prediction " which has in strictness no special concern with the future, but merely with the addition to knowledge as such.

and the right valuation of achievements and civilisation prior by ages even to that period.   All this, no
doubt, gravely affects the life of to-day and of the
days to come.   But the fact that it is so only shows
more conclusively how that which concerns and
interests us is not essentially something still to
come, but inherently is the comprehension and
valuation of the whole in which we are members.
It is the future that will amplify it ; but what it is, is
the vision of the whole.   Whether the future is to
afford us individual creations of the mind greater
than any of the past is a question beyond the
possibility of prediction, and perhaps unmeaning.
In a sense, no doubt, it must transcend the past ;
but whether by inclusion or by repulsion, whether
lifted by it to a higher plane or pursuing a new
track on the level, seems impossible to determine on
general grounds.   It is not even easy to be sure of
the meaning of the expressions.   One thing seems
to me certain.   The expression of the Absolute
cannot be wholly reserved for the future.   The
past must have had its share.   What else can it
have been than such an expression?   And something is certainly dropped as we proceed, by the
nature of finiteness, though it is open to any one to
argue that what is added must be of greater value.
Therefore our progress, though progressive in a
sense, cannot be an absolute advance in all respects.

iv. But, as the result of our whole argument, we
are clear, I believe, about what really matters.
And this is what I want unequivocally to affirm.
It follows from our consideration of the finite-infinite
being that what really matters—what alone, in the
main, the future can conceivably have to offer—is

*What really matters in progress is the deeper and more general self-recog- nition, i.e.*

the re-
ligious con-
sciousness. to begin with, no doubt, an increased wealth and harmony of finite existence, but further, because of and along with this, a profounder sense of the worthlessness of the finite creature in and by himself, and a deeper union, through will and conviction, with the perfection of the whole; in other words, a religious consciousness more widespread and more profound. All progress, all civilisation, all transvaluation of values, must ultimately be tested by this double criterion.[1] The finite being's grasp of the world is the measure at once of what he has to renounce as his own, and to affirm as his in the whole.

Illustra-
tion : two
suggestions
about past
and future
respect-
ively. 4. In order, then, to convey some definite impression of the direction in which views like ours project our outlook and interest, I will try to embody our results of principle in two illustrative suggestions ; first, as to what changes have been most important in the history of our race down to the present time, and secondly, in what sort of modification—however brought about—our doctrine of values would teach us to look for the most important changes of the future. What I am trying to indicate is a sense of values ; and I ask to be interpreted by the intention of the argument in this respect, and not to be judged merely by defects of historical knowledge or imagination.

---

[1] This double criterion, of a positive gain, the magnitude of which has its main value in facilitating its own absorption in the whole, obviously repeats the two sides of the logical criterion, comprehensiveness and coherence, in which the main value of comprehensiveness is that it makes contradiction at once more profound and more possible to overcome. The satisfied self, in possession of a vast social and intellectual world, has more to give up than a simpler being, and yet, as we saw, is more likely to feel the strain of holding on to it, and has more, a deeper faith, to gain by self-recognition.

i. The most important changes in the past history of mankind, whom I take as the type of finite self-conscious beings, have been, on our view, all those that have affected their freedom in the most inclusive sense of the word.  It has very many senses, but for us they all culminate in that recognition of its own true nature by the finite-infinite being which I have spoken of as the religious attitude and the sense of the Absolute.  This recognition, as we have seen, is highly complex.  The unity of the finite-infinite is in one sense diminished[1] and in another sense advanced by the conflicts and contradictions which set man against himself and his world.  The expression "the unhappy consciousness" is applied in a famous philosophical classic[2] to a particular phase of mind which is there associated with the failure of Stoicism and Scepticism and the birth-pangs of Christianity, a phase of yearning, isolation, and sense of loss, in the individual mind. " It is the bitter pain which finds expression in the words, God is dead."  In a kindred sense the name might be applied to the condition of any and every consciousness that has lost its hold on its own spiritual foundation, especially in ages of social and intellectual unrest.  In the present day a similar phenomenon seems to prevail, associated on a large scale with pessimism.  And therefore the idea urges itself upon us, that so far from the advance in a scientific and practical mastery of Nature being in

*The most important changes in past history those connected with man's "freedom" or recognition of his full nature. Part played by "the unhappy consciousness."*

[1] See Cornford, *From Religion*, p. 77, on the idea of an original unbroken unity of feeling in which the tribal group included external nature—so unbroken that it could hardly be called conscious or religious.

[2] See Hegel's *Phenomenology of Mind*, Parts iv. and vii., Eng. Tr., vol. i. 219, vol. ii. 762.

316 THE GATES OF THE FUTURE LECT.

itself a guarantee against the unhappy consciousness, it is, taken by itself, merely a fresh source of contradiction, and a root from which, in the bewilderment of the individual mind which has lost itself[1] in the labyrinth of things, new forms of evil are bound to spring.

The suggestion seems inevitable that the unhappy consciousness, the sense of the division between mind and the universe, and therefore between mind and itself, is *prima facie* rather intensified than set at rest by the vast material and. intellectual advance of mankind. The principal benefit, then, derivable from the more tangible and verifiable advances of civilisation would lie, I do not say wholly in the demonstration of their own worthlessness, but in a very intricate combination of spiritual results, in which such a demonstration is a considerable factor. On the one side there is actually an intensification of the unhappy consciousness, through the tendency of the individual spirit to lose itself, and incur recurrent disappointment, in the alien order of a mechanical universe, reflected in satisfactions which do not satisfy, and in falsification of values throughout all social relations. On the other side there is the contribution of this very form of consciousness itself to the depth of the reconciliation which a true sense of the finite-infinite nature now as always involves. And the transvaluation of values belonging to this latter insight, so far as attained, must react on the external order so far as determined by man. Hence human freedom, the

---

[1] Cf. Rousseau in the *Discours sur les Sciences et les Arts.* His anticipation, for good and evil, of the anti-intellectualist attitude of to-day, is most remarkable.

formal conception of which had been won by the self-experience and self-recognition of mind, but has tended to be practically lost again in the mechanical order with its jarring of fragmentary aims, has begun, and must, we hope, continue, to assert itself substantially—*not* in direct proportion to material and scientific progress, *but* in proportion to such progress so far as accompanied by the insight, won by sad experience of its failures, into the insignificance of its value *except as controlled by a consciousness which is aware of that insignificance and of its relation to what in truth makes life worth living.*

This hard-won insight into the nature of finite mind and its satisfaction, establishing as it must what we have called the stability and security of the finite self, with the true sense of values reacting on external conditions, may be described in general as the sense of human worth and freedom.   And its acquisition seems to be the most important modification of life which the past has bequeathed to us. It is substantially one with what we have called above the religious consciousness : the mind's recognition of its own true nature and the conditions of its strength and weakness.

I will venture to illustrate the position by citing from a distinguished writer an illustration of the unhappy consciousness as it exists to-day, and then attempting to point out how, from our standpoint, facts which need not differ in their tangible aspect from those there rehearsed, will lead us to an attitude of polar opposition to the ideas there advocated.

I cite from Mr. Russell's remarkable essay, " The

Free Man's Worship."[1]    The whole essay should, of course, be read :—

"To Dr. Faustus in his study Mephistopheles told the history of the Creation, saying, 'The endless praises of the choirs of angels had begun to grow wearisome, for after all did he not deserve their praise? Had he not given them endless joy? Would it not be more amusing to obtain undeserved praise, to be worshipped by beings whom he tortured? He smiled inwardly, and resolved that the great drama should be performed.'

"For countless ages the hot nebula whirled aimlessly through space. . . . And [man] gave God thanks for the strength that enabled him to forego even the joys that were possible. And God smiled; and when he saw that Man had become perfect in renunciation and worship, he sent another sun into the sky, which crashed into Man's sun, and all returned again to nebula.

"'Yes,' he murmured, 'it was a good play; I will have it performed again.'

"Such in outline, but even more purposeless, more void of meaning, is the world which Science presents for our belief. Amid such a world, if anywhere, our ideals henceforward must find a home. That Man is the product of causes which had no prevision of the end they were achieving; that his origin, his growth, his hopes and fears, his loves and his beliefs, are but the outcome of accidental collections of atoms; that no fire, no heroism, no intensity of thought and feeling, can preserve an individual life beyond the grave; that all the labours

[1] Hon. Bertrand Russell, *Philosophical Essays*, p. 59 ff.; and compare quotation from Wallace, p. 238, above.

of the ages, all the devotion, all the inspiration, all the noonday brightness of human genius, are destined to extinction in the vast death of the solar system, and that the whole temple of Man's achievement must inevitably be buried beneath the débris of a universe in ruins—all these things, if not quite beyond dispute, are yet so nearly certain, that no philosophy which rejects them can hope to stand. Only within the scaffolding of these truths, only on the firm foundation of unyielding despair, can the soul's habitation henceforth be safely built."

Here we have the unhappy consciousness in the plainest form. And it is very noticeable how in these deepest depths it finds a foundation on which, while affirming it with the mind's whole force to be despair, it succeeds in building a valuable and positive structure. No one, I think, could compare the passage just cited with the corresponding transition in the philosophical classic to which I have referred [1] without observing an affinity of principle between the modern writer's firm foundation of despair with all that he builds on it, and Hegel's transition from the unhappy consciousness to the self-confidence of reason. The affinity turns upon the familiar point that every negative rests on an affirmation, and we touch bed-rock, the "firm foundation," the confidence of reason, when we commit ourselves to our faith in inclusive reality and repudiate the flattering idea of our private substantiality and importance. It seems plain that the essayist's position is capable of further affirmative development. But the purpose of my reference is not to renew at the eleventh hour an argument about the Absolute.

[1] Hegel's *Phenomenology*, *l.c.*

It is rather to point out that such views as I have advocated demand no conditions, of a kind to be criticised by science, at variance with those which the author of the passage assumes.[1]  We interpret, as we think, the whole of the appearances more pregnantly.  But the author's pessimism, and the facts on which it rests, so far as they go, are positive parts of our case, and they, or something of their kind, are the foundation on which a genuine optimism must take its stand.  There is no stability nor security of the finite self which has not in principle[2] drawn its confidence out of the ultimate despair.  Freedom, then, we say with the author of " The Free Man's Worship "—but in a sense which as we think makes man more profoundly free of the universe—is, so far as achieved, the main achievement of mankind in the past.  And its profoundest element is the spiritual induction by which our accumulated finite acquisitions convince us of their worthlessness and nullity, except in so far as renounced in themselves, and received only as graces from the supreme will.

This is not the place to work out a historical and social study, but it will be found that the sense which I have given to freedom includes all its expressions, both formal and substantial.

---

[1] In saying this I must make a caveat against such a phrase as " accidental " collocations of atoms.  But this can hardly be called a tangible or verifiable fact.  Obviously, again, I cannot pledge myself to any particulars of scientific prediction, any more than to the prophecies of those who believe in some far-off divine event.  All I say is that to an absolutism which knows its business the former make no difference, and the latter bring no support.

[2] By saying " in principle," I mean merely to guard myself against asserting that all experience which goes to make a mood must be personally gone through by every individual who is to participate in the mood.  Obviously, in these matters we can reap where we did not sow.  The world wins moods for us.

ii. In the future of our race there will no doubt be enormous material changes; and especially it is important not to underrate those which will naturally arise from the transvaluation of values. For example, all genuine social improvement depends on the right valuation of the things which are increased by sharing as compared with other values. But this will only be part of the spiritual change, the recognition of man's own full nature with all its consequences; and this, we believe, will be the most important change in the future, as it has been in the past. The main result of our obvious "progress" will be, if I am right, through forms of the unhappy consciousness, to bring us to a sense of its worthlessness *per se*, which sense alone, it would seem, can enable us to control and subordinate it to the true values of life. It is worth noticing as an illustration that the happiest results of mechanism and applied science are those which, often through very complex processes and discoveries, bring us back to extreme practical simplicity. The bicycle,[1] electric light and power—especially when worked by a waterfall, as you see it in rough settlements of the U.S.A., or in a peasant village on the St. Gothard—the conditions of healthy living as aimed at in town-planning and house-building, are modest but very suggestive

*(marginal note:)* The most important change in the future history of our race will be to learn, through experience of material progress, the dependence of values on the renunciation involved in self-recognition. A typical anticipation of a much improved society, and the problem of its valuation.

[1] The very fascinating writer known as Vernon Lee has somewhere made this observation about the bicycle. I may remark on the essence of the opposite character, as developed, for example, in the technique of luxury. The point here is not primarily selfishness; the point is letting ourselves get interested in contrivances to secure trivial satisfactions, forgetting to enquire whether the whole affair is worth while, judged by the real values of life. Then, before we know it, we are in the hands of a Frankenstein's monster, and have to learn, sadly, the relative worthlessness of the whole mechanism of our lives

examples of simplicity and subordination to natural needs emerging from the highest technique of mechanism and discoveries of biological science. This, I say, is mechanism at its best, when it, so to speak, undoes its own complication and brings us back to simple means directed to high and indubitable values.   But the mere increase of comfort, convenience, and physical security, even if taken, as must be presupposed, to extend to all classes, will not bring us any nearer satisfaction.   In saying this I am illustrating my argument by supposing an impossibility, for I do not believe that such a triumph over mechanism is conceivable without a considerable advance in the transvaluation of which I am speaking ; and, in so far as such a spiritual change is realised, the conditions of a more profound satisfaction would be attained.

It is a pleasure to me to elucidate my position by a prolonged quotation from the late William James, the more so as I made use of a similar quotation to express an acute difference from him at an early point of the previous course of lectures.   I will read a passage which helps me to bring my argument before you in what seems to me a very striking way :—

" A few summers ago I spent a happy week at the famous Assembly Grounds on the borders of Chautauqua Lake.   The moment one treads that sacred enclosure, one feels one's self in an atmosphere of success.   Sobriety and industry, intelligence and goodness, orderliness and ideality, prosperity and cheerfulness, pervade the air.   It is a serious and studious picnic on a gigantic scale.   Here you have a town of many thousands of inhabitants, beautifully laid out in the forest, and drained and equipped with means for satisfying all the necessary lower and most of the superfluous higher wants of man. You have a first-class college in full blast. You have magnificent music—a chorus of seven hundred voices, with possibly the most perfect open-air auditorium in the world. You have every sort of athletic exercise from sailing, rowing, swimming, bicycling, to the ball-field,[1] and the more artificial doings which the gymnasium affords. You have kindergartens and model secondary schools. You have general religious services, and special club-houses for the several sects. You have perpetually-running soda-water fountains, and daily popular lectures by distinguished men. You have the best of company, and yet no effort. You have no zymotic diseases, no poverty, no drunkenness, no crime, no police. You have culture, you have kindness, you have cheapness, you have equality, you have the best of what mankind has fought and bled and striven for under the name of civilisation for centuries. You have, in short, a foretaste of what society might be, were it all in the light, with no suffering and no dark corners.

"I went in curiosity for a day. I stayed for a week, held spell-bound by the charm and ease of everything, by the middle-class paradise, without a sin, without a victim, without a blot, without a tear.

"And yet what was my own astonishment, on emerging into the dark and wicked world again, to catch myself quite unexpectedly and involuntarily saying 'Ouf! what a relief. Now for something primordial and savage, even though it were as bad

---

[1] For base-ball, I presume.

as an Armenian massacre, to set the balance straight
again. This human drama without a villain or a
pang ; this community so refined that ice-cream soda
is the utmost offering it can make to the brute
animal in man ; this city simmering in the tepid
lake-side sun ; this atrocious harmlessness of all
things—I cannot away with them. Let me take my
chances again in the big outside worldly wilderness
with all its sins and sufferings.'" What was lacking,
he found, was " the element that gives to the wicked
outer world all its moral style, expressiveness, and
picturesqueness—the element of precipitousness, so
to call it, of strength and strenuousness, intensity,
and danger." [1]

Assume this picture to include, as it could not
to-day, all social classes, and the processes of industry made easy and pleasant by invention, and
still the fundamental defect would not be removed.
I would willingly incorporate in this concluding
lecture the whole argument of that remarkable
paper. [2] As we have seen, the chapter of accidents,
the world of hazard and hardship, and the being
recast as if in the furnace, [3] are inherent belongings
of finiteness ; and we can have no good without evil.
The self-satisfaction of the finite is the portal where
hope vanishes—the sin against the Holy Spirit.
There is no true optimism, we saw, which has not
absorbed renunciation into itself, and learned to look

[1] James, *Talks to Teachers on Psychology and Life's Ideals*, p.
268 ff.

[2] Note the subsequent reference to Tolstoi's view of the labouring
class, who in hardship and danger seem to him to have mastered the
secret of existence. For us, of course, these also are only factors.

[3] In this metaphor throughout I have had in mind Ibsen's man
with the ladle in *Peer Gynt*, who comes to recast those who have not
proved themselves to possess a self really of their own.

for strength and security to its union in will and conviction with the whole in which it is rooted. Then, and then alone, when their worthlessness, *per se*, is seen, can its finite possessions and acquisitions claim value as embodiments of the supreme will, or as contributions to the Absolute. The universal recognition of this, with its consequences, is, in my belief, the main thing that the future has to bring us.

"In this solid and tridimensional sense, so to call it, those philosophers are right who contend that the world is a standing thing, with no progress, no real history." So William James observes in this same paper.

5. I will finally summarise the doctrine of these lectures in two passages—the voices respectively of the ancient world and of the new. The first, from a writer of Aristotle's school, shows us the effect of such a recognition as we call religious on the framework and constitution of life; the second, from a great teacher of your own country but lately passed away, indicates the depth and universality of that secure optimism which we have endeavoured to correlate with the inherent value and destiny of the finite individual.

The *Eudemian Ethics*, written by an Aristotelian moralist of the fourth century B.C., teaches us :—[1] "So whatever choice or distribution of worldly resources, whether of bodily qualities or of wealth or of friends or of other goods, will be most helpful towards the contemplation of God, that is the best, and that is the most beautiful standard of organisation ; and whatever arrangement, whether by defect

*Marginal note:* Conclusion : the reaction of a profound self-recognition on the apparatus of life, and the absoluteness of the security which it involves. Identification with ultimate individuality, which can only be through religious self-recognition, constitutes the worth and destiny of finite beings.

[1] Ar. 1249 b 16-21.

or by excess, hinders men from glorifying God and enjoying him, that arrangement is to be rejected."

And the great Scottish teacher reminds us that "it is a significant fact that no one has ever brought such an accusation [as that of treating evil too lightly] against the greatest optimist whom the world has ever seen. And the reason seems to be that in the life and death of Jesus the consciousness of suffering and of evil, not as a far-off subject of reflexion, but as an immediate and personal experience, is raised to the highest conceivable point of intensity. It is this certainty of ultimate triumph, this combination of the despair of pessimism with an optimism that overreaches and overpowers it, nay, that even absorbs it as an element into itself, which constitutes the unique character of the religion of Jesus."[1]

It will be noted that the words "the certainty of ultimate triumph" seem literally to indicate some reference to a future event or attainment. If they are to be so taken, the present argument could not endorse them. For it the triumph is in the Absolute, and the total expression of it within the temporal series is inconceivable. Nor can we suppose that all which is to come in that series is nearer to perfection than anything which has gone before. Our answer to any such problem has previously been explained.[2] It remains solid ground that the security of the finite is fully to recognise its own nature, and that in this recognition a given self-conscious race must naturally tend to advance.

I said at the beginning of the previous course that our results would be nothing startling or extra-

[1] Caird, *Evolution of Religion*, ii. 109 ff.    [2] P. 313.

ordinary.  I have tried to aim throughout at sanity and coherence—at showing what the universe inherently must offer to the finite being, at what price, and why.  Consider, as a final example, only the case of love—the typical self-transcendence.  No doubt it is the best thing, in a sense the only thing, in the world; but most certainly it is not to be had for nothing.  That is the essence of our argument in this second course of lectures.  And the first had endeavoured to exhibit the relation to its own full nature—to the full individuality—in which the self-transcendence lies that actually constitutes the so-called or finite "individual."

The atmosphere of our pilgrimage has necessarily been sombre.  It is not the business of philosophy to praise the universe or to exalt the satisfactions of goodness.  The framework of our theory has been the logical structure of the real; and our attempt has been to connect in a single view the inherent factors of self-transcendence.  Thus we hoped and intended to exhibit the perils and troubles of the finite self as essential elements of the whole in which its value consists—its union with the ultimate individuality.  In such an analysis the hindrances, the causes of friction and collision, necessarily attract theoretical attention.  They call for explanation, while what primarily satisfies is readily welcomed.  None the less, I trust that our portrayal on the whole has done justice to the higher obvious experience, of which we spoke at starting as the medium in which alone a sound logic could be satisfied.  The at-homeness in the whole, the strength and vitality, which the very perils of the finite presuppose, and the fuller types of experience so persistently reveal, are not dwelt upon at large for theoretical purposes. But such experience, I hope, has been sufficiently indicated to exhibit the general nature of the value—the perfection of the ultimate individuality—which the fragmentariness and the conflicts of finite existence are the means of manifesting and sustaining, and his degree of identification with which constitutes the worth and the destiny of every finite individual.

# INDEX

THE END

*Printed by* R & R. CLARK, LIMITED, *Edinburgh*

# THE GIFFORD LECTURES FOR 1911

# THE PRINCIPLE OF
# INDIVIDUALITY AND VALUE

BY

## B. BOSANQUET, LL.D., D.C.L.

*8vo.*   *10s. net.*

## SOME PRESS OPINIONS

## MACMILLAN AND CO., LTD., LONDON.

9 781330 798096